Dear Brewster

Trust this will help pass the time along your road of recovery

M.S.B.

INTERPRETATIONS
1931–1932

THE MACMILLAN COMPANY
NEW YORK · BOSTON · CHICAGO · DALLAS
ATLANTA   SAN FRANCISCO

MACMILLAN & CO., LIMITED
LONDON · BOMBAY · CALCUTTA
MELBOURNE

THE MACMILLAN COMPANY
OF CANADA, LIMITED
TORONTO

INTERPRETATIONS

1931–1932

BY

WALTER LIPPMANN

SELECTED AND EDITED
By ALLAN NEVINS

NEW YORK
THE MACMILLAN COMPANY
1932

973.9
L

PRINTED IN THE UNITED STATES OF AMERICA
NORWOOD PRESS LINOTYPE, INC.
NORWOOD, MASS., U.S.A.

Gratefully to

HELEN ROGERS REID

and

OGDEN MILLS REID

who made possible the writing of these articles

INTRODUCTION

SOME months ago I received a message from my friend and former colleague, Walter Lippmann, which said in effect: "I have a number of letters asking for a book of my articles published in the New York *Herald Tribune,* and Macmillan is ready to publish it. I do not know what is stone dead and what is still alive in all that material, and anyway no man is to be trusted to select his own writing. Would you be willing to do the choosing?" I was glad to do it because of our old association on the New York *World* and also because these articles have dealt with a singularly fascinating period of modern history.

The years 1931–1932 have been interesting and critical. They are the years in which, after a false and delusive recovery from the World War, all mankind seemed to fall into a deeper gulf than ever. Depression was universal throughout the globe. Revolution swept almost all of South America. Only desperate measures stayed the tide of political upheaval in Germany. Great Britain, so long the strongest financial power in the world, fell from the gold standard and carried half of Europe with her. In the United States the number of unemployed approached ten millions. Mr. Lippmann could not have entered upon the latest phase of his journalistic work at a time which gave more opportunities to his pen. When he began his labors, Great Britain was just plunging into one of the severest crises of her modern history, a crisis with which her people found only a coalition or national government could cope. The immediate sequel of the European disorders was a partial panic in the United States, with new evidences of economic collapse and fears for even the financial safety of the government. While the western world was still trying to gain some temporary security there came the news of the Japanese seizure of Manchuria, involving Japan and China in virtual war and throwing the heaviest strain upon the peace machinery which the nations had been trying to build up since the Treaty of Versailles. It was a time of bewilderment for everyone; for not merely the average man but those who called themselves exceptionally well informed. This bewilderment had much to do with the eager attention that met Mr. Lippmann's articles, and the earnestness with which they have been discussed.

There are two reasons, in the editor's opinion, why it is worth while to present a selection from the articles of 1931–1932 in book form. The primary reason is that they expound a set of general ideas which have permanent values; which can be extricated from their temporary application, and which deserve more than the evanescent currency of newspaper print. Like all editorial writers, Mr. Lippmann has penned much that was dead the day after he wrote it. Like all journalists, he has set down some false judgments and has expressed opinions which have been confuted by events. But any reader of these articles will perceive that he has expressed a number of ideas that have been signally vindicated by time. In two of his early articles on the Chino-Japanese situation he suggested the principle which Secretary Stimson a number of weeks later embodied in his note of January 7, 1932: the principle that the Western Powers might checkmate Japan in Manchuria by simply refusing to recognize any arrangements there in violation of the Nine Power Treaty. It will be noted that Mr. Lippmann was insistently calling for a program of budget-balancing as a first and fundamental step toward recovery before any of our political leaders did so. It will be noted also that the idea he expressed upon the proper form and scope of Federal relief were those which, after much advancing and retreating, were finally embodied in Congressional legislation. Above all, it is to be noted that there runs throughout these articles a series of basic ideas upon world relations and the best means of repairing the shattered economic fabric of the world which, if they have any validity at all, have a permanent validity. The fallacy of the early American view of our self-containment, for example, and the contradictory nature of our general economic policies, are forcibly exposed—and the right way pointed out.

The second and lesser reason for this collection is simply that it affords a peculiarly interesting record of a year of turmoil and anxiety. We shall have, in time, much fuller and exacter records of a factual nature—year books and contemporary histories. With such works this volume makes no effort to compete. But it does offer a record of the ideas prevalent during the recent series of world-shaking events—of the themes for discussion that were uppermost in the minds of thinking Americans. It indicates the nature of the atmosphere of opinion that surrounded the news of the day; it tells what people were debating, and why and how. Such records of discussion and opinion, in any convenient form, are rare. To obtain anything of the kind, readers usually have to search formidable and dirty files of newspapers and magazines. Here the discussion has a special quality of penetration. The *significant* ideas of the day are better extricated than they would be elsewhere. Any reader who follows the articles from the fall of the British Labor Government to the success of the Lausanne Conference, from the meeting of Congress in 1931 to the launching of the Presidential campaign in 1932, will have a fair insight into the most interesting subjects of public anxiety in two hemispheres. A record of this kind has a certain lasting value.

The editor of this collection was confronted with not far

from two hundred of Mr. Lippmann's articles, short and long, dead and alive, on a hundred topics, and of course in no order except that of time. He has arranged what he believes to be the most important and vital articles under a dozen headings. These topics have themselves a rough chronological sequence. The articles under each heading have usually been disposed chronologically, but by no means invariably; for the main attention of the editor has always been to the flow of ideas. New titles have frequently been invented for the articles, and sub-headings have been supplied for all of them. Enough notes have been added to explain names and facts which would otherwise gleam somewhat darkly in the text. Perhaps most readers, in taking up a volume of this nature, will be irresistibly tempted to browse here and there. But some of the deeper values of the collection will hardly appear unless the various papers are read in the sequence in which they are here presented, with the logic of the author developing as he pursued his subject.

COLUMBIA UNIVERSITY   ALLAN NEVINS
    July 20, 1932

CONTENTS

INTERPRETATIONS
1931–1932

· I ·

THE DEPRESSION IN THE UNITED STATES: ITS CAUSES AND NATURE

I. THE PARADOX OF POVERTY AND PLENTY [1]

A solution found for the problem of scarcity; the next problem that of distributing our plenty

EVERYONE is aware of the paradox at the heart of all the present-day suffering—the sensational and the intolerable paradox of want in the midst of abundance, of poverty in the midst of plenty. This is the first great economic depression in which every thinking person has been conscious of such a paradox.

It is often said that this depression is not unlike the great depressions after 1837 and 1873. There are indeed many common elements, and if our knowledge of these other crises were more reliable than it is we should probably have more practical wisdom at hand for meeting our problem. But in the mentality of the people there is a profound difference between this crisis and all its predecessors. This is the first time when it is altogether evident that man's power to produce wealth had reached a point when it is clearly unnecessary that millions in a country like the United States should be in want. In all previous crises there was some doubt as to whether the wealth of the nation was sufficient. That doubt no longer exists.

[1] This article was an address before the National Conference of Social Work at Philadelphia, May 20, 1932.

Man has invented and organized the power to produce wealth on a scale which allows us to say that the most ancient of human problems—the problem of scarcity—has been solved. It has not been solved in all parts of the globe. It has not been solved in China or in India and not yet, I think, in Russia. There men are still under the dominion of scarcity; the wealth, no matter how fairly it may be distributed, does not exist, to liberate the peoples from the menace of want. There the problem is still the ancient problem—the problem of scarcity, of famine due to the shortage of food and other goods.

But in our Western world, and above all in the United States, this problem is solved. Not only do we know how to produce all the wealth needed for a decent standard of life for everybody, we actually do produce it in great abundance.

It has taken about 300 years to arrive at the point where we can definitely say that the problem of scarcity is solved. It has required the development of modern science, the overthrow of feudalism, the liberation of personal energies through the democratic destruction of caste, and the widespread popularization of knowledge to accomplish the result. But it has been done. It is in any large perspective a great achievement.

We who stand at the culmination of this epoch can see today that in order to reap the results of this achievement, in order to translate the power we possess into a secure and ordered civilization, we have to do something which is extremely difficult. We have to tamper with the motives which made the achievement possible. For if we are realistic we must acknowledge that the moving force behind the stupendous material work of the nineteenth century was the acquisitive instinct stimulated to tremendous energy by the prospect of enormous personal profits and personal power. The supreme social problem of the twentieth century, and perhaps for a longer time than that, is to find energies as powerful and as persistent as the acquisitive and the competitive which are disinterested and coöperative in their effect.

If I read correctly the recent experience of Russia it is being demonstrated there how difficult it is to solve that problem. For the Russian system starts with the premise that the acquisitive motive shall be outlawed. But the Russian experience seems to show not only that the acquisitive motive is difficult to suppress, but that without it the energies of men to produce wealth are at present insufficient. That is why the Russians, when they find the output of wealth insufficient, are compelled, temporarily at least, to mitigate their pure doctrine and make concessions to private acquisitiveness.

I mention this, not by way of criticism, but because it seems to me to show the essential difficulty met by men who are making the most radical experiment with a problem which confronts all mankind. Their experiment shows thus far, it seems to me, that a technology for the production of wealth brought into being under the stimulus of strong acquisitiveness will not easily be maintained and mastered by disinterested and coöperative motives alone.

It seems probable, therefore—indeed, I think we may say it is certain—that as it took several centuries to solve the problem of scarcity, so it will take long generations to solve what we may call the problem of the management of plenty. The solution of that problem depends upon changes in human motives as great as those which distinguish a feudal peasant from the modern business man. I do not say this in the spirit of those who tell us that nothing is possible because human nature is unchangeable. Human nature is changeable in the sense that the informed idealist has in mind. The change that has come over human nature in the West since the fifteenth century has made possible the capitalist system. The modern business man is the descendant of peasants, and if his human nature is unchanged from that of his ancestors, the motives which actuate him and the energies which he shows are at least a radical rearrangement and displacement of the ancient pattern. If the descendants of the modern business man are to operate a social order in which personal initiative is to be combined with public responsibility, his motives will have to change as radically in the next centuries as they have in the past.

We are not, however, able to wait until human motives have been transformed. The pressure of events compels us to make experiments in the management of human affairs, for which in fact we lack adequate human material. We do not have the wisdom and disinterestedness to manage with any assurance the volume of credit which determines the rhythm of economic enterprise. We do not have the wisdom and disinterestedness to make the world secure against war. We do not have the wisdom and disinterestedness to plan and arrange the growth of our cities or the future of agriculture or the balance between agriculture and industry. Nevertheless we have to attempt all these things, and many more besides, for which we are unprepared and inadequate. For the world in which we live, the world which our achievement in production has created, is a world which is so complicated, so dependent upon agreements and upon foresight that a policy of laissez-faire has become utterly impossible. We have to attempt the management of it, though we know so little how to manage it. We have to learn by trial and error, since the whole truth is not revealed to us and we cannot spin it *a priori* out of our minds.

Therefore, the Ages of Discovery are not over. We are entering a new one in which the problems are as fascinating and the issues as momentous as any with which man has dealt. The voyage of Columbus opened up a new world to the European spirit, and within those widened horizons men accomplished miracles of invention and human organization. The solution of the problem of scarcity is a discovery like that of Columbus. It has opened a new world in which the human spirit can and will expand with hopes and energies and invincible ambitions for a better order of life than men have ever known before.

May 21, 1932

II. MAGICAL PROSPERITY

Revolutionary character of the depression; the fallacy that the prosperity of 1928 was normal and can be automatically restored

It is now two years since hard times reached this country, and it is no longer open to serious question that we are in the midst, not of an ordinary trade depression, but of one of the great upheavals and readjustments of modern history. A dozen governments have been brought down by it. In all the five continents it has upset the normal expectations of men by which they had been planting and making, buying and selling, borrowing and lending. In all the vast confusion which has resulted one thing at least is certain—the world, when the readjustments are made, cannot and will not be organized as it was two years ago. The post-war era of the Nineteen-Twenties is over and done.

As individuals living through this tremendous experience most of us know this with our heads and feel it in our bones. But as a people, in our corporate capacity, we have not yet begun to acknowledge the reality of the change and to formulate our national purposes for dealing with it. As a nation we continue to stand just where we stood two years ago, refusing in any responsible fashion to consider whether the increasing political insecurity of the world (which is reflected in mounting armaments), the increasing obstructions to trade, the desperate complications of debts and reparations, are a probable foundation for the restoration of prosperity. Thus far our national response has been to stand pat in all such matters, and to believe that in sixty days, ninety days, or six months, the dove would return with the olive branch, the flood would recede, and business would go on as usual.

In anticipation of this happy event the stock market has now, I believe, indulged in five separate little bull movements, and it would be cruel to recall the number of times our authorized prophets have announced that the turn was at hand. The chief effect of all this prophesying and waiting for a turn has been to divert the minds of the American people from honest consideration of their problems, and to substitute for the stern business of facing the facts the wholly frivolous business of fortune-telling.

As a result we who pride ourselves on being a people of great practical energies are today absurdly demoralized, so demoralized that we actually look upon the assembling of the next American Congress not as an opportunity for collective action, but as a nightmare. For, having failed to organize our minds and feelings in any resolute and coherent fashion, it is no wonder that our nerves are frayed, and that our vitality is low. Men can endure much when they are up and doing, but it gives most of them the jitters to sit and shiver.

Why should we be in this state? It is, I think, because we entered the depression with a false set of ideas and have never shaken them off. They have obscured our vision and paralyzed our will. We have been and are even now under the spell of an illusion, a kind of popular superstition of a type common enough in history. It is, in our case, a belief in the magical restoration of prosperity. Whereas up to the autumn of 1929 we had dreamed that depressions were abolished, we have since clung with passionate faith, worthy of some better object, to the idea that a boom and a crash and a recovery follow each other, like winter and summer, in a fixed cycle.

This belief in the automatic restoration of prosperity has made us for the time being a nation of fatalists. We have told ourselves in a thousand public statements that if winter comes spring cannot be far behind. We have looked upon our troubles, not as problems to be solved, but as so much bad weather in which the chief thing to do was to sit in front of the barometer and wait for a change in the wind. Thus we have become more interested in prophesying the future than in preparing for it, in guessing than in governing, in statistical curves than in statesmanship, in wishing than in willing.

Now, however true it may be that depression, revival and prosperity tend to follow each other in rhythmical sequence, it is a fatal misunderstanding of the theory to suppose that the economic cycle proceeds regardless of human decisions. In fact, the essence of the theory is that the prelude to any recovery is to liquidate and cancel the accumulated miscalculations of the preceding boom. Therefore the one sure way to prolong a depression is to resist it by trying to stand pat, rather than to carry through the ultimately inevitable adjustments in as cool and orderly a way as possible. Early in the depression, however, the American people, encouraged by all the front page prophets, got it into their heads that they would not have to readjust their affairs and that the magical force of the business cycle would bring everything back to normal.

The prophets encouraged them, moreover, to believe the preceding boom was normal. The automatic restoration of prosperity meant, it was therefore assumed, a resumption of everything at the levels prevailing two or three years ago. It followed that the policies in vogue then must be maintained until the present unfortunate interruption is over.

That surely is a dangerous illusion. For such prosperity as we enjoyed appeared in a time when the international economy of which we are a part was passing through epoch-making changes. Slowly but steadily since about the turn of the century, violently and spectacularly since 1914, the whole world has been drawn into one of the greatest read-justments among continents, nations and classes of which there is any record. It is a marvel, looking back upon it now, that we could ever have so complacently thought that a boom under such treacherous conditions was permanent. It is more marvelous that so many should still think so, and should still mistake for solid metal the golden bubble we managed to inflate, when for a brief moment there was a lull in the storm.

September 8, 1931

III.   THE FALSE BASIS OF POST–WAR PROSPERITY

*The mania to borrow and lend; our cheap-money
policy and the failure of the Federal Reserve Bank
to control inflation*

It is a sign of returning sanity that the Administration has at last decided to begin paying its way by economy and taxes rather than by contracting more and more debts.[1] The decision is important from the point of view of government finance. It is, perhaps, even more important as an example

---

[1] President Hoover announced on November 6, 1931, that the budget to be presented to the coming Congress had been cut about $350,000,000; and

to the nation which has yet to unlearn the bad financial habits acquired during the war and the era of inflated prosperity. For our troubles today are in very large part due to the theory that anything our hearts desired—from a diamond brooch to a battleship, from an icebox to a motor highway— could be had painlessly and promptly by borrowing money.

In the fifteen years between 1914 and 1929 the whole world, ourselves well at the front of the procession, has been piling up debts. The nations borrowed to pay for the war. They borrowed to reconstruct what the war had destroyed. Then they borrowed in order to finance prosperity. Then they borrowed in order to finance the depression. The borrowing mania ended for Germany last June, for Britain last September. For us it should at least begin to end now. President Butler does not overstate the matter when he says that the towering structure of public and private debt is "the result of a habit and a policy which, unless checked, may readily bring the people of the United States face to face with the same grave financial crises as have just now confronted the peoples of Germany and of Great Britain."

It is hard to end the debt habit. The ease with which governments borrowed money to carry on the war convinced officeholders and voters that anything could be done by the simple process of floating a bond issue. The ease with which corporations and individuals borrowed money in the five years preceding the crash has almost obliterated public knowledge of the fact that what is borrowed has to be paid for by somebody. We are still living in a kind of amiable stupor induced by the intoxicating effects of the war and the post-war inflation.

---

that the appropriations already made for the current year would be cut about $280,000,000. The government's deficit at this time was already well over $600,000,000. Press dispatches reported that the President was studying the sales tax as a means of increasing the Federal revenues.

It is so long a time since governments, states, cities, and individuals ceased paying for what they bought when they bought it, that the notion has got itself implanted that there is an infinite reservoir of credit which can be drawn upon. Hence the innumerable projects for covering deficits, for raising prices, for creating work, for stimulating purchases, based almost invariably on the theory that the money somehow can be manufactured out of hand and then borrowed.

It is now fairly clear that the inevitable demoralization of war finance was greatly aggravated by the reckless character of post-war finance. The mania to borrow was brought on by the mania to lend. From 1924 to 1929, the era of the blessed boom, the United States, having an excessive supply of gold, expanded bank credits and embarked on a cheap money policy. The result was that banks had more money than they knew how to invest, and it was during this period that they sent agents all over the world begging governments and corporations to borrow. It was then that loans were poured into Latin-America, into Germany, into Central Europe, into American cities, counties, and states, into mergers and new corporate issues and into instalment buying. It was then that the high pressure salesman flourished in the land with his thousand tempting proposals for letting people possess things by paying only about five dollars cash.

It is clear, too, that the ultimate responsibility for letting this mania to lend get out of hand lies in Washington. For the record shows that it was the Federal Reserve Board in Washington which stood in the way of the effort of the banks to reverse the cheap money policy, stop the inflationary process, and keep credit within bounds. From July, 1928, to August 9, 1929, the board in Washington refused to approve any requests by the Reserve Banks to raise their discount rates. It even ignored the recommendations made by its Advisory Council on May 21, 1929, that the rates be increased. During the last wild year of utterly demoralizing speculation and debt creation the Board in Washington stood firmly against use of the accepted method of controlling such evils.

Its objection was that practical measures to control speculation would cause legitimate business to contract. Perhaps this was just sheer foolishness. But let us remember that in July, 1928, when the Board took this position, the Republicans were about to notify Mr. Hoover of his nomination, and that Mr. Hoover was running on a platform of "prosperity." Let us remember that the period when the Board was forbidding the Reserve Banks to stop the inflation was the period of the Presidential election, the inauguration, and the beginning of Mr. Hoover's term. This may be mere coincidence, but the Federal Reserve Board is a political body appointed by the Administration.

In any event, to the Board which was in office during 1928 and 1929, whatever its motives, neither the country nor the world at large has any reason to be thankful.

November 18, 1931

IV. THE PREVAILING CONFUSION: INFLATION OR DEFLATION?

The agony of deflation; why the prospect of its continuance is unnerving; the duty of the government to pursue a resolute policy

Robert Louis Stevenson once said that "the obscurest epoch is today," and I imagine that most of us in the face of our perplexities would say amen to that. It is the obscurity of events, rather than the actual painfulness of them, which is demoralizing us. For the human animal can endure suffering far better than he can endure uncertainty; he will face a known danger with a stout heart, but his courage is not equal to prolonged aimless wandering in the unexplored darkness.

The anxiety which has gripped the American spirit is not due primarily to the actual losses which almost every one has suffered. Apart from those who are unemployed and destitute—a large number absolutely but a small number relative to the whole population—the problem is not as yet one of actual privation or even of a serious reduction in the standard of life. The problem is one of fear of what is to come: the fear of the wage-earner that his wages will be cut or even that he will lose his job entirely, the fear of the employer that he will not be able to meet his obligations, the fear of men that they will not be able to pay their taxes, or the interest and instalments on mortgages, the fear that savings will be lost, and so on and so forth. These individual fears spread like an hysteria in a crowd which is trapped in an inclosure and cannot find the exits, and the hysteria itself accelerates the very evils which men fear.

In such a time it is the duty of those to whom the people look for guidance, the financial and political leaders of the nation, to dispel the obscurity by making clear what are the choices open to the people. They hesitate to do this, of course, because they themselves are so preoccupied with the relief of specific situations resulting from the general crisis and also because they themselves are perplexed. None the less, a beginning must be made so that public discussion may at least free itself of mere futile exhausting palpitation and set itself to deal with the real alternatives which confront us.

Reduced to its simplest terms, what has happened is that wholesale prices have fallen about 30 per cent since the beginning of the depression, the cost of living has fallen about 15 per cent, the earnings of labor have fallen in the mass about

40 per cent, and the cost of labor to the employer has fallen about 10 per cent. These figures, which are rough but will do for the purpose of the argument, enable us to state the problem. The seller of goods at wholesale gets seventy cents for a product which in 1929 brought him a dollar. He pays for the labor of making the product ninety cents. He, therefore, does not see how he can pay his rent, which may still be a dollar; his taxes, which are at least a dollar; his interest charges, which are still a dollar, and go on paying ninety cents to labor. So he thinks about cutting wages. There he runs into the wage-earner, who, even if he is getting the same rate of wages, is getting a much smaller amount of wages, and has perhaps only sixty cents to live on where in 1929 he had a dollar. Since it still costs this wage-earner eighty-five cents today to buy what cost a dollar two years ago, he has to cut down his purchases or default on his mortgage or his installment payments or his rent.

Now the problem facing us is this: if wholesale prices are to remain what they are, other incomes cannot remain what they are. They will have to adjust themselves to the lower level. The word adjustment is an easy word to use but it really represents an agonizing process. It means a drastic reduction of wages and salaries, it means also an interminable series of foreclosures, bankruptcies and defaults. Let us not deceive ourselves. The effort to bring the whole economic system into balance at the present price level cannot be carried through automatically. It involves struggle step by step on the way down to it, and a multitude of personal tragedies, not to speak of social disorders, accompanying every phase of the long-drawn-out process. For our whole capital structure, our whole wage level, our whole standard of life, is posited upon a much higher price level. Theoretically, we should all be just as well off if *everything* were reduced to the lower level now prevailing. But practically we cannot get everything down to this lower level without infuriating labor and defaulting upon a considerable portion of private and public debt.

The demoralization which now prevails is due to the growing realization among the people that we are for the present committed to this long, dangerous, and painful process of deflation. They do not acquiesce in it. On the contrary, they resist it, and in their resistance they are encouraged by the teachings of the Administration and of most of the popular economists who have convinced them that a recovery of business means a return to the levels of 1928–1929. These teachings are meaningless, in fact they are the cruelest kind of deception, unless it is the purpose of government and finance deliberately to raise prices again. This, since it involves inflation and all the enormous dangers of that policy, responsible men shrink from doing.

Thus the American people are utterly confused. They are taught to believe in a future which involves inflation, and they are actually living through one of the great deflations of modern times. Is it any wonder they are demoralized? Is it any wonder they have lost confidence? Is it any wonder their hopes have been dashed so often that they are losing hope? We say one thing and we do the other, and, of course, nothing happens as we expect it to happen.

The time has come to make up our minds as to which way we intend to go. We cannot go both ways at once. We cannot go one way and pretend to go the other. Either we must deflate and pay all the costs of that policy and face all its dangers, or we must inflate and pay all the costs and face all the dangers of that. Both policies are costly and dangerous: but either one resolutely, intelligently, deliberately pursued is better than stumbling around in the dark.

October 2, 1931

V. THREE PHASES OF DEPRESSION: THE ATTEMPT TO STOP FALLING PRICES

The early belief in a quick return to old levels; the later belief in a moderate readjustment; the mobilization of public credit to salvage the capital structure

In days like these ideas lag behind events so that by the time the leaders of thought and the mass of public opinion have come around to a policy, it is often found that the policy is no longer adequate. The remedies have been evolved more slowly than the situation has developed. As a consequence the remedies have been not only insufficient at the time when they were applied, but at many crucial points they have by their insufficiency aggravated the problem.

It may be that at the present stage of human knowledge we are not equipped to understand a crisis which is so great and so novel, and that this is the explanation of the failure of our political, financial and industrial leaders to justify themselves. Is there anyone who foresaw the whole crisis and predicted its course? I do not know of anyone. I know that there is a roll of honor on which there are a very few names of men who saw a little of the future and spoke out bravely. But nowhere in the whole world has there been a prophet of whom it can be said that his teachings were comprehensive and prompt and sufficient. It has been said that this is a crisis of over-abundance. It is also a crisis of the human understanding, and our deepest failures have not been failures arising from malevolence but from miscalculation.

Our need is to determine where we are and where we can go, and then on this fog-bound sea to steer not by the winds and not by the whims of the passengers but by the compass.

To attempt this we must take to heart the recent admonitions of Mr. Justice Brandeis that "if we would guide by the light of reason, we must let our minds be bold."

It is easiest to see where we are by looking back over the way we have come. We have come, it seems to me, through two phases and are now in a third.

The First Phase was dominated by the ideas of the preceding boom. Its fundamental assumptions were that the economic structure erected in the twenties was normal and sound. It was held that the capital charges, the public and private debts, the volume and distribution of profits, the level of retail prices, rents, salaries and wages, the rate of public expenditures and taxation, were in a proper equilibrium. It was believed that the fall in world prices which had upset this equilibrium was not only temporary but self-correcting. This phase, which lasted through most of 1930, was an era of standing pat and waiting for prosperity which was just around the corner. The dominant ideas were those of the New Era in economics and the obituary of that era was written by Mr. Edward Angly in that devastating classic entitled "Oh Yeah!"

The principal error in the thought of this period was the failure to realize that world forces had been set in motion which were causing a drastic deflation in gold prices. It was this deflation of prices that threw the whole system out of balance, made business unprofitable and produced the immense unemployment.

The Second Phase began somewhere around the spring of 1931. The dominant idea then was that a reasonable fall in gold prices had become inevitable and that a readjustment to this lower level was equally inevitable. It was believed that if retail prices, salaries, wages, and costs could be deflated moderately, and that if at the same time international trade could be revived by political settlements, a restoration of confidence, and resumption of lending, prices would rise enough to make the main body of debts and fixed charges liquid again. The objective in this period was to stabilize somewhere below the 1929 level of prices but not so far below as to make the capital structure of 1929 insolvent.

This was the period, then, of the Hoover moratorium, of the standstill agreements, of moderate wage cuts, of economies in operating costs, and of urgent pleas to governments and parliaments to settle debts and reparations, reduce tariffs, limit armaments and make peace. It was accompanied by a willingness to let the more obviously insolvent concerns on the fringes of things liquidate themselves through bankruptcy.

This period ended in September, when Britain and many other countries fell away from the international gold standard. The reasons for the failure of the plans on which the hopes of that period were based are intricate and by no means clear. The fact is that the governments and the peoples rejected these plans and nothing came of them. In the longer view it may be the verdict of history that the reason why this view of the crisis failed is that it was essentially an attempt to restore a pre-war world of free exchange in a time when capitalism had become rigid and inflexible by the development of immense fixed charges, fixed price controls, fixed tariffs and fixed wage rates.

It is plain enough that so rigid a system can be solvent again only if prices would rise not only to the level of 1929 but indeed above it. For only rising prices could make the load of fixed charges tolerable by reducing their real burden. But instead of rising, prices fell still more. By the autumn the spiral of the deflation of gold prices had become vicious.

We entered the Third Phase some time about October. By that time the fall of prices had become so great that no mere readjustment by reducing costs and by clearing the way through separate bankruptcies was adequate. Too great a volume of indebtedness then rested upon assets whose earning power was insufficient. At this point in the crisis public credit was mobilized to save the existing capital structure.

It was soon realized, however, that these emergency measures could not of themselves cure the situation. They could only postpone the issue in the hope that in the interval prices would rise. They have been followed, therefore, by a policy of deliberate action on the part of the Federal Reserve System which is designed to cause a rise in prices.

The central question of the moment is whether the policy will succeed. We are in the midst of an effort to make good the great mass of all debts, public and private, by forcing an expansion of bank-money, a rise in prices and a reduction in the value of gold. What those who are in positions of responsibility need to consider is whether in adopting this policy they are implementing it adequately. They are making money cheap. They are filling up the reservoirs of credit till they overflow. Will this be enough, or is it necessary at the same time to stimulate the demand for credit and put the credit to work by a large program of capital investment on the part of public and private agencies?

There were cogent reasons some months back why such a program could not be undertaken, the chief reason being that the banking system was then too inelastic and the Federal budget was then too hopelessly unbalanced. But the very reforms which have made it feasible for the Federal Reserve System to embark on an expansion of credit have robbed these two objections of their principal force. The time has, therefore, come to reconsider frankly, without prejudice, without obstinate pride of previous opinions, whether the logic of the present policy of credit expansion does not call for a program of public and private works.

It is by no means certain that a cheap money policy plus a works program can raise gold prices to a level at which indebtedness can again be thawed out. But if these two measures cannot do it, then, barring miracles which we have no reason to expect, the structure of indebtedness will have to be scaled down in any one of the many ways in which unmanageable debts have so frequently in the past been scaled down. There will be in one form or another a modern version of the Biblical Year of Jubilee.

April 29, 1932

VI. THE WAY FORWARD

The crisis grows worse; three great reasons—economic warfare, tension over war debts and reparations, and internal conflict in France, Germany, and America; the need for unified effort

That the deflationary movement has not yet been stopped is attested by the fact that during the month of March the value of all shares on the New York Stock Exchange declined another eleven per cent and wholesale prices have continued to decline. This is a negation of the policy which Congress, the Administration, and the banks adopted at the beginning of the year, when they established the Reconstruction Finance Corporation, passed the Glass-Steagall bill, and declared for a balanced budget.[1] Our declared policy is to stop the deflation of credit and thus to arrest the fall in prices

---

[1] In January, 1932, on the initiative of the Hoover Administration, Congress passed a bill to establish the Reconstruction Finance Corporation with available funds of $2,000,000,000. This, the Administration's foremost proposal for economic relief, was intended to furnish credit to save hard-pressed banks, railroads, and other business organizations. By midsummer of 1932 it had loaned more than a billion dollars, the largest part of which

and lay the foundation for a rise in prices. We are compelled to ask ourselves why this policy is not more effective.

It is fairly evident that although the Federal Reserve System now possesses the legal and technical means to do its part in executing this policy, the necessary confidence is lacking to carry it out boldly. A policy of credit expansion depends not merely upon the will of the central bankers to create credit, but also upon the willingness of commercial bankers and business men to use it. The question, therefore, arises as to what are the controlling causes of this lack of confidence.

They are to be found in part, we may suppose, in an indecision within the Federal Reserve System due to divided counsels. A policy of deliberate credit expansion is not orthodox banking, and if current reports are reliable there is within the Federal Reserve System itself important opposition by reputable but ultra-conservative individuals. This hesitation is reinforced, we may assume, by the fact that although the policy of expansion in the United States is ardently desired by most of the outer world, the Bank of France is believed to be controlled by old and highly orthodox gentlemen who are greatly alarmed at the idea. Their power to withdraw gold is still sufficiently great to make their opposition embarrassing.

Thus it may be said that the policy is stalled by the failure as yet to arrive at unanimity in the central banking circles of France and America.

But this position, this resistance by the very orthodox, is not merely theoretical, is not merely devotion to ancient principle, and is not selfish calculation. It is due essentially

---

had gone to small banks throughout the country. The Glass-Steagall Bill, signed late in February, was designed to broaden the acceptability of commercial paper for rediscount by the Federal Reserve Banks, and to make about $750,000,000 of the gold supply of the Federal Reserve System, previously used to support the currency, available for other purposes.

to fear arising out of wider and deeper causes. The policy of credit expansion has for its aim the resumption of production and purchasing. Everywhere in the world governments are pursuing policies which destroy trade, deflate prices, and make the payment of debts difficult. Not much hope can be placed in a policy of expanding credit while the nations are engaged in the suicidal efforts to strangle the trade which would justify the use of credit.

On the part of the debtor nations the difficulty of meeting their old obligations at current prices has forced them into a drastic curtailment of their purchases abroad. An extreme illustration of the plight of the debtor countries is provided by Bulgaria: in 1931 the weight of her exports was nearly doubled over 1929 but their value in gold was actually less. The only way for the debtors to keep relatively solvent is to cut down their purchases. On the part of the creditor nations, like the United States and France, the doctrine that the home market should be monopolized has produced an unwillingness to buy. It has, of course, been followed by an inability to sell. With every nation, debtor and creditor alike, trying to cut down imports the exports of all nations have been cut down too. For, though it is hard for the average voter to understand it, each nation's imports are the exports of other nations. If all nations simultaneously attack foreign imports they are bound collectively to bring world trade to a virtual standstill.

There is, in short, an economic war raging in the world and during a war men have little confidence for enterprise. What each man aims at is security and liquidity for himself, which means simply that he will not buy or lend if he can avoid it, and prefers to indulge in some one of the many forms of hoarding.

The economic war is accentuated by the political tension arising out of the uncertainty as to what Europe will do about reparations and the United States about the war debts. For while it is perfectly possible for the governments and voters to say that they will not compromise and settle, the price of this irreconcilability is the destruction of confidence.

Finally, the tension is increased by the fact that in the three nations which occupy a central place in the situation today—in France, Germany, and the United States—the people are deeply and bitterly divided by sectional and class conflicts which paralyze them in trying to make national decisions. The most dangerous division is, of course, in Germany, where, until the Prussian elections at the end of the month have been decided, the very existence of the Republic is in doubt. The French position is not remotely of the same order. Nevertheless, the impending elections are being fought with increasing bitterness and, therefore, cause great uncertainty as to the future. Finally, there is the situation in Congress, which undoubtedly reveals the pent-up sentiment of the country, and there it has been shown since the collapse of Mr. Garner's leadership that in the absence of a national program which inspires hope for the future there is a strong disposition to resort to vindictive and punitive measures.

Only the boldest and most resourceful leadership all along the line can open a way out of this destructive deadlock. On the main objective there is general agreement: there must be an expansion of credit based upon a restoration of confidence, which in its turn must rest upon the prospect of an economic and political truce. To say that is easy. To achieve it is hard. For in order to achieve it bold and generous actions have to be taken simultaneously and in coördination on several fronts: by the bankers in the realm of credit, by business men in the realm of enterprise, by Congress in the realm of commercial and fiscal policy, by the State Department in the realm of political security, and by the President as the field marshal of the whole campaign. The problem has to be seen as a whole. The task is to justify credit and to provide it, and this cannot be done by sitting around and waiting for someone else to move. All the responsible agencies need to move together if their separate actions are to take effect.

A unified effort of this sort is possible only among a people who have taken themselves in hand, have written off the losses of the past, and have seen that their common concern in so great a crisis transcends all their separate interests. In the name of patriotism much evil has been done in this world. Yet there come periods in the history of peoples when they must resort to their common loyalties and there remember that beneath all their differences is a common life. This is such a period. This is a time when the nation is at war not with an enemy outside but with encroaching disorder and chaos, and it may well be asked of every man that he keep order in his own spirit, and shut the door in no other man's face.

April 8, 1932

VII. THE LONG WAR

The rôle of war debts and reparations in the crisis; war wreckage and the new generation

Not long before the war, when to a young man all things seemed so simple and so progressive, I was permitted to join a seminar conducted by Graham Wallas, one of the truly great teachers of our time. The subject of our study was the change wrought in human life since mechanical inventions had compelled men to work and think and feel in an environment vaster and more complicated than that of any previous civilization. Among the things Mr. Wallas kept pushing us to consider were the effects of a great war under modern conditions. I can well remember feeling that this part of the course was academic and uninteresting, and when Mr. Wallas read us the draft of a chapter which appeared later in his book "The Great Society," I was astounded and entirely incredulous at hearing him say that if a European war broke out— "the war perhaps between the Triple Alliance and the Triple Entente, which so many journalists and politicians in England and Germany contemplate with criminal levity . . . it may, after the first battles, smoulder on for thirty years." I am no longer so incredulous on this the eighteenth Christmas when it must be confessed of the nations that "the way of peace they know not; and there is no judgment in their goings: they have made them crooked paths."

For here once again we have a report, this time from a committee at Basle,[1] telling us in language muffled by the world's fears and prejudices, how a little step may be taken to bring a little nearer its end the long drawn-out war. Now that the experts have spoken, the politicians will confer once more, seeking some new adjustment towards a still distant peace. It will be the fourth great occasion when the belligerent powers have met in a peace conference. They met in Paris in 1919 and wrote the Treaty of Versailles. They met in Paris in 1924 and wrote the Dawes Plan. They met in Paris in 1929 and wrote the Young Plan. They will

[1] The Bank for International Settlements called together an advisory board of experts at Basle on December 7, 1931, to investigate Germany's capacity to pay reparations under the Young Plan. German representatives protested that the burden, under existing conditions of depression, was preposterous. On December 17–18 the advisory board issued statements showing that the payment of the scheduled reparations in 1932 was absolutely impossible, and advocating formal acknowledgment of the fact. On December 23, a report to this effect, calling upon the nations to which reparations were due to make a drastic revision of the Young Plan, was issued.

meet somewhere or other next month and write another plan. The greatest difference between what they are about to do and what they have done in the past is that on each of the other occasions they thought the settlement was final, whereas this time they are more humble and expect only to devise another armistice.

I do not say this in order to cast disparagement upon the work of the Basle Committee. The full text of its report is not available as this is written, and when it is available, it will be necessary to study it carefully before its full import can be understood. But as we prepare to read it, I think it useful to remember that it is nearly eighteen years since the war began, and that what we are studying is a proposal to bring the end of the war a little nearer.

That, so it seems to me, puts the matter in its true perspective. The financial details, the statistics, the juridical theses, the economic analyses, the proposals and counter-proposals, which the report will engender are all the outward manifestations of the central fact, that here it is Christmas of 1931 with the war of 1914 unfinished.

All true wisdom on the fantastic entanglement of reparations and debts consists in remembering the simple fact that there will not be peace in the world until we decide to end the war. I know there are solemn documents in existence, duly signed and delivered, which say that this thing must go on for the rest of this century, that the war of 1914 must not until 1987 be allowed to pass into history. I do not believe these documents. I do not believe mankind will be insane enough to keep alive the memory of the war for two more generations. It may suit us today to swear that we shall never forgive and forget till the last red cent is paid, but these declarations for a future we shall not live to see are braggarts' boasts, mere wind and air and emptiness.

The great war will have to be ended in the generation

that made it. That is the history of such things. For when the war generation is gone, the profit to be reaped by waving the bloody shirt stops. The new young people will have other hopes and other plans and they cannot be bothered with the cantankerous inheritance of their fathers. It was thus after the Civil War. The ghost of Thaddeus Stevens walked until the nation was sick of him. Then he vanished. He walks again today, incarnate in Hiram Johnson. In time, when the nation is through with its rancors and has turned its face toward the business of living well, all that will be left of these debts and reparations, of these declarations and recriminations, will be a few shabby pages of printed matter about which some professor will write a book explaining how completely some Americans of the 1920's and 1930's forgot the lessons of the 1860's and 1870's.

Let us hope he will not overlook the fact that in the carnival of unreason there were, nevertheless, multitudes who were prepared to pay the price needed to have on earth peace, good will toward men.

December 25, 1932

VIII. FALSE GODS: NATIONAL MORALE IN THE DEPRESSION

Demoralization the principal peril; the moral apathy of American leaders

From what source come these unmanly fears that prevail among us? These dark forebodings? This despairing impotence? What is it that has shaken the nerves of so many? It is the doubt whether there exists among the people that trust in each other which is the first condition of intelligent leadership. That is the root of the matter. The particular projects which we debate so angrily are not so important. The fate of the nation does not hang upon any of them. But upon the power of the people to remain united for purposes which they respect, upon their capacity to have faith in themselves and in their objectives, much depends. It is not the facts of the crisis which we have to fear. They can be endured and dealt with. It is demoralization alone that is dangerous.

A demoralized people is one in which the individual has become isolated and is the prey of his own suspicions. He trusts nobody and nothing, not even himself. He believes nothing, except the worst of everybody and everything. He sees only confusion in himself and conspiracies in other men. That is panic. That is disintegration. That is what comes when in some sudden emergency of their lives men find themselves unsupported by clear convictions that transcend their immediate and personal desires.

The last ten years have been a time of exceptionally drastic change in the underlying convictions of Western men. For reasons which it is not easy to state briefly or even clearly to discern, it seems as if in this decade the change in life brought about by science and machinery and the modern city, by democracy and by popular education, had struck with full impact and with cumulative force against the traditional morality, the social conventions and the ideals of the mass of men.

That a period of profound spiritual bewilderment had to ensue was inevitable. But this bewilderment has been greatly aggravated in the United States by what I believe may truthfully be called the moral apathy of those in high places. At the beginning of the decade the national government was attacked by brutal and conspicuous corruption. No clear word about it was spoken by those in high places. On the contrary, they sat silent, hoping that the people would forget, calculating that the evil would be overlooked. Is it surprising that public spirit weakened when it was demonstrated from the highest places that the corruption of government was not something that the citizen ought to care deeply about?

During this decade the country has been making the experiment of outlawing an ancient and general human appetite. Those in high places have known quite well how badly the experiment was working, what stupendous lawlessness and corruption the prohibition law was producing. Yet in all this time no candid word, no straightforward utterance, no honest inquiry about this matter has come from any high place. The problem has been muffled in hypocrisy, in miserable ambiguities, and in equivocation, to a point where any open, public debate of the matter has become impossible.

During this same decade those in high places have steadfastly preached to the people that it was their destiny to have two-car garages and eight-tube radio sets. That was the ideal they held out before the people, to be acquisitive, to seek feverishly to become richer and richer, to prostrate themselves before the Golden Calf. To read today the rhapsodies which issued from the highest places during the last decade is to find the main reason why now, when the nation must call upon all its resources in integrity and magnanimity and public spirit, a clear devotion to the national interest is not surely available.

For if you teach a people for ten years that the character of its government is not greatly important, that political success is for those who equivocate and evade, and if you tell them that acquisitiveness is the ideal, that things are what matter, that Mammon is God, then you must not be astonished at the confusion in Washington, or the nonchalance of James J. Walker, or the vermin who in a hundred different ways exploited the tragedy of the Lindbergh baby.[1] You cannot set up false gods to confuse the people and not pay the penalty.

Those in high places are more than the administrators of government bureaus. They are more than the writers of laws. They are the custodians of a nation's ideals, of the beliefs it cherishes, of its permanent hopes, of the faith which makes a nation out of a mere aggregation of individuals. They are unfaithful to that trust when by word and example they promote a spirit that is complacent, evasive, and acquisitive.

It is not only against the material consequences of this decade of drift and hallucination, but against the essence of its spirit that the best and bravest among us are today in revolt. They are looking for new leaders, for men who are truthful and resolute and eloquent in the conviction that the American destiny is to be free and magnanimous, rather than complacent and acquisitive; they are looking for leaders who will talk to the people not about two-car garages and a bonus, but about their duty, and about the sacrifices they must make, and about the discipline they must impose upon themselves, and about their responsibility to the world and to posterity, about all those things which make a people self-respecting, serene, and confident. May they not look in vain.

May 20, 1932

[1] Colonel Charles A. Lindbergh's twenty-month-old son was kidnapped from his home near Hopewell, N. J., on the night of March 1, 1932.

· II ·

SPECIAL PROBLEMS OF THE DEPRESSION

I. HANKERING FOR SUPERMEN

Folly of the demand for abnormal political methods;
simple statesmanship of a high order the only need

IT is indeed a sign of the times that a resolution should be
submitted to the American Legion and already adopted, declaring that

> the principal causes of the present situation are in general
> such that they cannot be promptly and efficiently met by
> existing political methods.

For while it is not made very clear just what the authors of
this resolution would like to see done, their general feeling
is plain enough. They are impressed with the "unrest, indecision and dissatisfaction . . . prevalent among the people,"
and they would like to see a strong central agency, like a
revivified Council of National Defense, take the situation
in hand. They do not expressly say, but it is implied, that
they would like the President and the Council to assume war
powers and somehow to dictate national action to overcome the depression.[1]

The proposal is frankly a counsel of despair. Quite evi-

---

[1] The American Legion held its national convention in Detroit on September 21–23, 1931, and was addressed by President Hoover. It passed
resolutions of which a part are here quoted.

dently it is a reflection of popular resentment against the deadlock between Congress and the Executive, and the political demoralization which has ensued. Proposals of a similar kind have been put forth in almost every country in the world during the last decade, but particularly during the last two years, and as normal political methods were found inadequate, have been adopted. In Europe south of the Alps and east of the Polish frontier dictatorship is the prevailing method of government. Germany has a semi-dictatorship in which legislation is carried on by decree. England has had to resort to a kind of coalition government and to deal with its budget by Orders in Council. In France the Laval ministry has hastened the adjournment of the Chambers so as to be free of parliamentary pressure. In the United States Mr. Hoover, with the approval of a large part of the nation, is deferring to the last minute allowed by the Constitution the meeting of the Congress elected in November, 1930. The resolution adopted by the Legion comports with a general tendency to supersede the normal methods of popular government.

But although there are these striking analogies, they are, I think, misleading examples for us. If the authors of the resolution will study the circumstances which have caused other countries to resort to a suspension of normal popular government, they will find in each case, I think, that the "emergency" which had to be dealt with was not general and complex, as ours is, but specific and immediate. Some particular thing had to be done, such as balancing the budget, which could not wait for legislative debate. That certainly is the history of the Bruening government in Germany and of the National government in England.

In our case circumstances are quite different. The Hoover Administration has not, at least as far as anyone knows, any specific program or any specific objective on hand which it requires the exercise of war powers to put into effect. Suppose Mr. Hoover did declare a national emergency and asked Congress to vote extraordinary powers to himself and the Council of National Defense? What would be done with these powers? In a war the objectives are concrete and simple. You have to mobilize men and munitions at a point where you can force the enemy to sue for peace. The whole nation is agreed on the objective, and minorities are silenced.

In the emergency which confronts us there are no simple objectives. The depression, we know, is a world-wide dislocation of productive energies and a sudden profound maladjustment of the relations between costs and prices, debts and the capacity to pay debts. This means that we are in the midst of tremendous changes in the relative income and earnings of all classes, occupations, geographical sections, and continental masses in the world. We do not have, as in war time, a common aim. We have, on the contrary, to face radical issues, involving divergent vital interests.

It is an alluring notion to picture a conclave of great executives meeting at Washington to formulate a "constructive" plan to re-create prosperity. One can imagine the committees and the conferences and the publicity. But if the assembled supermen were to do more than assemble and confer, they would at a minimum have to produce definite recommendations affecting wages, prices, tariffs, taxes, the budget, reparations and debts, the working of the gold standard, armaments, our political relations with the outer world. Is it conceivable that Congress and the voters would abdicate their power over these matters in favor of the President and a committee, or that men could be found who were wise enough to do the job and rash enough to try it?

It is no good hankering for supermen. The supermen have not yet been born. We might do very well with our "existing political methods" if we made up our minds to use them. All we need for the present is that our political leaders should fix their attention on this emergency rather than on the next election, that they should propose definite measures which they judge to be right, rather than to wait to see what seems expedient.

There is no need to be afraid of debate if those in authority will lead and clarify it. There is no need to be afraid of Congress if the Executive will give sober and informed opinion inside and outside of Congress definite measures around which to rally.

September 25, 1931

II. WAGE–MAINTENANCE AND THE HOOVER ADMINISTRATION

Hoover's empty talk of preventing wage-cuts; wages to be kept static only if prices are re-inflated; if we inflate, it should be by plan

One of the curious illusions which the Administration has fostered for a long time now is that until Monday afternoon it had managed to maintain wages.[1] If you listen, for example, to the Secretary of Labor, Mr. Doak, you would suppose that until the steel companies cut wages 10 per cent their

[1] Repeatedly during 1930 and 1931 President Hoover issued statements declaring that the Administration was opposed to wage-cuts. In many of these statements he implied that such cuts were being successfully prevented. The fact was that early in the depression part-time virtually cut wages in many industries, and that later direct wage-cuts became general. On September 22, 1931, it was announced that the United States Steel Corporation, the Bethlehem Steel Corporation, and the General Motors Company had all cut wages; and in the next few days other large corporations also announced reductions—usually of ten per cent.

employees had been receiving the wages they received before the depression. Nothing could be further from the truth.
He has only to look at the figures published by his colleague,
the Secretary of Commerce, Mr. Lamont, to see that since
the peak of June, 1929, the payrolls of the steel industry had
already been reduced about 40 per cent. The *rate* per hour
or day had been the same, but the number of hours or days
on which the men have been employed and could earn the
rate had already been cut tremendously. Now a man cannot live on a *rate of pay*. He lives on the actual money he
receives, and the steel workers have been receiving about
40 per cent less money.

The actual reduction of workers' earnings varies from one
industry to another, and even from one plant to another, but
with practically no exception workers' earnings in the mass
have been reduced throughout American industry. It is
juggling with words to talk as if an elected providence in
Washington had been able to maintain the purchasing power
of American labor unimpaired, and it is astonishing that
labor leaders should talk as if they believed it. The purchasing power of American labor, including labor protected by
the strongest kind of union contracts, has been seriously reduced in the last two years. The proof lies not in the theoretical wage rate but in the actual content of the pay envelope.

To what end is this illusion persisted in? I do not know.
But it is easy enough to see how it started. It started after
the stock market crash of November, 1929, when almost
everybody from the President down believed that there was
not going to be a real depression and that prices and business
activity were going to return within sixty or ninety days to
the level of the boom. On that assumption there was good
sense in saying that since nothing else was going to be
deflated, employers ought to bind themselves not to deflate
wages. The assumption was wrong. The notion that there

would be a quick recovery to the 1929 level was wrong. The notion that business would soon be proceeding as usual was wrong. Production fell off and with it the earnings of labor. But the Administration in Washington and the spokesmen of the trade-unions have gone right on talking as if they had maintained the purchasing power of labor.

What they have actually succeeded in doing is to divert attention from the real problem and to establish a passionate interest in an unreal problem. For the most likely effect of this concentrated interest in wage *rates,* if it has any effect, will be to provoke costly and useless strikes. The real interest of a wage-earner today is in the amount of money he has at the end of the week. That is already drastically reduced, and it cannot be restored without a restoration of business activity. The question is whether it has to be reduced still further, and that question can be answered only by knowing in the case of each particular employer whether with present costs and present prices and present demand for his goods he can or cannot keep his plant running on the existing schedule. If he has to lay off more men, or cut the working hours of the men, the maintenance of the rate of wages keeps up the cost of labor in his product but does not help the workers. Their income is cut when they have less work to do.

The real problem is whether American industry can revive at a lower price level while the costs of production remain at the boom level. If the Administration must regard itself, not merely as a government, but as the ultimate source of industrial, economic, and financial policy, that is the problem it ought to be talking and thinking about. For two years it has held the ground that the boom level was normal. It has resorted to every device within its powers, and to some that strain its powers, to maintain that level. The insistence on wage rates is one phase of it. The attempt to push up agricultural prices is another phase of it. The pleas from Washington against short selling and for various kinds of pegging of prices are other phases of it. The tariff, in its present guise, is still another. What does all this mean? It means that the Administration has been staking its hopes on a rise in prices. For nothing but a great recovery of prices will again make business profitable at the 1929 level.

It follows that the Administration's attitude in this depression makes sense only if it proposes to produce an inflation. That, I take it, is its secret and unavowed hope. For only by an inflation of prices can the real overhead charges of industry be reduced without tampering with the rate of wages and the nominal return on preferred stocks, bonds and bank credits. That the mind of Washington is tempted by this remedy is suggested by the undercurrent of pleasure with which it is greeting the beginning of inflation in Great Britain.

That inflation has great possibilities of danger and that it works cruel injustices is certain. Nevertheless, it may be assumed that the demand for it will grow tremendously strong from now on. For the device has instant and overwhelming appeal to all producers and to all debtors, and they are the great majority. Inflation is least painful to those who can protest the most. The labor leaders who will resist to the bitter end a 10 per cent reduction in the rate of wages would be the first to acclaim a 10 per cent rise in prices. Thus the social momentum behind the inflationary method may very well be irresistible. For the attempt to adjust at a deflated level calls for a long agony of wage cutting and bankruptcies, and defaults and foreclosures which a modern democracy may not willingly go through.

Now if inflation is to be the policy of the government, and no other solution is consistent with its conduct, then the country ought not to be allowed to drift or be pushed into it unprepared. It is always a dangerous policy, and only the most resolute control can keep it from engendering worse evils than those it is designed to cure.

There are various kinds of inflation, and much depends on which is chosen and how it is done. If inflation is the remedy to which we are to turn, then it is better to inflate deliberately, and according to a definite plan, and with the government's finances in order and its budget balanced, than to cherish the secret hope that inflation will somehow happen but do nothing to prepare for it.

September 24, 1931

III. INDUSTRIAL PLANNING: MR. GERARD SWOPE'S PROPOSAL

The stabilization of industry to regularize production and employment; industrial planning and government price-fixing; the desirability of experimenting with one large industry

On Wednesday evening the president of the General Electric Company, Mr. Gerard Swope,[1] made public a plan designed to prevent unemployment in the electrical manufacturing industry, and, when it cannot be prevented, to insure the workers against the consequences. The plan is definite enough, and it already has enough support from the large and the small companies to be called a concrete proposal for action. Steps could be taken immediately to give it a trial if the electrical manufacturers were free to proceed

[1] Mr. Gerard Swope has been president of the General Electric Company since 1922. On September 16, 1931, in a speech before the National Electrical Manufacturers' Association, he offered an elaborate plan for the stabilization of industry.

with a demonstration. But they are not free to do so under existing laws, and those laws will not be amended until Congress and the voters are satisfied as to what Mr. Owen D. Young called "the grave questions both of public and of business policy lying at its very foundations."

For Mr. Swope's proposals bring us face to face with the fact that under our existing laws, and perhaps even under the Constitution as it now stands, it is not possible for an industry composed of many companies to stabilize production, regularize employment and provide effective insurance for its employees. Our laws commit us and condemn us to an uncoördinated, unplanned, disorderly individualism which inevitably produces alternating periods of boom and depression. Any serious attempt by a whole industry to substitute coöperative planning involves the risk of prosecution under the anti-trust laws.

Mr. Swope's plan brings this issue into clear relief. For the electrical manufacturers it disposes of the charge that as responsible heads of important companies they lack the will or the intelligence to deal with the insecurity of the capitalistic system. It is, of course, by no means certain that the Swope plan could make electrical manufacturing secure. It may be that the foresight of man is not adequate to achieve that at present in an economic system which is world-wide in its extent, and in rapid motion owing to the incalculable effects of invention, technical improvement, and changing human standards.

But it can be said that if within the framework of the United States a beginning can be made towards the stabilization of industry, it would not be possible to find a more promising place to begin. For the electrical manufacturing industry, being new, is relatively free of the accumulated bad habits of the older type of industrial management. The continual contact of its executives with the work of the research laboratories has, moreover, instilled them with much of the liberality of mind and courageous realism which applied science requires. The industry happens, also, to be led by men of exceptional talent for organization and with wide experience of human affairs. These executives happen, too, to be engaged in an industry which is not, like agriculture, at the mercy of natural forces, or, like clothing or amusement, at the mercy of fashions and the public taste. If, therefore, any group of men could make a fair trial of the proposal to have at least one industry coöperatively planned and socially responsible, it would be the men for whom Mr. Young, Mr. Swope, and Mr. Robertson speak.

Yet this plan cannot be inaugurated without a radical change in the established industrial policy of the United States. For in order to put it into effect the Federal government must encourage all the competing units of the industry to work through their trade association for a common pool of information "on the volume of business transacted, inventories of merchandise on hand, simplification and standardization of products, *stabilization of prices* [italics mine], and all matters which may arise from time to time . . . to promote stabilization of employment . . ." I am assured that Mr. Swope does not believe that for the electrical industry this implies price-fixing. But, of course, whatever his intentions may be, he would admit, I suppose, that such close coöperation of a whole industry would normally tend to mean agreement on the volume of production and the price. Thus while he does not contemplate going that far in his own actions, he recognizes the inevitability of the issue by providing that these trade associations shall be "supervised" by some Federal agency.

There is no escape, I think, from the conclusion that any effective plan to stabilize industry would require ultimately a Federal control of prices. The hard core of the matter is that one cannot have industrial planning without a highly centralized control of production and of prices. The Swope plan does not say this, but to my mind it implies it inescapably. What is more, it is, I think, beyond the wit of man to devise a system of planned industry which does not imply it. Centralized control is of the very essence of planning. For how else can "a plan" be put into effect? By publishing a plan and then hoping that the competing units of an industry will be simultaneously inspired to abide by it? That would be sheer utopianism. Planning involves, as Mr. Young so clearly pointed out, "the voluntary surrender of a certain amount of individual freedom by the majority and the ultimate coercion of the minority. . . ."

The Russians have accepted coercion as inherent in planning and are proceeding under a dictatorship with the most gigantic experiment in centralized control in all human history. The question for us is whether the advantages of planning can be had without paying so terrible a price for them. In considering that question we may, I think, confidently take the Swope plan as an illustration of the irreducible minimum of surrender required to inaugurate a stable and socially responsible industrial order on the foundation of capitalism and political democracy.

If we were a rational people in our public affairs we should not try to judge the practicability, the value, and the disadvantages of such a proposal by arguing abstractly and consulting our feelings. We should accept the tender of the electrical manufacturers to make the experiment, and we should find a way under our laws of guaranteeing them immunity from prosecution while they adhered loyally to the principles of their plan. I do not know whether our political system is flexible enough to permit one industry to offer itself up for a public demonstration; but it would be a highly enlightened proceeding if, by some kind of treaty between the electrical industry and the government, the experiment could be made. It would teach us more than we can ever hope to learn in any other way.

September 18, 1931

IV. THE RAILROADS AND THE DEPRESSION

The hard experience of one industry where government price-fixing rules; wisdom of the I.C.C. decision against a general freight increase; either bondholders or unions must make a sacrifice

It has been estimated by Professor Slichter of Harvard University that the government now fixes the price of goods valued at about thirteen billion dollars a year, and that half of this is in the railways. That means that the income on something like one-eighth of the productive wealth of America is regulated by the government.

This officially regulated part of the national income has a peculiar importance. Partly because it comes out of fundamental and necessary services, and partly because the properties which produce it are so closely supervised by government, it has been the custom of savings banks, life insurance companies and other institutions which are trustees of other people's money to invest their funds in the bonds of railways and other utilities. As a result the safety of funds which ought to be safe beyond all question is dependent upon the solvency of the railroads. Now the depression has cut tremendously the traffic, and, therefore, the earnings of the railroads. This has made doubtful the ability of many railroads to pay interest on their bonds. This, in turn, has imperilled financial institutions which hold the bonds, and in consequence the whole credit structure of the country has been weakened. It is clear, then, why the problem of the railroads is so tremendously important.

I am no expert in these matters, but it does not require much expertness to see why the railroads are particularly vulnerable in the face of a great depression. They are vulnerable in the way that governments are vulnerable, because they cannot easily reduce their expenditures to balance the reduction in their revenues. According to figures, which I suppose are reliable enough, that part of the railroad's expenditures which is fixed has been steadily increasing in the last twenty years. Wages, which are protected by contracts, have risen nearly 100 per cent. Taxes have risen over 40 per cent. But most striking of all has been the increase in the indebtedness of the railroads. In twenty years their common stock outstanding increased by much less than a billion dollars, but their funded debt increased by much more than three billion dollars. The public, in other words, was willing to take mortgages on the railroads but it was not willing to go into partnership with them. In the era when the public was in a frenzy to own common stocks, it still had little faith in anything but the bonds of railroads. As in the German economy the American railroads had to finance themselves by going into debt. Now debt charges are fixed regardless of earnings.

So with wages fixed by contract, with taxes fixed by law, with debt charges fixed in the bond, from half to two-thirds of every dollar earned is earmarked. The possible economies out of what is left, on purchase of supplies, on repairs, and by cutting down employment, are limited. Something, therefore, has to give way. The railroads as a whole cannot pay all their fixed charges, including wages, on their present revenues.

Their first move has been to seek an increase in revenues by applying for permission to increase all freight rates 15 per cent.[1] This move must be regarded as a strategic maneuvre rather than as a serious proposal. For it is obvious that in a period of drastically fallen prices, one industry on which all others depend cannot successfully swim up Niagara and raise its prices. It was to be expected, therefore, that the Interstate Commerce Commission would refuse, not out of bad will towards the railroads, but as a matter of common sense. For a general increase of railroad rates would be equivalent to an increase of the fixed charges on industry, and fixed charges, as a result of the deflation, are already unbearably high.

The Commission has, however, allowed increases on certain kinds of freight, provided the railroads pool the increases and use them to help the weaker railroads. The Commission has evidently tried to select particular commodities, which either have not fallen in price as much as others or are so bulky and necessary that they have to be carried on the railroads anyway. From the shippers of these selected goods it hopes to extract about a hundred and twenty-five million dollars in order to support some of the bonds of railroads which would otherwise collapse. The proposal is a kind of emergency tax aimed at those who cannot escape it.

But barring a general recovery of prices and business activity, this emergency measure leaves the real problem unsolved. It is whether the bondholders or the unions are to make the sacrifice which is necessary to balance railroad budgets. There are roads in which the choice is between default in the bonds and a wage-cut, and the application for a general rate increase and its rejection has served chiefly to uncover this underlying problem. We may expect, therefore,

[1] On June 17, 1931, the principal railroads of the country filed with the Interstate Commerce Commission a formal plea for a 15 per cent increase in freight rates. After prolonged hearings, on October 20 the Commission announced its conclusions. It denied the blanket increase which had been sought, but offered partial increases in freight rates if the railroads would establish a credit pool by which the stronger lines could help the weaker.

that an effort to cut railway wages will now begin.

If all the railroads were in the same position the problem could be dealt with wholesale. But since some roads are still strong a wage reduction which was just sufficient to save a weak road would give the strong ones an unnecessary benefit. Therefore, if the wage problem is to be handled wisely, and it will not be easy to do it, it will have to be dealt with not by a wholesale decision but piecemeal, according to the needs of each railroad system.

Looked at in a larger perspective, the railroads present the most important examples of the economic, social and political perils which result from making an industrial fabric rigid with fixed charges and then subjecting it to a violent deflation of prices. Their plight raises the question whether the capital structure we have erected in the last generation, and the social standards we have imposed upon it, are practicable if we do not learn how to protect ourselves against great fluctuations in the general price level.

October 22, 1931

V. THE BALANCE OF INTERNATIONAL PAYMENTS

A basic truth; England's experience; balancing of international payments as a prerequisite of recovery

The work of reconstruction might proceed if the general public here and abroad could be made to understand a basic truth which they persistently ignore. It is that nations, as well as governments, corporations, and individual householders, have to balance their payments. I believe that much of the confusion of mind about war debts, reparations, tariffs, commercial and investment policies, and the gold standard, arises out of a failure to grasp this one simple idea, and that a man who takes the trouble to understand it will find he has an altogether new understanding of what is going on about him in the world today.

Let us begin with a concrete illustration: that of England. Each year for the last seven years England has bought from foreigners more goods than she has sold to foreigners. In round figures the difference was about 1,800 million dollars each year. England has had, of course, to find these 1,800 millions somewhere. Where did she find them? Up to 1929 she got about 1,400 out of 1,800 millions from dividends and interest on her foreign investments made before the war. She got another 600 million or so from her shipping. These in-payments took care of her out-payments with, say, 200 million to spare. These extra funds plus another 300 millions which came into England out of insurance commissions and interest on short loans, she lent abroad. Now the essential thing to notice is that England managed to pay her bills only because she had inherited a large income from investments.

Then came the depression: it cut down what England could sell abroad much more than it cut down what England bought from abroad. At the same time it cut down the return on her investments and her shipping, etc. In 1930, the first full year of the depression, England's bill for goods was a little larger than in the last year of prosperity, but her income was smaller by 400 million dollars. By 1931 her bill for out-payments was still about as large as ever, but her income had been reduced still more. How could England as a nation pay her bills? She couldn't. And that is why she had to go off the gold standard and is now paying her bills, apart from certain special debts, in depreciated money at about 80 cents on the dollar.

Here then is a clear and dramatic illustration of the basic fact that a nation has to balance its payments somehow.

Let us now look at our own national balance sheet in the

last full year of prosperity, which was 1928. We sold about 850 million dollars more goods abroad than we bought. We also had coming to us that year about 200 millions on the war debts, and about 600 millions net return on our foreign investments. How did our foreign customers and debtors get those 1650 millions to pay us? They got 660 millions from the tourists. They got 220 millions from immigrants here who sent money home. That covered about half what they owed us. Where did they get the rest of it? They got it out of the 970 millions which we loaned to them that year.

In other words, the only way we were able to sell so much more than we bought was by lending the outside world the money to make up the difference.

The same analysis applied to Germany will show that she has paid reparations and for her excess of imports out of money we and others lent her. Now what does all this mean? It means that even before the depression the three greatest industrial nations in the world, Britain, Germany, and America, were leading a crazy economic existence. The British were living on their inheritance. The Germans were piling up debts to pay their debts. We were piling up loans to pay ourselves.

How did we come to do these things? We drifted into them by ignoring the warnings of every responsible economist in the world and by adopting national economic policies which have thrown all three national economic systems out of balance. The Germans were saddled with the reparation debt. The British were hemmed in on all sides by tariff walls. And we set ourselves the impossible task of collecting the money for our surplus exports and the money on the war debts and the money on our foreign investments while we raised a prohibitive tariff. Other governments did equally unworkable things, and the combination of all of them has produced not a mere cyclical depression, but a radical dislocation of the economic structure of the whole world.

The root of the trouble is the popular delusion that a nation does not have to balance its payments. In England it took the form of selling too little and buying too much. In America it took the form of selling too much and buying too little. The misconception is the same in both cases: it arises from the inability of the voters to understand, and of their representatives and leaders to make them realize, that a nation cannot buy without selling, or sell without buying, that in the long run a nation cannot cover deficits by borrowing or lending.

The idea is elementary: yet our existing tariffs and debt policies utterly ignore it; our publicly discussed official plans for dealing with the crisis continue to ignore it. The President and the leaders of both parties in Congress, and a very influential section of the press, proceed as if they had never heard of it. Men talk of "recovery" from the depression by some manipulation of credit, when here before their eyes lies a world prostrated by governmental policies, which are no more intelligent, and no more workable, than perpetual motion machines or the alchemists' devices for turning base metal into gold.

It is difficult for individuals to learn that they must either balance their expenditures or get into trouble. It is even more difficult for governments to learn it, as the fiscal history of states teaches us. It is perhaps the most difficult of all for nations in all their complexity to learn that they too have accounts which must balance if they are to be prosperous and secure. But difficult as the idea is, it is now indispensable that we should grasp it. For it provides the fundamental clue to the world problem, and we ignore it at our peril.

October 9, 1931

VI. THE TARIFF, FOREIGN TRADE, AND THE DEPRESSION

Naïve tariff theories; selling abroad impossible without buying abroad

The other day the New York *Sun,* discoursing on American statesmen with "the low tariff complex," complained that "they do not tell us what foreign manufactured articles they would like to see admitted to successful competition here with the equivalent American made articles." It then proceeded to put to them "in a brief if rugged way" the following question: "Which American industries do you wish to see put in bankruptcy first?"

This has the appearance of being an absolute poser, disposing once and for all of a problem which has exercised the mind of the world for a long time. It would seem as if there were nothing more to be said now that the editor of the *Sun* has settled the tariff question. For if any reduction in any schedule means bankrupting the industry protected by that schedule, a general horizontal cut of all the rates such as the Democrats contemplate, would mean the general bankruptcy of the nation. If the *Sun* is right in its reasoning, the only proper tariff policy is an embargo against all foreign goods which compete with American. If the only way to avoid bankruptcy is to stop competition, why bother with a tariff? Why not prohibit imports, with the exception perhaps of a few articles like rubber, which cannot be produced here and are absolutely irreplaceable? Thus we might prohibit the import of silk from Japan and compel people to use rayon and cotton. We might prohibit the import of coffee from Brazil and either grow coffee in hot-houses or drink sarsaparilla for breakfast.

No high protectionist would go quite that far, though

it has been proposed to stop the import of bananas so that people would eat more apples. But every high protectionist has a feeling that imports are bad for the country and should be discouraged, that the less we buy from foreigners the more prosperous we shall be. Your high protectionist does not believe in foreign trade. He believes in selling American goods to foreigners, the more the better. But he does not believe in buying from foreigners if it can be avoided. He believes in the sale of goods but not in the exchange of goods.

Now it is an indisputable fact, capable of overwhelming proof, that a nation cannot sell abroad unless it buys the rough equivalent abroad. For a time a nation may sell more than it buys and make up the difference by lending money to foreigners. Or it may make up the difference, or part of it, by sending tourists abroad who buy hotel accommodations, goods, railroad tickets, wine and so forth. But in the long run and in general the only way to sell goods abroad and get paid for them is to buy goods of about the same value.

The Secretary of Commerce, Mr. Lamont, has just published his annual report, which illustrates this quite clearly. He gives figures of American foreign trade before the war, that is, the average for 1910–1914; for the post-war period, the average for 1922–1926; and for the year of the depression ending June 30, 1931. The figures show that the value of all our exports, that is to say of our sales to foreigners, doubled from the pre-war to the post-war period. During that time our imports, that is our purchases from foreigners, doubled and a little over. Exports and imports went up together in roughly the same proportion. Then came the depression. As compared with the average of 1922–1926, exports fell off about one-third and imports fell off about one-third. Here then we see in concrete form what is meant by saying that selling and buying are two sides of the same process of trade. We see both exports and imports double and then we see both decline one-third at the same time. Can there be any doubt then that to export we must import and to import we must export?

Now if this is true, and there is no recognized economist in the world who would question it, what becomes of the *Sun's* theory that the way to be prosperous is to discourage imports? The theory comes down to this: That in order to protect some American producer from foreign competition it is necessary to destroy the foreign markets of other American producers. The low tariff theory on the other hand is that by increasing the volume of trade, both imports and exports, the whole business of the country would be stimulated, that the more foreign trade there is the more domestic trade there will be. For what the domestic producers lose by the competition of foreign imports they can more than make up by greater sales to those Americans who are profiting from the sale of exports. The theory is quite simple once it is admitted that trade is desirable, that trade is not a monopoly of the right to sell, but a continual exchange of goods.

December 4, 1931

VII. THE STOCK EXCHANGE

The public and the stock exchange; recklessness in marketing securities; need for internal reform and self-discipline

It would simplify matters greatly if it were possible to believe that the bear market has been caused by bear raids. For then it would be possible to stop the bear market by catching the bears. Unhappily, the facts lend no support to this theory. The records show quite clearly that taking the bear market as a whole, the fall in the prices of stocks corresponds very closely with the reduction of earnings. It is impossible, therefore, to believe that the bears have been making the market. Plainly, it is the market which has been making the bears.

It is difficult, however, for the public to believe this. There is, to begin with, a natural human tendency to ascribe events to dramatic and personal causes rather than to prosaic and impersonal ones. Our ancestors thought that many of their troubles were caused by the evil eye. This disposition to believe in malignant powers is always aggravated in times of strain and confusion. For in the absence of clear and compelling explanations and of a general conviction about what needs to be done, men sink back into their more primitive habits of mind, and superstition flourishes among them. The notion that bear raiders could produce such a market as this is nothing but superstition. The notion, held even in some high quarters, that this market is the product of Democratic bears trying to ruin the Administration, is a surprisingly curious bit of naïveté.

What gives to the idea its persistent vitality is the fact that though neither the bull nor the bear speculators can determine the general direction of the market, they do undoubtedly accentuate the direction in which it is going. Thus Mr. Richard Whitney's statement before the Senate Committee that the bull market was "indulged in by 120,000,000 people of the United States" is not truly responsive to what the critics of the stock market have in mind.[1] What they are thinking about, as they remember their losses, is the extent to which they were encouraged by

[1] In the spring of 1932 the Senate Banking and Currency Committee began an investigation of short-selling and other alleged abuses in the operations of the New York Stock Exchange, and called numerous witnesses. Richard Whitney, president of the Exchange, testified on several occasions between April 11 and April 21.

brokers and bankers to indulge in bull speculation during the boom. They believe, and I think rightly, that those who were presumably in a position to know, did not adequately protect them. It is true that the American people ignorantly and greedily indulged in bull speculation. But what sticks in their minds is that they were encouraged, often by the methods of high-powered salesmanship, to give themselves up to this folly.

The present resentment against the New York Stock Exchange is the aftermath of the collapse of the bull market. It is therefore regrettable that so able and high-minded a spokesman as Mr. Whitney does not speak more realistically on the main point which interests the public. According to the newspaper reports he was asked by Senator Brookhart about the bull market of 1929, and this colloquy took place:

Q. Led by the New York Stock Exchange?
A. I deny that, sir.
Q. It does not lead anything?
A. It is a market-place.

I am afraid that Mr. Whitney's replies are literally rather than substantially true. Literally, he is right in saying that the Stock Exchange is merely a market-place, and his remarks would be substantially true as well if the members of the Stock Exchange were merely the mechanical agents who executed their clients orders. But in fact the stock brokerage firms act as financial advisers to their clients and by their market letters they undertake to guide the individual who enters the market. The real question, which Senator Brookhart, with his customary muddleheadedness, failed to bring out, is how responsibly, how disinterestedly, and how competently the members of the Stock Exchange have discharged their responsibility as advisers.

That is the question which men like Mr. Whitney ought

to face in a far more searching fashion than they have yet done. For the Stock Exchange bases its claim to immunity from public regulation upon the thesis that its own capacity for self-government and self-discipline are a better protection to the public than any laws which could be enacted. That thesis is true when the self-discipline is courageously applied. Has it been? That is the main question. In the last fifteen years the general public has come into the stock market. There has been a distribution of securities without any parallel in all history. This distribution of securities has produced a condition where there is an enormous gulf between the actual owners of corporate property and the directors of these properties. It has become impossible for the public who own securities to arrive at sound judgments about the position of their property. They are entirely dependent, therefore, upon advice, and in the nature of things they are dependent to a very great degree upon the advice of their brokers.

It is not enough to say that the Stock Exchange is a market-place. It is a collection of firms which advise the investor what to buy or sell in that market-place. This is a grave responsibility. It is more than an academic question whether the responsible firms which have sound traditions behind them have had the power and the courage to discipline the old pirates and the considerable number of irresponsible amateurs who rushed into the stockbroking business during the mad days of the inflation. There is a general impression that the responsible men lost control, that things got out of hand, that greed destroyed judgment, and that the ignorant trust of the public was exploited.

There is, consequently, a wide and sharp feeling in the community that, in addition to defending the Exchange against vindictive and destructive attack, the reputable interests which Mr. Whitney represents need fairly soon to demonstrate that they appreciate the evils of the recent past and that they intend to protect the Stock Exchange by internal reform and self-discipline.

For the Stock Exchange has become the greatest popular market in the world, and its members have the duty to regard themselves collectively as trustees of an immense public interest.

April 13, 1932

VIII. AMERICAN INVESTMENTS ABROAD

Foreign loans: the need for thorough investigation; our position as chief creditor nation and its meaning

For the long run the best thing Congress can do now is to continue its investigation of foreign financing until the whole matter has been thoroughly explored.[1] An understanding of the nature of these loans, of the manner in which they were made, of the reasons for them and of their effects, is basic to the development of a sound national policy for the future and of enlightened public opinion to support it. Our experience during the last decade cannot be studied too much. For the appearance of the United States as the leading creditor power of the world is one of the turning points of modern history, and the consequences involve every important item of our national policy.

If the investigation is to bear fruit, it is necessary that the Senate and the public should have a clear idea as to what it

[1] The Senate Finance Committee held an investigation of foreign loans during January, February, and March, 1932, which revealed much recklessness in the flotation of foreign bonds by American banking houses, the actual bribery of high officials in Peru in connection with one issue, and the use of misleading or mendacious statements to American investors. Denunciatory speeches were made by Senator Hiram Johnson and others.

is that is being investigated. In order to have a clear idea it will be well to begin by remembering that until 1914 the United States was a debtor country. In the first hundred and twenty-five years of its existence as a republic, the American nation borrowed capital from the Old World. In 1914 the American debt to Europe stood, according to the best estimates, at about two thousand million dollars.

The World War radically altered this position. In a very short time the European powers became our debtors, and in the fifteen years following 1914, the United States, which had been a net debtor to the extent of two thousand millions, became a net creditor to the extent of about eighteen thousand millions. Of this amount about seventy-five hundred millions is the present value of the War Debts figured at 4¼ per cent. The rest are American private long-term investments in all parts of the world minus foreign long-term investments in the United States. The figures come from the Department of Commerce.

What the Senate is investigating is this lending of ten or eleven thousand millions of private money during the period from the war to the depression.

The investigation, if it is thorough, will undoubtedly show some bad banking in the course of these huge operations. It will reveal inexperience, poor judgment, some folly, and some greed. All of this should be brought out in order to satisfy the public that nothing is being concealed, in order to fix blame where it specifically belongs and thus to re-establish confidence where it is deserved. Finally, it should be brought out in order that the lesson of the experience may be learned by bankers and investors.

But this necessary work of sanitation is only a part of what needs to be done. It is necessary that the American people should understand the epochal significance of their sudden rise as the chief creditor of the world. On this matter the

Democratic party has a peculiar duty and opportunity, and if it is led by its statesmen, it will take hold vigorously.

On December 2, 1919, President Wilson delivered his message to Congress, and in the course of it described prophetically the problem which now confronts us. I have space to quote only a few sentences:

> A fundamental change has taken place with reference to the position of America in the world's affairs. . . . Before the war America was heavily the debtor of the rest of the world, and the interest payments she had to make to foreign countries, . . . the expenditures of American travellers abroad, and the ocean-freight charges she had to pay others, about balanced the value of her pre-war favorable balance of trade. . . .
>
> During the war America's exports have been greatly stimulated and increased, prices have increased their value. On the other hand, she has purchased a large portion of the American securities previously held abroad, has loaned some $9,000,000,000 to foreign governments, and has built her own ships. Our favorable balance of trade has thus been greatly increased and Europe has been deprived of the means of meeting it heretofore existing.
>
> Europe can have only three ways of meeting the favorable balance of trade in peace times: by imports into this country of gold or of goods, or by establishing new credits.

Since those words were written a Republican Congress has twice raised the tariff against the import of foreign goods. After the first high tariff was established, the country experienced the great boom and a great expansion of its exports. How was it possible to expand exports and have the debts paid under a high tariff? It was possible because, as President Wilson predicted it would be necessary to do, the country imported gold and exported dollars in the form of loans. It is no accident, but the very essence of the matter, that gold piled up here and that dollars were lent lavishly abroad at a time when the export trade was booming and the tariff was so high.

Thus what the Senate is studying when it examines the post-war financing is the unconscious effort of the world to adjust itself to the unheard-of paradox presented by a nation trying at one and the same time to stop imports, collect debts, and expand exports. Because our debtors could not sell enough of their goods for dollars, they had to sell us their gold and lure dollars abroad by offering speculative returns. The American public was seduced by the speculative returns and devoured the bonds. Many bankers, utterly inexperienced in these matters and without sound banking traditions, rushed forward to supply the demand. That follies and scandals ensued should surprise no one. A radically unsound national policy, derived from a total misunderstanding of how the war had altered America's position in the world, produced the conditions which have resulted in all the things the Senate is so distressed about.

December 23, 1931

IX. BALANCED BUDGETS AND THE DEPRESSION

The A B C of the deficit; balancing the Federal accounts the central problem in combating the depression

For the first time within the experience of most of us the United States government has a serious financial problem. Most Americans are accustomed to the comfortable belief that the Federal power is inexhaustibly rich. It financed the great war lavishly. In the post-war decade it was able for many years to reduce taxes and yet accumulate fat surpluses. It is hard for the country to realize that this era of easy finance is over, and that we are left today with greatly diminished incomes, greatly increased current expenditures, and most of the war still to be paid for. In respect to government finance, as in respect to so many other things, Congress and the people of the country have radically to readjust their minds.[1]

It is well to get the fundamental figures clearly fixed in our minds, and for that purpose round numbers are all that it is necessary to remember. Let us see then what the Federal government is spending this year, remembering that when we speak of the government's financial year we mean the twelve months from July 1, 1931, to June 30, 1932.

We are spending 4,500 million dollars. On what? 1,000 millions goes to pay interest and principal on the debt. It is chiefly the cost of the last war. Nearly another 1,000 millions goes to the veterans of former wars. A little over 700 millions goes to the army and navy. This accounts for half of our expenditures.

The actual running of the government, of Congress, the courts, the executive departments, commissions, bureaus, and civil pensions cost a little more than 400 millions. This includes a postal deficit of 156 millions.

On various kinds of public services, public works and subsidies we are spending another 1,000 million. This includes

[1] At the time this article was written Americans were just becoming aware of the huge size of the impending Federal deficit. On January 4, 1932, it was announced that the government had ended the first half of the fiscal year 1931–1932 with a deficit of $1,385,500,000. In the same period the public debt had increased $1,024,000,000. The estimate at this time was that at the end of the fiscal year (June 30, 1932) the deficit would be about $2,122,000,000.

small expenditures on such things as education and public health, huge expenditures of more than 200 millions to help agriculture, of nearly 150 millions to help the merchant marine, and of more than 500 millions on public buildings and public works.

Finally we are spending about 250 millions on miscellaneous items such as refunds, administering the District of Columbia, and so forth.

The figures may be put in another way in order to remember them. The cost of running the executive, legislative and judicial branches of the government is one-tenth of the total expenditures. Of the remaining 4,000 millions about one-quarter goes to the debt, one-quarter goes to the veterans, one-quarter goes to public works and subsidies, three-sixteenths to the army and navy, and one-sixteenth to sundries.

Let us look now at the revenues for this year. We have only estimates, for the year is only half over, and it is not possible to predict exactly what can be collected in the remaining six months. But the Treasury estimate is that the government will receive about 2,360 millions. This is just about enough to pay for the debt, the veterans, and the navy. For the army, the whole cost of the government, and all the public works and subsidies, there are no revenues. They have to be paid for by borrowing. If we regard the debt, the veterans, and the navy as our first fixed national charges, then it may be said that the Federal government's revenues this year will just meet their fixed charges, and for everything else it is compelled to borrow.

The next thing to fix in mind is the immediate reason for this financial position. It can be put most clearly in this way: since the last full year of prosperity, which was the year ending June 30, 1929, the government's expenditures have *increased* more than 16 per cent and its revenues have *decreased* more than 40 per cent. The increased expenditure during the Hoover Administration is not fairly measured by this 16 per cent. For the dollar in terms of purchasing power is worth about 10 per cent more, which means that the expenditures this year, measured in purchasing power, are about 25 per cent heavier than at the beginning of this Administration.

To meet this increasing weight of expenditure we have a tax system which is peculiarly vulnerable to a depression. Being based largely on incomes and capital gains and on customs, it has no stability in a depression. The Under Secretary of the Treasury, Mr. Mills, said on Monday night, that whereas the government collected 1,000 millions from corporations in 1930 it will collect only half that much this year. When the figures for income tax this year become really available, it will be shown that it is a deeply unsatisfactory basis of revenue as it is now arranged.

The people of this country face in really serious and practical form the problem of reducing the cost of government and of increasing the revenues of government. All other projects revolve about this central question of how to balance the Federal accounts.

December 16, 1931

X. WHAT OFFICEHOLDERS MUST FACE

The deflation of government; urgency of financial reform in the nation, states, and cities

It is evident that officeholders have been the last great group of people to realize that the New Era is over. One of the major tasks of the next few months will be to change fundamentally their whole state of mind. Every other section of the people now realizes that the boom is over and that it is necessary to bring costs and prices into balance at a much lower level than that of 1928–1929. All except the office-holders. They are still at the stage where most of us were two years ago, the stage of explaining why they cannot cut or why they can cut so little. For they have not yet adjusted their minds to the fact that they must cut, and that if they must they can.

Take, for example, three of our largest governmental agencies: the Federal government, the State of New York, and the City of New York.

The President has explained that out of the total appropriations less than half "is available for consideration in seeking means to curtail our expenditures." How does he arrive at such a figure? He does it by adding the cost of the debt, which is a quarter of the cost, to the expenditure on the veterans, which is another quarter. These he calls "fixed charges." But there is nothing "fixed" about a thousand million dollars for the veterans, which is as much money as the whole government cost before the war. These thousand millions are "fixed" only by political fear, not by the real and undeniable needs of the veterans. It is an absolutely safe assumption that, without depriving any veteran of his just due, the sum could be cut considerably by eliminating waste. It is simply inconceivable that it can cost such a gigantic sum as is now spent to provide for the veterans of an army of whom only about a quarter were ever within sound of the enemy's guns.

Passing by the veterans and the public debt, there still remain expenditures twice those before the war. Admittedly, governmental activity has had to expand. Still, the fact is that business and agriculture are adjusting themselves to a level of incomes a good deal nearer the pre-war than the post-war level. How can the Federal government seriously maintain that it is facing the realities of the present critical adjustment when it is still handing out enormous subsidies, making huge unproductive expenditures, and is failing to reduce salaries?

These are not pleasant subjects to talk about. But this is a very unpleasant depression, in which we are gradually learning that our notion that we had suddenly grown fabulously rich was the illusion of inflation, that, after making up the losses of the war, we are at best somewhat but not very much richer than we used to be, and that we are compelled to bring our greatly expanded governmental expenditures into some reasonable relation with our real wealth.

From the Governor of New York we hear the same explanations as from Washington. He has a budget in which "well over two-thirds cannot readily be reduced either by the Governor or the Legislature unless they decide to ignore the established order and urge, as a matter of policy, that the state withdraw its support from commitments already made or discontinue established activities which are rendering distinct services to the social welfare of our citizens." Everybody knows that official expenditures cannot "readily be reduced." The question is whether they can be reduced, and the failure to discuss a reduction of official salaries is prima facie evidence that Governor Roosevelt, without impairing the essential obligations of the State to those in need, might very well save more money than he is saving.

The point is that the official mind has not yet adjusted itself to the situation, and a real will to reduce does not yet exist. Nobody is proposing to cut relief for the unemployed —in fact it may have to be increased—or on the care of the state's wards. But that the State could reduce elsewhere if it had the mind to may be asserted. It spent less money ten years ago and it could spend less today.

The City of New York is the most unregenerate of our examples, and Mayor Walker is a prize specimen of the happy-go-lucky spender of the boom period. The Comptroller's summary of New York City's finances for the five years, 1926 to 1930, offer a perfect illustration of what went on during the bad old good days of the inflation. The annual cost of the debt has been increased 50 per cent, the administrative expenses of the city have increased about 33⅓ per cent, taxes have increased 40 per cent. What supports these borrowings and expenditures? The answer is real estate. The assessed valuation was jacked up nearly 40 per cent. In other words, the city borrowed and spent and taxed on the basis of the boom in real estate. The boom is over. Yet when it is suggested to the Mayor of New York that he cannot go on borrowing and spending as if real estate values were booming, he complains to high heaven and the Senate that the bankers are squeezing him.

What is squeezing him is the same thing which has been squeezing farmers, manufacturers, railroads, wage-earners, investors and bankers, namely, the fall in prices which will not permit anyone to borrow and spend at the boom level.

The officeholder is so slow to learn the truth about what is going on because in a time like this he is specially protected and does not, like other men, have to face the music. His job is safe; his salary increases in value through enhanced purchasing power, and is tax exempt. His employer, the government, can obtain money. The Federal government, the State and the City of New York can obtain income if they have to, for they have the power to tax. Therefore, these officeholders are the last body of men to abandon the old inflationary mentality. But the time has come for them to abandon it. All over this country the states, municipalities and villages, have now to go through what agriculture and business have gone through. They have to deflate. It is estimated that state and local governments have increased their expenditures eightfold in the last twenty-five years. The American nation is not eight times as rich. Therefore, the reform of government finance is one of the urgent inescapable tasks in the program of recovery.

January 15, 1932

· III ·

MR. HOOVER: HIS TASK AND HOW HE
DEALT WITH IT

I. MR. COOLIDGE AND MR. HOOVER

*Mr. Coolidge's clear but narrow conception of
Presidential duties; Mr. Hoover's lack of purpose in
political fields and excess of activity elsewhere*

IT is one of Mr. Coolidge's most engaging traits that he
has never had the slightest delusion of grandeur. He has
managed somehow to pass unscathed through the fierce
flattery and exaltation of a successful political career, and is
able to look upon himself calmly as a former President rather
than as a hibernating messiah.

This gift for honest self-appraisal has now protected him
against a temptation to which most men in his position would
have yielded. Mr. Hoover is in the worst straits that any
President has been in since 1912. He faces the opposition of
the Western Progressives and he has to a startling degree lost
the confidence of the Eastern Conservatives. Mr. Coolidge,
as he himself admits, has been hearing from many quarters
that he alone can save the party or the country. He must
have heard also, not once but many times, that if he will not
run again he might at least allow his name to become the
rallying point for public sentiment and for delegates, in
order to exercise a deciding influence at the next Republican
convention. All these temptations he has put definitely aside,
and with a lack of egotism which is really exceptional in

65

public men, has relieved Mr. Hoover and his managers of at least one major embarrassment.

Although Mr. Coolidge's action is highly magnanimous, the manner of his doing it must be a little depressing to Mr. Hoover's more ardent admirers. There is no mention of Mr. Hoover's name. There is no word that implies approval, much less enthusiasm, for anything that Mr. Hoover has done. There is simply a statement of the theory that party discipline must be maintained. Many an unhappy Republican will read the article and feel that the high, cold path has been pointed out, that Duty and not Pleasure is the order of the day. There is no concession to human weakness in Mr. Coolidge's utterance, no indulgence of those who would like to feel some glow of personal satisfaction while they practice virtue. Mr. Coolidge, in fact, has carried his restraint to such excess that instead of an indorsement of Mr. Hoover he has produced an abstract argument to the effect that the authority of the Presidential office can only be maintained if the party in power refrains from considering the qualifications of the man who occupies the office.

Now it may be the duty of former Presidents to ignore the qualifications of the man and think only of the office. But the people generally will, I think, continue to take the less abstract view that the Presidential office is very much what the man makes it. They are bound, therefore, to be interested in the personality of the individual who through his office wields the greatest power on the face of the earth.

It is often said these days that Mr. Coolidge was a very lucky President and that Mr. Hoover has been a very unlucky one. If immediate popularity is the measure, that is true enough, for Mr. Coolidge did not make the prosperity and Mr. Hoover did not make the depression. It is also true, I suppose, that the period of bad times has subjected Mr. Hoover to tests which Mr. Coolidge never had to meet.

Nevertheless, there is something deeper than luck which divides the two men and accounts for the profound difference in feeling toward them among conservative Republicans.

The clue to that difference can be found in Mr. Coolidge's article. He appears, there, as a man who has thought out and arrived at a clear, a well-ordered, rather narrow, if you like, but entirely consistent set of convictions about the functions of the President, his duties and his limitations. There is no confusion in his mind as to what the office of the President is. Thus one may disagree with Mr. Coolidge's principles, but they remain the definite principles of a man who believes what he believes.

Mr. Hoover's deepest difficulty, it seems to me, is that he has no well-considered conception of his office and of his own purposes. That is why you will hear Republicans accuse him of doing "nothing" and in the next breath of trying to do too much. It seems absurd at first that men should complain that Mr. Hoover won't make up his mind to act and then that he is too active. Yet if you examine the complaints in detail the seeming paradox disappears. It turns out that what his critics complain about is that Mr. Hoover is indecisive and hesitant in dealing with political issues and extraordinarily fertile, impulsive, and energetic in trying to influence matters that lie outside his duties and his powers.

Thus in meeting this depression he has in respect to those elements which are governmental and require his leadership —like tariffs, debts, reparations, political stabilization— been extremely disinclined to act and greatly bewildered by political opposition and public criticism. He does not seem to know how the political functions of the President are exercised effectively, and to be rather dismayed at not knowing. On the other hand, he has had the utmost confidence and boldness in attempting to guide and oversee the industrial life of the country, initiating major policies as to wages, purchases of raw materials, capital investment and what not. Scarcely a week passes but some new story comes out of Washington as to how Mr. Hoover has had somebody on the telephone and is attempting to fix this situation or that.

Thus he spends his energies lavishly in fields where under our political system the President has no powers and no responsibility: he is unable to use his energy successfully on the major political tasks where he alone has the power of leadership and the consequent responsibility. This is the reason why he has fallen under the double criticism that he is both inactive and meddlesome, and that is the reason why his advisers are alarmed at the lack of confidence now so commonly felt about him in high Republican circles.

It may be a little late in the day for Mr. Hoover to acquire perspective on his office and a clear working philosophy of its functions and its limitations. But in view of what the winter is to bring he ought to make the effort. He might succeed if only he would give himself the chance: if he would take a real vacation—if he would relax, if he would establish leisure to reflect, if he would do less conferring and less telephoning, if he would read fewer newspapers, and would care less what journalists say—if only he would find time to clear his mind and compose his spirit.

October 1, 1931

II. A BASIC FALLACY OF THE ADMINISTRATION

The belief that the price levels of 1929 might be restored; no business of a President to fix wage and price levels

In the month of November two years ago the Administration laid down a policy for dealing with the depression. That policy was based on the theory that the collapse of prices in Wall Street need not and should not be followed by a general deflation of prices and dividends and wages. The Administration's view was accepted by Congress and by the industrial leaders of the country. Pledges were given and taken not to disturb wages or employment. The Farm Board set itself the task of holding up agricultural prices. Mr. Ford raised wages. The Steel Corporation declared an extra dividend. Congress reduced the income tax. The assumption was that the 1929 level of prices, wages, profits, was normal, and that a resolute concerted effort should be made to maintain it.

The national policy, initiated by Mr. Hoover and consented to by the country, consisted of what Mr. H. G. Wells likes to call an "open conspiracy." It was an open conspiracy not to deflate.

We are now in the later stages of the failure of that whole policy. It has not been possible to maintain the 1929 level of prices, profits, or wages. Experience has shown that government, finance and industry have not had the power to maintain the old price level. There has been a relentless movement down to a new price level. But the movement has not been uniform. For some prices and some wages are protected by a kind of monopoly. They have come down more slowly than unprotected prices and unprotected wages. The result is that today the whole economic system is out of adjustment because the relationship between all kinds of buyers and sellers, employers and workers, borrowers and lenders, are radically different from what they were two years ago.

The basic premise of the Administration has been that the old adjustment would and should be restored. This has meant, if it meant anything, that for two years the Administration has been hoping and praying for an inflation to restore the price levels of 1929. On no other theory does the Administration's stand against the reduction of prices and wages make any sense. For obviously, if the prices of farm products and of raw materials are going to stay down somewhere around the pre-war level, it is not going to be possible to hold up rents, retail prices and wages far above that level. Therefore, unless the Administration can produce an inflation of wholesale prices, it can only prolong the maladjustment by opposing the deflation of retail prices and wages.

The inflationary remedy was a tempting one until about two months ago. It is no longer tempting because it is no longer safe to fool with it. The financial crisis following Britain's abandonment of the gold standard, a crisis which has apparently been weathered, made an inflationary policy impracticable. Since that time there has been no real alternative but to work out a readjustment of all costs by deflation.

This is what has actually been taking place. But the process of deflation is obviously not completed. The prices received by farmers have fallen 50 per cent. The prices paid by farmers have fallen only about 20 per cent. Farm wages have fallen 35 per cent, wages in factories perhaps 10 per cent, wages on railroads not at all. Retail prices have had a very uneven deflation: clothing has been reduced about 20 per cent and food about 12 per cent, but rent only about 8 per cent. The conclusion is inescapable that the prices of manufactured goods at wholesale and retail have still to come down some, that rents have still to come down considerably, that wages which have not come down will come down, and that over-extended capitalization and credit have to be written off.

While the deflation is in process uncertainty is bound to prevail. Consequently, the more quickly it is done the better. The time has come, therefore, for the Administration to acknowledge that the policy of standing pat at the 1929 level, which it adopted two years ago, is no longer feasible, and that, therefore, its moral and political resistance to the deflation is no longer justified. The policy has failed. It should be abandoned, and the Administration should return to a position of neutrality.

It never was the business of a President to determine wage and price policies, and Mr. Hoover's experiment had been a failure. Persistence in it now simply prolongs the agony by raising false hopes and encouraging a futile resistance to the inevitable. The great inflation which began with the war has run its course and is ending, and no good whatever can come from acting as if the abnormal monetary structure of the war and post-war era were sacred. The structure has collapsed in all its essential parts, and the few tottering remnants of it which remain are useless and dangerous. They will have to come down before reconstruction can confidently begin.

November 24, 1931

III. THE PRESIDENT'S ANNUAL MESSAGE, 1931

Self-containment theory of the message its principal weakness; why we cannot return to the artificial economic era of post-war days

On the important matters the President's message[1] is in the nature of an introduction to a series of messages which

[1] The first session of the Seventy-second Congress met at the beginning of December, 1931. Mr. Hoover sent his annual message to Congress on December 8. He recommended in general terms increased taxation to balance the budget by 1934; cuts in government expenditures; a revival of the War Finance Corporation; the creation of home loan discount banks; the liberalization of the discount requirements of Federal Reserve Banks; and avoidance of any tariff revision. A supplementary message on foreign affairs was sent to Congress on December 10.

are to follow it. Thus the subject of government finance will be dealt with in the budget message. Foreign relations are to be discussed at greater length later. The railway problem, which the President recognizes as of great and immediate importance, is the subject of negotiation at the present time and cannot be discussed realistically until the results are known. The widely heralded proposal for reviving the War Finance Corporation as "Emergency Reconstruction Corporation" is approved in general terms but no specific plan is submitted. There are many lesser recommendations and suggestions and opinions on various questions, all of which can best be discussed when definite proposals are put forward. The weight of the message lies in the President's effort to make clear to the nation his underlying policy and attitude towards the depression.

The crucial statement of his attitude is in a sentence which reads as follows:

> Although some of the causes of our depression are due to speculation, inflation of securities and real estate, unsound foreign investments, and mismanagement of financial institutions, yet our self-contained national economy, with its matchless strength and resources, would have enabled us to recover long since but for the continued dislocations, shocks and setbacks from abroad.

This conception of ourselves as a self-contained nation prevented from recovering by the outer world has evidently dominated the President's mind.

It has two major effects on his practical action. The first has been to make him believe that the problem at home was to devise emergency means for resisting the shocks from abroad, chiefly by mobilizing credit to enable banks, corporations and individuals to ride out the deflation. Thus it has been no part of his philosophy to believe that a genuine readjustment of domestic costs and domestic prices was necessary. The greater part of his emphasis throughout has been upon furnishing credit to make such readjustment as little necessary as possible.

The second effect of the President's thesis has been to make him unwilling to raise the question whether the post-war policies under which we fell into this depression, our tariff policy, our debt policy, our foreign policy, have had any bearing upon the depression. His assumption is that they have not had any bearing. They are assumed to be sound. It is taken for granted that they do not need in any fundamental sense to be reconsidered, and that two years hence—that is the date Mr. Hoover now sets for complete recovery—we can resume prosperity under the same policies which were in force before the depression.

The President's theory that we are a self-contained nation capable of recovery but for shocks from abroad is on the face of it paradoxical. If we are indeed self-contained, why should shocks from abroad prevent us from recovering? If they do, what justification is there for calling us self-contained? A truly self-contained nation would be one which was immune from the impact of foreign conditions. A nation suffering as we are from what Mr. Hoover declares to be the effect of foreign conditions is plainly not self-contained but in high degree interdependent with other nations.

It is true, of course, that the American nation possesses most though not all of the resources of economic existence. But that does not make us self-contained. For we have organized an economic system on those resources which is not prosperous, and therefore cannot provide remunerative employment to the whole population, unless certain surpluses can be exported at a profit. It is a misunderstanding of the nature of our economic system to say that we are self-contained because we can, for example, raise all the wheat and cotton we need. As we are at present organized we have to sell surplus of wheat and cotton abroad or suffer dire distress in great sections of the country. The same condition applies to many major industries. They can produce what we need for our own consumption, but they are so organized, so capitalized, so arranged that they cannot produce successfully unless they can sell more than American consumers need.

We might conceivably be more self-contained than we are. Had the Republican party in the last two generations not overstimulated the industrialization of the country by tariffs, had it set itself the task of diversifying agriculture, had it avoided the great post-war inflation which overexpanded all manner of production for quick monetary profits, we might be more self-contained than we actually are. But as matters stand we are not self-contained. We have made ourselves highly dependent upon world markets, and we must either revive them in our own interest by promoting the international exchange of goods or we must liquidate those parts of our agricultural and industrial interests which produce surplus for export.

In either case we shall not return to the highly artificial and utterly unstable economic arrangements of the post-war era which have now collapsed.

December 9, 1931

IV. MR. HOOVER AND THE BUDGET

Temporizing nature of the budget message; importance of a balance

The budget message presented to Congress on Wednesday is based on the theory that it is not necessary to balance the budget until the fiscal year ending June 30, 1934.[1] There was a huge deficit last year. There is a still larger deficit this year. The budget is not to be balanced next year. Only in the year after next does Mr. Hoover intend even in theory to balance the budget.

Since no one can predict what prices and incomes will be two years hence, it may be said that the Hoover Administration is not seriously trying to set the government's finances in order. It offers the spectacle of the government of the richest country in the world unwilling to economize enough and unwilling to tax enough to balance its accounts. The financial practices we have so often condemned when resorted to in Latin America or in Central Europe we now resort to here.

The assumption at the bottom of the whole thing is Mr. Hoover's favorite notion that the depression is temporary and that we shall soon be back somewhere about the level we were on when he was elected. His present guess seems to be that this will have happened about two years from next July, for he says that the recommended increase of taxes "shall be definitely terminated in two years from next July." How can he possibly know what taxable incomes and custom receipts will be two years from next July? How can he possibly know whether more or less taxes will be needed then? He cannot know. He is guessing on his hopes. And because of these hopes for the future he is willing to temporize with the present, with this year's budget and next year's, piling up deficits, putting no effective brake upon expendi-

[1] Secretary Mellon's annual report to Congress was made public on December 9, 1931, and on the same day the President sent in the annual budget message. The Administration made proposals designed to balance the budget in 1934. These included the levy of taxes on amusement tickets, automobiles, radios, checks and drafts, and telegraph messages; and higher taxes on tobacco, estates, corporation income, and personal income. But Mr. Hoover hardly went beyond generalities in asking for economy.

tures, and adding to all the uncertainties of the time the uncertainties of the government's finance.

The figures for the present year show how impossible it has been thus far for Mr. Hoover to calculate the effects of the depression. His original estimates of receipts were 1,700 million dollars greater than what has actually been collected. They are only a little more than half of what it was believed they would be. That being the fact, what confidence can the country have that the taxes of 1924, which were so productive during the Coolidge boom, can carry the country through its greatest depression?

All that the President claims for his taxes and economies is that they will reduce this year's deficit about twenty cents on a dollar, and that next year they will meet current expenditures except for statutory debt retirement. This leaves no real margin of safety. It is a pure gamble on the theory that expenditures won't rise and that revenues can be calculated to a nicety in times like these. The least that could be expected is that the Administration would provide taxes and economies to balance the budget next year, including the statutory retirement of the debt. This would allow it a margin of safety in case its calculations are wrong. In view of the fact that the calculations were wrong by 1,700 million for this year a margin of 450 millions or thereabouts would hardly be excessive in an era of tremendous deflation.

It may be asked why it is important for the government to balance its budget at a time like this. It can borrow. Why should it tax and economize?

The greatest reason is that in resorting to such shoddy fiscal policies the Administration offers the worst possible example to the world. In the days before the depression the world piled up debts with absolute recklessness. Governments, cities, corporations, individuals, borrowed on such a scale that when prices collapsed and monetary incomes de-

clined they found themselves burdened with fixed charges
that were in many cases intolerable. All of the excess of
these debts cannot perhaps be liquidated now, but surely
it is of prime importance that unproductive indebtedness
should not be increased.

The Government of the United States does not have to go
into debt to pay its bills and it does not have to suspend
the retirement of its debt. If it deliberately refuses to do its
fiscal duty, it lends the enormous force of its example to all
other governments, to the states, to cities, to counties, to
corporations and individuals, who, rather than face the
music, would like to borrow and temporize and gamble
on their hopes. With the Federal Government setting the
example Mr. Hoover offers, the chances of obtaining the
needed readjustments and reforms elsewhere are greatly
diminished, and by that much the actual economic recovery
delayed.

But the policy adopted is not only bad as an example. It
is bad in itself. The government's credit is good. But it is
not infinite. By taking the position that it is not very important to balance the budget, the Administration has deprived itself of any real check upon expenditures. If it
insisted that next year's budget must balance, it would
have an unanswerable argument with which to meet the
enormous expenditures that Congress will wish to make.
As matters stand now it has forfeited its argument and
surrendered its best defense. Having admitted that it is
not necessary to balance last year's, this year's, or next year's
budget, it has thrown open the doors of the Treasury.

For if Congress has to appropriate within the framework
of a balanced budget, the appetite for spending is automatically checked by the distaste for taxing. But if Congress can appropriate in an unbalanced budget there is
nothing to check it except Mr. Hoover's veto message. He

may not find these messages so very effective on the eve of a Presidential election.

December 10, 1931

V. THE GENERAL QUESTION OF PUBLIC WORKS

The resumption of investment; self-sustaining projects as a means of encouraging it

In the determination of policies for dealing with the depression, the most difficult and controversial problem is that which centers upon proposals deliberately to stimulate economic activity. There is a great variety of opinions. On one extreme there are those who think it unwise to intervene at all; on the other those who offer plans for immense bond issues to do public works. The debate is conducted with much heat and, it seems to me, with more dogmatism than patient desire to arrive at an understanding.

Yet if the arguments are examined, it is clear enough that, as between Senator La Follette, who desires a great program of capital expenditure by the government, and his orthodox opponents, there is common ground. Both see that for a recovery there must be a resumption of investment in enterprises that create employment and profits. Both see, too, that this resumption of investment depends upon a restoration of "confidence." Then they diverge.

The heretic school believes that the lack of confidence is really a subjective condition among business men, bankers and investors, and that, therefore, the government, which can afford to take risks that private individuals are afraid of, should temporarily fill the vacuum left by the absence of private initiative.

The orthodox school believes that the lack of confidence is due to real causes, and not merely to a mental depression: that there is a genuine scarcity of good borrowers who could use credit profitably; that there is still a considerable readjustment of costs to be made; that a great program of public works will add to these costs by increasing the weight of taxes to carry the loans; and that in view of the precarious condition of governmental budgets the flotation of another huge bond issue would ruin the bond market and imperil institutions which have large holdings of bonds.

Now, if it were necessary to make a flat choice between these two schools, I do not see how the force of the orthodox argument could be denied. For if great new bond issues have to be superimposed upon the public borrowing that is now unavoidable owing to the state of the budgets, they will certainly depress bond prices. These new issues will also add to the dead-weight burden on the budgets. On the other hand, if it is true that the readjustment of costs in private industry is not sufficiently advanced to have prepared the ground for a revival, no public works conceivable can create a revival. This was amply demonstrated in 1930, when a great deal of money was unsuccessfully spent by public authorities and by corporations to fight the depression. For it is a vain hope to think that a major deflation can be stopped by the relatively small influence of the most grandiose public works scheme. Those who think that have not studied the experience of other countries or really grasped the depth and magnitude of the depression we have been passing through.

But admitting the full force of all this, it does not seem to me that we are entitled to sit back and dismiss the problem from our minds. For the fact remains that though credit is being created there is not yet a resumption of investment. The fact remains that private investors are suffering from severe shock and that the objective facts are made considerably worse by a loss of nerve. It is true that there is a paralysis of private initiative which is more severe than a cool appraisal of conditions warrants. Therefore, it is very desirable that the problem of stimulating a resumption of investment should be explored more deeply.

I venture to suggest that it be explored on the following principles: that no money be raised which entails a charge upon any governmental budget, that an inquiry be instituted to determine what socially useful projects could be started which would be self-supporting, which would not be destructively competitive with existing enterprises, which could be constructed at low costs, which would create a demand for labor and materials. Projects which meet these specifications would not be open to the objections of the orthodox school. They would not put new burdens on the budgets. The bonds to pay for them would not add to existing volume of government securities. They would not destroy private enterprises which are struggling to survive. They would be economically sound in that they would be constructed when costs are low. They would add to the permanent wealth of the community. They would provide a little immediate relief, and they might stimulate by example and effect the spirit of private enterprise.

The question is: Are there such projects? Can projects be found which meet all these specifications? That some projects of this sort could be undertaken I feel certain. Take, for example, the City of New York. There is urgent need of a vehicular tunnel under the East River to connect Manhattan with Long Island. Such a tunnel, by charging tolls, could certainly be made self-sustaining. There is a partially completed express highway on the west side of Manhattan. That could be completed and made self-supporting by charging tolls. The only real objection to these two projects arise from the inefficiency of the Walker Administration. If Mayor Walker could be put aside, if the Legislature would create a public authority divorced from the city government and empowered to cut red tape and sweep aside obstructions, what possible objection can there be to undertaking these two projects?

I cite them only for purposes of illustration. They indicate the type of enterprise which, it seems to me, ought promptly to be studied. As long as we adhere to the principle that the project must be essentially non-competitive and self-sustaining, honestly self-sustaining in the opinion of disinterested experts, the orthodox objections to a public works program do not hold. Another field of enterprise which should be studied is slum clearance. Here the principle that the project should be non-competitive may be invoked. Yet I should suppose that housing built by semi-public corporations on land occupied by slums would not add to the oversupply of housing; it would merely replace bad housing. Certainly this is worth examining at a time when land is cheap and building costs at a point where contractors and unions might be willing to take lower rates in return for fuller employment.

There should be explored, too, the possibility of capital loans to private corporations where those corporations have a capital structure that is reasonable and sound. I do not know the merits of the proposed loan by the Reconstruction Finance Corporation to the Pennsylvania Railroad to enable it to proceed with the electrification of its lines. But assuming that this is a sound idea in the sense that it would be adopted if business were better, then it seems to me that a loan of this sort should be made now. For surely productive loans of this type are far better risks than loans to carry frozen assets. If the government can lend money for any purpose to private institutions, it can well afford to lend it for enterprises that will earn money and create new business.

The main thing is that we should begin to think about the resumption of investment. It is a bad thing to rest in an attitude of negation. The very effort to explore this problem and to work out solutions would be a healthy tonic. For it would give the spirit of enterprise some badly needed exercise. It would remind us that we used to have the habit of initiative, and it might help us to recover it.

There comes a time in every depression when the way to resume is to resume. That time must be approaching, and it would be well to prepare for it.

May 12, 1932

VI. MR. HOOVER AND RELIEF THROUGH PUBLIC WORKS

Various plans for public relief; Mr. Robinson's plan and Mr. Hoover's; the Wagner-La Follette-Smith plan; the two questions of principle

There are three plans to be considered.[1] The first is that of Senator Robinson, which was set forth on Wednesday of last week. He described it as follows:

With assurances that the budget will be balanced and with emergency assistance in sight for those in distress, a well-considered construction program may be promptly authorized and entered upon by the issuance of, say,

[1] Proposals for relief legislation had been offered in Congress as soon as it met. Senator Copeland brought forward a bill to permit the Reconstruction Finance Corporation to make loans to cities for relief; and on January 11, 1932, it was defeated in the Senate 28 to 45. In February was brought forward the Costigan-La Follette bill providing for loans of $375,000,000

$2,000,000,000 of tax exempt bonds, *to be spent upon self-liquidating or profit-making enterprises,* such as tunnels, bridges, and the destruction of slum districts in the great industrial centers. In instances where their credit resources have not been too far depleted and where authority exists or can be promptly obtained the States and the cities desiring to carry forward construction programs which have been suspended because of lack of credit should deliver to the government their own tax-exempt obligations, *and the revenues from the undertaking should be impounded to pay, first, the running expenses, and, second, interest and sinking fund to the Government.*

The second plan under consideration is the President's, made public the day following Senator Robinson's statement. There is only one important difference between the two plans. Both agree that the Federal credit should be pledged only to "income-producing and self-sustaining enterprises." But the President proposes that the Federal Government make loans to private corporations as well as to public bodies.

The third plan is that originally sponsored by Senator Wagner and by Senator La Follette. It is backed by ex-Governor Smith. It proposes to undertake public works without requiring that they be self-liquidating.

Thus, among those who wish to take positive measures, the debate centers on two questions:

---

to the States for relief. It was defeated in the Senate by a vote of 35 to 48. At about the same time the House passed a bill offered by Representative Almon of Alabama, 205 to 209; it increased the Federal allotments for highway construction by $132,500,000. Early in May an earnest effort was made to bring a really feasible plan for relief legislation into shape. Among those who took a hand in the work were Senators Wagner, Robinson of Arkansas, and Pittman, the President, and ex-Governor Smith. The situation as it stood in the middle of the month is dealt with in this article.

1. Shall the enterprise be limited to self-liquidating projects, which entail no charges on the budget for interest, sinking fund, operation, or maintenance?

2. Shall private enterprises be included or shall the projects be confined to public enterprises?

These are the questions of principle to be discussed. These questions have to be answered before a program can be agreed upon.

Before seeking an answer we must first of all consider the case of those who object to any positive program of this character. The *Herald Tribune* objects. Passing over the fact that the *Herald Tribune* has confused the Robinson-Hoover plan with the La Follette-Wagner-Smith plan, the crux of the objection is that the new credit applied to enterprises will not in a period of "debt-paying," that is of deflation, "set in motion a series of stimuli which spread gradually throughout the country. For after one or two changes of hands . . . it returns to the banks, where it merely ceases to be, like any other credit that is not needed." This argument assumes that the money received by employees and firms engaged in the work would be used by them, or by those from whom they in turn made purchases, to repay loans at the banks, and that the banks would make no new loans. This, I take it, is what is meant by saying that the new credit would quickly cease to be.

The argument assumes that the time has not yet come for a resumption of investment, that debt-paying, or in other words, deflation, has not gone far enough. Those who argue this way can point to the fact that although the Federal Reserve Banks have been creating credit on a large scale, the member banks continue to call loans and to deflate. The banks do not want to invest, and therefore, it is argued that a positive program of credit creation and public investment must fail.

Now it would be admitted, I suppose, that the essence of recovery would be a resumption of investment. If tomorrow morning the bankers announced that they had sold successfully a bond issue, let us say, to electrify the Pennsylvania Railroad, and the next day that they had sold successfully a bond issue to construct a large power plant, the objectors to the Robinson-Hoover idea would unquestionably hail the news as most encouraging.

Now what is it that stands in the way of such undertakings? Is it a belief that the country will never again need capital improvements? Hardly. Is it a belief that capital improvements cannot yet be made profitably? Yes. Why can't they be made profitably? Some would say because the costs of materials and labor are still too high; others that the volume of business is not great enough to make any enterprise profitable. The objection as to costs is a matter for negotiation with contractors and with labor; the objection as to volume is a question of being able to wait for an improvement in business. For this waiting means uncertainty in the mind of the investor. He wants to be very sure that the money he invests will be safe as to capital and interest.

The fundamental argument for the Robinson-Hoover idea is that it is a plan to overcome this initial hesitation of the investor by giving him the assurance that the national credit is pledged. Let us take a concrete illustration. Suppose the Port of New York Authority undertook to build a vehicular tunnel under the East River. Suppose it issued bonds for that tunnel which were guaranteed as to interest and sinking fund by the tolls of the tunnel. Suppose then that the Federal Government announced that it would buy those bonds at par whenever offered. I am no bond expert but I should suppose that private investors would be glad to get such bonds and that actually the government would not have to buy many of them. Now if this happened, an actual increase of investment would have taken place.

Those who object to this idea on the ground that the money received by contractors and employees will simply be deflated out of existence by the banks take a very ominous view of the present situation. They imply that after the most drastic deflation of prices and credit of which there is any record a still more drastic deflation is impending. Now it may be granted that there is still considerable scaling down of inflated capital structure to be gone through with. But it is perfectly possible, or at least it has been perfectly possible in the past, for investment to be resumed in enterprises which have been deflated while others lag behind and are passing through receiverships and foreclosures.

There is no certain sign which everybody recognizes as the signal for resumption. It is legitimate, therefore, to assume that some resumption is possible at this time, and that it would occur if the nerves of bankers and investors had not been shaken by the harrowing experiences through which they have passed. It may be that the Robinson-Hoover scheme will not work great results. No one can guarantee it. But the risks of the attempt are small. The country will not be worse off, come what may, for having made some investment in useful and revenue-producing projects. On the other hand, the risks of not doing anything, of sitting and letting the vicious spiral of deflation spin, are very great.

There is the risk that "debt-paying" will become impossible. There is also the risk—no, I should say the certainty —that the country will not endure the consequences of continuing deflation, and that Congress will resort to really inflationary devices to cure it. The Robinson-Hoover plan is, therefore, a truly statesman-like effort to deal by sound principle with a problem which will otherwise surely provoke the adoption of entirely unsound principles. If the people are to bear what they are suffering, they must be convinced that those who claim to be sound are also willing to take all the positive measures which informed opinion can justify. The Robinson-Hoover plan can be justified by informed opinion; though no one is finally expert in these matters, it can be said confidently, I think, that there is sufficient weight of expert opinion behind the scheme to warrant the experiment.

If it succeeds in some measure everybody will rejoice. If it fails, it will be because the forces at work are greater than we are able to cope with, and they will run their course in spite of us. But at least we shall not have to reproach ourselves with having been unwilling to do what we could with such light as we have.

May 18, 1932

VII. BOND ISSUES AND PUBLIC WORKS

The debate about public works; principal question its effect on private recovery; validity of Mr. Hoover's self-liquidating plan

In his criticism of the President's public works program ex-Governor Smith said that "the main thing overlooked by the President . . . is the need of finding immediate productive employment for millions of people." I do not suppose that Mr. Smith meant to be as unfair to Mr. Hoover as these words, taken literally, appear. For whatever else may be said about Mr. Hoover, however much one may disagree with his policies, it cannot be said that he has overlooked the need of restoring employment. Mr. Hoover's concern with the problem has been quite as sincere and his efforts to deal with it quite as persistent as those of any man living.

The question of ways and means can best be debated, therefore, by assuming that the only differences among responsible
men arise out of differences of judgment in a matter where
there is no certain knowledge based upon tested experience.

Ex-Governor Smith's statement is founded on the assumption that a large public works program can produce "immediate productive employment for millions of people." Those
who differ from him, and they include Mr. Owen D. Young,
Senator Robinson, and the President, do not believe that any
public works program conceivable can provide enough work
to make any important impression upon the existing volume
of unemployment. They start from the fundamental assumption that the only way in which jobs can be provided for
millions is through a recovery of business. Only in business
are there enough potential jobs for the unemployed workers.
Therefore, the test of every program is whether it will promote or retard the resumption of private business. The government cannot itself provide the jobs which private business
is not now providing.

Thus, Mr. Hoover cannot be substantially wrong when
he points out that the proposed subsidy of $132,000,000 for
state highways construction would provide direct employment for 35,000 men and indirect employment for perhaps
20,000 more. This would mean that it requires about $2,500
of public money to employ a man for as long as it takes to
build a highway. On this basis a $2,000,000,000 program
would provide temporary work for less than ten per cent
of the estimated unemployed.

The British, who have been experimenting with public
works programs for the last ten years, have had somewhat,
but not very much, better results. A report made to Parliament in 1930 estimates that they have gotten about twice as
much employment out of their experiments as Mr. Hoover's
figures show. This is due in part to lower wages. But even

assuming that the British results could be obtained in the United States under our higher rates and more wasteful methods, there is no ground for believing that a public works program as such can really absorb or even substantially alleviate the present volume of unemployment.

That being the case, any program of government intervention must be looked upon not as a method of providing work immediately on public projects, but as a device which will either stimulate or hold back the resumption of private investment and ordinary business. The immediate problem of relief is not involved; there is no longer any difference of opinion that for the fourth winter of the depression Federal money, as well as state, local, and private, has to be provided. The matter which the President and ex-Governor Smith are discussing has to do with recovery and not with relief.

Now, if the test of any program is its effect on the recovery of private activity, then it is hardly "hairsplitting" about "fine spun theories of financing" to inquire what effect great bond issues would have on public and private credit. For we are suffering from a violent contraction of credit which has drastically lowered all prices.

If we look at the prices of long-term Federal bonds as they stand in Wednesday's papers we note that the first six issues on the list stood at par or better. The last six were selling at a discount down to ten points. We note, too, that all the issues which are at par or better are from 4 per cent bonds or better, whereas the discounted bonds are less than 4 per cent. The weakest bonds, selling at 90.4, are the 3 per cent bonds which were sold last autumn.

Here in all probability lies the explanation of why the Administration and the financial community are so much opposed to a new large issue of long-term Federal bonds. Such an issue would probably have to carry a fairly high rate of interest, certainly at least 4 per cent, and the offer of it would certainly depreciate further Mr. Mellon's 3 per cent bonds, which are already down to 90 and have been as low as 82.3 within the year. These bonds are held by banks and other financial institutions which would suffer heavy losses.

It seems fairly certain that the Treasury in recent years has gravely misjudged the rate of interest. But if it was a mistake it has been made and we are confronted with a condition and not a theory. It is highly undesirable that the Federal Government should issue a new large bond issue which would depreciate the outstanding issues and force the banks, whose assets would be that much impaired, to contract their loans. It is literally true that a big government bond issue would actually increase unemployment and depress prices.

That is a principal reason why the Young-Robinson-Hoover program has as its essential principle that the public credit should be extended only to self-liquidating projects. The theory is that if municipalities, states or private corporations can offer bonds, which are self-sustaining, the government could underwrite them without actually being forced to sell a large issue of new bonds of its own to compete with its existing obligations. The plan, if it works at all, should result in issues of local and corporate bonds which the investing public would be glad to buy.

If the plan worked, the Federal Government would, of course, have pledged its credit—that is to say, its power to tax—but it would not actually need to sell its own long-term bonds or add new burdens to the budget. Such a scheme, if intelligently administered and if received with good will by the financial community, should not impair the national credit or by increasing taxes add to the overhead costs of business.

The scheme limited in this fashion is, of course, open to the criticism that it will not accomplish much. That remains to be proved. Its great merit is that it may, if the time is ripe, inaugurate a resumption of private investment by those who, lacking confidence in ordinary bonds and stocks, are hoarding money or keeping it in short-term notes. If the time is ripe, and judged by the extent of the deflation, we are entitled to assume that it is, a program of this sort might help to move the financial machine off dead center.

If it is to do that, the financial community ought to make an effort to help. It ought not to give way to gloomy forebodings because the plan is somewhat unorthodox. For in the last analysis, if the Young-Robinson-Hoover plan is not adopted, something much more drastic, something much more contemptuous of "fine spun theories of financing" will certainly be substituted for it.

May 26, 1932

· IV ·

CONGRESS: ITS TASK AND HOW IT DEALT WITH IT

I. THE NEW CONGRESS

*Congress takes its seat in a time of great crisis;
national insistence upon courage and candor*

THE Congress which is now assembled for the first time
was elected more than a year ago. Neither party has a
working majority in either house. Neither party has a clear
mandate from the voters. There is no set of promises to be
fulfilled by which the conduct of the individual legislators
have to be judged. They are called to act in the midst of a
crisis the nature of which neither they nor their constituents
foresaw when they were elected. They are uncommitted
upon the great issues before them. They are free for once
to consider themselves representatives of the nation and not
merely delegates from their districts.

The situation is one in which ordinary political practice
will not work. The task of this Congress is to see the country
through an exceptionally difficult period of its history. To
do that successfully this Congress is compelled to do the
very things elected politicians traditionally consider are most
dangerous to do. Normally, a man whose office depends upon
votes finds it politically profitable to spend government
money freely. This Congress is confronted with the largest
peace-time deficit in the history of the country. Normally,

elected officials hate to levy taxes on their own constituents. In this Congress no man possessed of a decent regard for the credit of the nation can avoid the obligation of laying taxes upon the whole mass of the people.

Normally, elected officials find it easiest to vote against the interests of foreigners. In this Congress no man who honestly faces the facts can escape the conclusion that the highest American interest lies in measures which will contribute to the stabilization and the recovery of the economic life of the world. The ordinary political habit of spending freely, shifting and avoiding taxes, and playing jingo can only deepen the depression and discredit democracy.

The ordinary politician has a very low estimate of human nature. In his daily life he comes into contact chiefly with persons who want to get something or to avoid something. Beyond this circle of seekers after privileges, individuals and organized minorities, he is aware of a large unorganized, indifferent mass of citizens who ask nothing in particular and rarely complain. The politician comes after a while to think that the art of politics is to satisfy the seekers after favors and to mollify the inchoate mass with noble sentiments and patriotic phrases. In easy times the politician is probably about right. Certainly he gets himself elected regularly by these methods.

But in really hard times the rules of the game are altered. The inchoate mass begins to stir. It becomes potent, and when it strikes, as it did in Britain the other day, it strikes with incredible emphasis. Those are the rare occasions when a national will emerges from the scattered, specialized or indifferent blocs of voters who ordinarily elect the politicians. Those are for good or evil the great occasions in a nation's history.

An occasion of this sort is probably forming itself here and now. For ten years the American people have been sunk first in the political lethargy of war-weariness and then in the stupor of the great inflation. They are coming out of it. There has been more thought and more feeling about public affairs in the last year than in the ten which preceded it. There is, too, a new generation at the threshold of authority, the generation which survived the war and the post-war era, and they have no emotional commitments to that past. They are tired of the old dull, calculating faces. They are tired of stuffed shirts. They are tired of the fawning and the flattery, of the evasiveness and the straddling, of the soft and the fat and the timorous, of the shoddy optimists, the ignobly self-indulgent, the greedy and the parvenu who battened upon the distortion of values which the inflation produced.

The Congress now assembled will work in an atmosphere very different from the one in which it was elected.

December 8, 1931

II. HARD TAXATION VS. EASY BOND ISSUES

Why should we be taxed?—Disasters certain to follow heavy bond issues; a depression-proof taxation the only real remedy.

Now that the discussion of the tax program is about to begin [1] it is necessary that we should attempt to understand clearly just why taxes must be raised and what must be accomplished by the new taxes.

[1] The tax bill took more of the time of Congress in the winter and spring than any other single measure. It was necessary to raise more than a billion dollars in new revenue, and Washington was filled with lobbyists of interests which did not wish to be taxed. The Ways and Means Committee started work on the measure early in January, and held extensive hearings on a plan recommended by the Treasury Department. It was generally understood that this plan would be drastically revised.

In the year which ended last June the Federal government spent about 900 millions more than it received. These 900 millions were borrowed from investors and were added to the national debt. In the year which will end next June it is practically certain that the government will spent 2,100 millions more than it receives. This also is being borrowed from investors and charged to the national debt. For the following year, beginning July 1 next, and ending June 30, 1933, the year for which Congress is now fixing what may be spent, the Treasury estimates that under the present tax laws and with the expenses approved by the Administration, there will be a deficit of 1,400 millions. This, too, would have to be borrowed and added to the debt unless expenses are reduced and taxes raised.

There are eminent economists who tell us that it is good policy for the government to borrow in a time of depression and to pay off its debt in a time of prosperity. They suggest, therefore, not only that the government should keep on borrowing to meet its deficits, but in some cases they even suggest that the government borrow great sums in addition, anywhere from 2,000 millions to 5,000 millions, to carry out a far-reaching public works program to create jobs and relieve unemployment. If this advice were followed it would mean that the government would, during the period of the depression, have to borrow somewhere in the neighborhood of 10,000 millions dollars. As the total net debt of the government in 1930 was 16,000 millions, the advice of this school of financial experts would call for the sale of five new bonds for every eight bonds now in existence.

What would it mean to add more than half again as many bonds to those already in the market? It would mean, obviously, that the price of all government bonds would go down. The supply of bonds would be 60 per cent larger and the demand, considering how people's incomes have shrunk, would certainly be smaller. Therefore, government bonds would decline. That this is no theoretical guess can be seen by looking at the present prices of government bonds. On Monday there were only two issues selling at par. All the rest were selling at prices which meant a loss to any man who bought them when the government originally sold them. The last two issues, sold during the depression, were down about 15 per cent, so that anyone who bought the new bonds of last September and sold them on Monday lost 15 dollars out of every hundred he invested.

Suppose, then, that under these conditions the government tried to sell 5,000 or 10,000 million new bonds. What would happen? The Treasury would see that the 3 per cent bonds were now worth 85 instead of a 100. Obviously, if it offered more 3 per cent bonds it could not hope to obtain more than 85 dollars on every hundred-dollar bond. The government would, therefore, have to increase the interest rate, how much I do not know. It would have to be enough to make the new bonds very attractive to an investor. Suppose it did that, what then? Then investors would try to sell the unattractive bonds they now have and buy the new, more attractive bonds. This would mean that the existing bonds would become still less valuable.

What difference does it make if government bonds lose value? Why is it thought to be such a bad thing? Why do men like Mr. Mills of the Treasury lay such stress upon maintaining the national credit; that is, on keeping government bonds at par? The reason is this: A very large part of these government bonds are owned by banks and insurance companies. Government bonds have always been considered the safest way to keep money. Now, if the bonds in which banks and insurance companies invest the depositors' money lose 15 per cent of their value, it is a serious loss. It means that the financial institutions, to whom every business man has to go to borrow money to conduct his business, are compelled to cut down their loans. When their best assets shrink, they do not dare to lend freely.

If banks and insurance companies do not dare to lend freely, railroads, corporations, all kinds of businesses have to keep cutting down their operations. Such a contraction of credit means the slowing up of business, the reduction of wages and the laying off of men. It follows that any one seriously interested in avoiding an increase of unemployment will wish to see the government credit jealously and absolutely protected. If, in addition to that, the credit of the railroads could be reëstablished, so that railroad bonds went back somewhere near where they were two years ago, it is no exaggeration to say that more jobs would be created, more business recovery accomplished, than by any other device now proposed.

The protection of the government credit is the first consideration, for only if that is indisputably secure, can the government hope to help railroads and banks, and through them the farmers, the business men and wage-earners. The only way the government can make its credit perfect is to stop borrowing to pay its expenses. It can do that in part by reducing expenses. It must do the rest by raising taxes.

What kind of taxes? There is no need now to go into details. We can wait for that until we have estimates as to how much money different sorts of taxes would yield. But the principle of the new taxation is clear enough. It must be taxation which is as nearly as possible depression-proof; that is to say, it must be taxation which will produce revenue without question in the next two years. That is the principle by which all proposals must be judged. It is right that income and inheritance taxes should be drastically increased. But let us have no illusions about these taxes. They are prosperity taxes, and will not yield nearly enough in a time of depression. They should be increased because it is just to increase them. Though they will not meet the needs of the government, high rates in the high brackets are the only effective way of justifying broader taxation to the voters. The rich are not rich enough to pay the deficit, but what they can pay they should be asked to pay first.

The quicker it is settled that high rates are to be imposed on the rich, the sooner Congress and the country can settle down to the real problem, which is to devise a tax program so broadly based, and so invulnerable to depression that there can be no further question about the adequacy of the government revenues.

For only when a certain flow of revenue is provided will the national credit be above suspicion.

December 30, 1931

III. THE STRUGGLE IN THE HOUSE OVER TAXATION AND ECONOMY

The Washington crisis; if Congress fails to show the needed public courage, a drastic expression of public sentiment will follow

Wherever governments by elected officials have been confronted with the iron necessities of governmental finance during the deflation they have begun, as Washington has begun, first, by postponing consideration of the problem, then by temporizing with it, then by approaching it reluctantly.[1] Only when the credit of the government was clearly seen to be imperiled have effective measures been proposed for pre-

---

[1] After the hearings on the Treasury plan for new taxation, the House Ways and Means Committee went into executive session and at the end of three weeks produced a plan of its own. It was based on a general manufacturers' sales tax, and carried a rate of 2.25 per cent applicable to

serving it. But in almost every instance these measures have encountered the hostility of a substantial majority of the legislature. For the normal reaction of popular assemblies the world over, once they discover that the necessary revenues cannot be obtained by taxing the very rich, is to feel as Mr. Crisp of Georgia, describes the House of Representatives as feeling now—that the "House is against reducing expenses, is in favor of increased appropriations and is against taxes."

Almost every country has had a large deficit and almost every country has begun, as we did, by borrowing money to meet it. For the alternatives to borrowing are to reduce expenditures and to increase taxes. In normal times both are politically dangerous. Against every specific proposal to economize or to tax there are arrayed a collection of powerful interests. Thus, if Congress touches the debt service, it collides with the investing classes and impairs the credit it is seeking to preserve. If it touches the veterans' payments, it collides with the soldiers' vote. If it touches government salaries, it collides with the office-holders, who are the backbone of the party machines. If it touches subsidies, it collides with sectional and class interests.

If, on the other hand, the government proceeds to raise taxes, it is soon confronted with the disconcerting discovery that in a period of depression and deflation the utmost taxation of the rich can not produce more than a small portion of the revenue needed. For the upper limit of taxation is the point at which capital will flee the tax collector: in Europe at the limit of taxation capital had taken refuge in foreign countries; in the United States we have provided a refuge

---

nearly all manufactured articles save the basic necessities of life. This plan was brought up in the House for debate on March 10, and it soon became evident that under Western and Southern pressure the House would reject it. On March 24, amid excited scenes, the House eliminated the general sales tax by a vote of 223 to 153.

by issuing some thirty thousand millions of tax-exempt bonds. But even if the rich would stand still and let themselves be taxed to the limit, they do not have in times like these a taxable income nearly sufficient to meet the deficits of federal, state, and local governments. Their total income is small in comparison with the total income of the mass of the people. As a result, every official who has honestly studied the problem, be he socialist or conservative, ends by realizing that if the money is to be raised, it must be raised out of the small contributions of the many.

Thus, governments, facing the necessity of balancing their budgets because they cannot continue to borrow without destroying the national credit, are inescapably compelled to retrench at the risk of antagonizing powerful interests and to levy taxes upon the heavily burdened masses of the people.

In no great country has an ordinary political assembly had the courage or the discipline to tax and to economize effectively. The whole habit of elected bodies is against so heroic a proceeding, for the sentiments of the voters are in the first instance invariably opposed to effective measures. Even when the voters understand the need of them they are at first more preoccupied with shifting the incidence of the sacrifice than in assuring the solvency of the government. Thus in all countries the politicians in office have temporized until the very last moment. It was not until June of last year, when capital was in full flight from Germany, that the Bruening government dared to take really drastic measures. It was not until midsummer, when the British credit was impaired, that Britain really began to take the matter in hand. It was not until about four months ago, when the American financial system had been badly shaken, that the Administration became a reluctant convert to the idea that it was vitally necessary to balance the budget.

In every country the eleventh hour effort to solve the problem has precipitated a political crisis of the first magnitude. No country has emerged from the crisis except by suspending the ordinary methods of partisan politics. In Germany there is government by decree. In Great Britain there has been what amounts to at least a temporary constitutional revolution. In no country where the problem has been as acute as it is here has it proved possible to govern according to the letter or the spirit of the established political system.

The real issue in Washington is not whether we shall have one kind of tax or another. It is whether in the ordinary proceedings of Congress elected representatives will impose the necessary sacrifices upon their constituents. For the retrenchments and the taxes must be laid upon large bodies of voters. There is no other place to lay them. The question is whether the existing parties can muster the courage and the discipline to conduct a government that is national in its purpose, and therefore superior to pressure and to clamor, that is strong and orderly and swift in its operation, and can thereby rally the country and command its allegiance. If it can be done, we shall have done what no other democracy has been able to do: we shall have surmounted the crisis without resorting to extra-legal measures.

If it cannot be done, if authority remains paralyzed, as it is today, so that no one is responsible who has power and no one has power who is responsible, the course of events here may not be unlike that in other lands. The nation will be brought to the brink of disaster. Then will come a reaction moved by a profound revulsion of national feeling. Somewhere and somehow the national spirit will assert itself. When it does, it will have small regard for parties and politicians, their platforms, their speeches, their exorbitant desire to be reëlected, or for the ambitions and prospects and nice calculations of candidates and party managers.

March 29, 1932

IV. THE BUDGET AND PUBLIC CREDIT

*Vote of the House to balance the budget; battle still
unwon; what is the precise meaning of the vote?*

There is, as yet, no real assurance that the new tax bill,
which has been so hastily contrived over the week end, will
really do what it is intended to do. The burden of proof is
on its sponsors. We know that in the considered opinion
of the Ways and Means Committee a very different bill was
called for, and something more than the emotions of Tues-
day afternoon are needed to prove that the new measure is
what it purports to be. The estimation of tax yields in times
like these is at best a very difficult and tricky business. A tax
bill hastily thrown together in the hysterical atmosphere
of the last few days must be looked at skeptically.

But even if we take the best possible view of the new bill
we cannot avoid asking for more specific assurances than
those which Speaker Garner persuaded the House to give.[1]
Did the House mean when the members rose from their
seats to declare in favor of balancing the budget that the
House will vote the economies which are part of the program? Did the House mean that it will vote no new appropriations beyond those in the program? Finally, how do
the members who rose in their seats square this pledge to
the nation with the report that 167 members are pledged to
the bonus bill, with another 177 listed as non-committal?

For if, in addition to the billion dollars the veterans are al-

---

[1] Speaker Garner, after the House defeated the general sales tax, took
the floor on March 29, and made a vigorous appeal for the passage of a tax
bill which would balance the budget. As a result of his entreaties, the
House by formal vote pledged the enactment of such a bill. It also immediately enacted eleven excise rates. But this restored only one-third of the
amount lost by the defeat of the sales tax, and left the prospects for an
adequate revenue gloomy.

ready receiving, Representatives vote them another two billions the pledge to balance the budget is sheer deception. The only question is: Who is to be deceived, the veterans or the country? If the payment to the veterans is to be made in some kind of scrip or depreciated paper, it is the veterans who are to be deceived while the country's credit is injured. If the plan is to vote the payments on the theory that the Senate or the President will save the country from the folly of the scheme, then it is cowardice as well as deception. If the plan is to be sincere with the veterans and really pay them this exorbitant sum, then the pledge to balance the budget was broken before it was given.

The prospect now is that there will be tedious and complicated debate and maneuver lasting many weeks before the financial policy of the government has actually been established. The problem is to maintain a vigilant and resolute public opinion in this interval. For it is our habit as a people to become quickly excited and no less quickly bored and diverted. The campaign which has to be waged will call for the utmost perseverance. For such a sustained effort in the face of all the plausible distractions which will be presented it is necessary to have firm and simple convictions as to the reasons why it is necessary to balance the budget.

The whole world, including America, is suffering from a stupendous fall in the prices of commodities. This fall took place after nearly the whole world, including governments, corporations, and individuals, had borrowed enormous sums of money at the old higher prices. Thus nearly all debtors everywhere are in great difficulty, and as a result almost all creditors are either in difficulty or at least deeply hesitant to lend any more money. So great is the volume of debts which cannot be paid at present prices that the private credit system of the whole world is almost immobilized.

There remains, however, the public credit of the United States, which rests, of course, on nothing but the fact that the American people still have enormous resources and that Congress has the legal right to tax them. With the drying up of private credit it has been necessary to mobilize the public credit in the effort to preserve a large part of the nation's economy from bankruptcy.

This use of public credit is obviously an emergency measure. It cannot cure the depression. For that steps will have to be taken which neither party in Congress has as yet seriously considered. All the present measures can do is to protect sounder enterprises from having to liquidate and by liquidation to depress prices and deepen the depression.

It follows that if the emergency use of public credit is to be effective the public credit must be beyond reproach. But if the government has to borrow great sums of money to pay its current expenses, if the government's own revenues are not enough to pay its bills, the government is deprived of the strength to support the private credit of the nation. It becomes another corporation in the red and by all odds the greatest. Therefore, the balancing of the budget is peculiarly necessary. The situation is the exact opposite of the war years, when the government was running huge deficits while business profits were booming. Today prices are collapsed and profits are largely deficits, and it is the government itself which must be solvent if private credit is to be tided over.

The balancing of the budget and the measures to sustain private credit cannot of themselves do more than prevent things from becoming worse. But it is necessary to do that if they are ever to become better. For if the government credit is impaired the situation will be lost to all central control and the world crisis will be liquidated here not by orderly adjustment and concerted and considered measures, but by a great financial and economic disaster. This is no alarmist prophecy.

This is the lesson of the experience of dozens of countries, and it expresses the judgment of experienced students.

The problem is understood better abroad than it is here, for since the war Europe has twice gone through the experience which now confronts us. When Europeans sell dollars on hearing that Congress may not balance the budget, when Europeans withdraw their deposits or start selling American securities, they are not moved by hostility to America. They have put their money in America because they hoped it would be safe here. When they take fright and start to withdraw it they are moved by the memories of the agonies they themselves have suffered because their legislatures lacked the courage to protect the national credit. They do not believe there is any magic by which the United States could escape the consequences of the same failure. Their action is, therefore, genuinely significant as a practical judgment on the merits of the question.

March 31, 1932

V. THE NEED FOR DETERMINED MEASURES

Washington wrestling with taxation and retrenchment; the problem can be only partially solved at present; but the attempted solution must be sincere and thoroughgoing

Washington, April 21, 1932.

No one can possibly follow in all their detail the controversies here about taxation and retrenchment.[1] Against every tax proposed there is a lobby. Against every economy pro-

---

[1] On April 1 a tax bill which few found satisfactory finally passed the House, 327 to 64. The problem then went to the Senate. The Finance Committee began public hearings on it and on the day this dispatch was written went into executive session to produce a new bill. There was a

posed there is a lobby. The arguments pro and con are interminable and inconclusive and not Solomon in all his wisdom could judge justly each complaint. The pressure from all directions is relentless. For the task of balancing the budget is a painful one: it consists in distributing not favors and privileges but burdens and sacrifices.

Only the strongest kind of party discipline backed by powerful national sentiment could possibly break the deadlock of lobbies and blocs and special interest. But in the last few months since the problem of public finance first became visible and acute the leaders of both parties have been too slow and too hesitant in their own actions and opinions to get command of the situation. On the Administration side the unconscionable delay in facing the question has impaired its prestige. On the Democratic side the leadership has been just plain stupid. The Democrats under Mr. Garner have not known what they were doing and hardly know now.

They found themselves with an uncertain control of the House, called upon to deal with a situation which meant retrenchment of hundreds of millions of dollars and the laying of a billion of new taxes. One would have supposed that as politicians the Democrats would at least have been shrewd enough to let Mr. Hoover take the responsibility of digging himself out of this hole. But no. The Democrats rushed forward and grabbed the shovel out of his hands. They would have their own tax bill. They would impose their own economies. Then to prove that they were newborn babes, they suspended party discipline so that every Congressman stood isolated and naked to all the blasts from all the four quarters of the heavens. The result is that the Democrats have drawn upon themselves most of the odium of

---

general fear that it would find the task really insoluble. Special interests were still represented by powerful lobbies, and there was danger of much trading and log-rolling.

the inevitable sacrifices, and in addition the odium of having alarmed the country by the exhibition of their own confusion.

Somehow or other a tax bill and some retrenchments will be agreed upon. It is in order for us to ask ourselves just what the real prospects are. It will transpire, I think, that the net result of the session's efforts will be to establish the idea that the effort to balance the budget is important, and a partial attempt to arrive at a balance will have been made. The problem will not have been solved. It will have to be dealt with again next winter. We might as well be candid about the situation. What are being talked about now are taxes and retrenchments which will just barely bring receipts and expenditures into theoretical balance provided business improves, provided no new expenditures are authorized, provided the European debtors pay in full. There is no provision for the sinking fund, there are certain to be deficiency bills in December, and full payment of the war debts is out of the question.

There is no use pretending. But equally there is no use getting panicky about it. The essential thing in this whole struggle is not the arithmetical balance of the budget on June 30, 1933, but an unequivocal testimony that the American people mean to bring the budget into balance. It is the sincerity of the purpose which matters most. It will not be disastrous to have a moderate deficit next year owing to miscalculation under exceptionally incalculable conditions. But it would be disastrous to confess by our actions that we do not much care whether we pay our bills or not and that we do not have the character to tax ourselves and make sacrifices. We could afford a deficit. We could not afford to show ourselves flabby and timid. For then our affairs would be out of hand and we should not trust ourselves or be trusted.

It follows that the essence of the matter is not statistical but political. The underlying question is whether the American nation acting through its party system can convince it-self that it is awake and determined. If that can be done, and it could be by a few bold and quick decisions in Wash-ington to pass a tax bill, accept the President's economies and kill the bonus by June 1, the immediately necessary will have been accomplished. The budget will not really be in bal-ance, but the government itself will be coherent and respon-sible. That is the important thing. For on such a demon-stration depends in good part the restoration of the confi-dence of the people.

Those who look ahead know that the fiscal problem will require much more far-reaching measures than are yet under practical discussion in Washington. How drastic they will have to be—how much further it will be necessary to go in broadening the base of taxation and in levying upon capital accumulation, how deeply it will be necessary to cut into the shocking anomaly of the veterans' subsidy—cannot be de-termined now. If political Washington has the good sense to show good faith and effective discipline now, the invig-oration of confidence may, in conjunction with the economic tides, relieve the pressure so much by next winter that easier solutions will be possible.

April 22, 1932

VI. A TEST OF GOVERNMENTAL PURPOSE

*The meaning of the budget struggle; only a tentative
balance possible; but the government can show that
it has the courage to tax and the courage to limit
expenditures*

The House has done to the Economy Bill what it did to the Tax Bill.[1] It has torn it to pieces. There is no cause for

---

[1] The House on May 3 finally passed an omnibus budget bill which greatly disappointed the country. In its original form the bill had offered

astonishment in this. All experience of legislative bodies shows that in a serious budgetary situation the ordinary representative who must soon face his constituents will not voluntarily vote for heavy sacrifices by taxes and retrenchments. The task is too great for political human nature. That is why every government facing a problem of the magnitude of ours has had either to balance its budget by executive decree or to obtain a special and overpowering national mandate from the people.

A candid view will show at once that if the Administration program of taxes and economies, or any other program now under discussion, were promptly enacted, the budget for next year—that is, for the year extending from July 1, 1932, to June 30, 1933—would not certainly be in arithmetical balance. Not only is there no provision made for the sinking fund, but the Treasury is counting upon full payment on the war debts; it has calculated the yield of taxes on the assumption of an improvement in business; nothing has been provided for unemployment relief, though that will certainly be necessary next winter; and the estimate of economies is optimistic and so deficiency bills are highly probable.

The truth is that all programs for balancing the budget depend upon the success of the effort to arrest the fall in prices and stimulate some recovery of employment and profits. That being the case, why is it so important to make the struggle now toward the ideal of a balanced budget? That

---

savings of more than $200,000,000; as finally passed the savings had been reduced to about $40,000,000. This was in spite of the efforts of President Hoover, who, after much delay, and after an unwise proposal on April 4 for the creation of a joint Congressional and executive board to frame economy legislation, had on April 16 sent the House his own draft of an economy bill, with a long and careful explanation. On May 5 he sent Congress another special message urging a speedy balancing of the budget. This article was written amid the confusion engendered by the long delay and the dark outlook.

struggle will obviously have to be resumed next winter even if Congress votes the taxes and economies now before it.

The answer usually given is that a balanced budget is necessary to maintain the credit of the United States Government, and that it is vitally important to maintain that credit at all times, but particularly at a time when private credit is so seriously impaired. That answer is correct, but it needs to be amplified if it is to be convincing to those who look at the present prices of government bonds and wonder whether there is any real doubt about the national credit.

The credit of the United States rests upon the conviction that the government can and will meet its obligations. This means two things: that the government will exercise its sovereign right to tax the people and that it will not tax them more than they can and will bear.

The first duty of the government, then, is to show that it has the courage to draw upon the resources of the people. If it has not that courage, its credit is at once impaired, for it is then demonstrating that it is not willing to place all the resources of the nation behind its obligations. If the government is afraid to tax the rich, if the rich are powerful enough to avoid taxes, then obviously for that government the fortunes of the rich are a frozen asset. If the government shows that it is afraid to tax the middle class in some fair proportion, then for the purposes of the government's credit the wealth of the middle class is a frozen asset. Therefore, in a time like this the best tax bill from the point of view of the national credit is one which fearlessly opens up to taxation, by one method or another, the whole range of incomes. That this taxation should be progressive, so that the larger the income the larger the rate, is perfectly clear and undisputed. But unless taxation is comprehensive as well as progressive the national credit has not been fully sustained.

The second duty of the government is to show that it can

control its own expenditures. If it has not the political courage to resist the pressure of lobbies, of organized minorities, of its own employees, then it cannot convince the taxpayers or the purchaser of its obligations that it can really perform what it promises. A government which cannot resist the pressure of the veterans has lost control of a very large part of its expenditures. A government which cannot reduce the pay of its own civil servants, when that pay has increased in real value, is not longer sovereign. A government which cannot reduce subsidies to special interests is under their heel.

Therefore, from the point of view of the national credit, those economies which are politically the most dangerous are for that very reason the most important. The actual savings which can be made provide relatively little relief. But a proof that the government can make them is of the utmost importance because it shows that there is no bottomless hole in any part of the budget.

May 3, 1932

VII. THE STRUGGLE IN THE SENATE

The attempt to reënact war-time rates on incomes;
both income taxes and consumption taxes required
to meet the Treasury's needs

The most decisive test of sentiment in the Senate thus far was the vote which defeated the Couzens amendment.[1] This

---

[1] The Senate was now struggling with the economy bill. On June 8 it passed a measure which was calculated to effect savings of about $150,-000,000 in the budget; an amount quite inadequate, but a great improvement upon the House performance. Of the $150,000,000 saving, about $100,000,000 was expected to result from a furlough plan for government workers urged by President Hoover.

was a proposal to reënact the highest war-time rates—those which were demanded under the Revenue Act of 1918. The general impression is that this was a measure aimed at the very rich, and it is known as the "soak the rich" amendment. An examination of the proposal will show that as compared with the Committee Bill the increase would have been considerable for incomes of $70,000 and over, but the really drastic increases would have been imposed on incomes from $3,000 up to $70,000. Thus under the Senate Committee Bill a net income of $3,000 would pay $3.75, whereas under the Couzens amendment it would pay $60. The Couzens amendment would have multiplied the lowest taxes fifteen times, medium taxes about twice, the moderately large taxes about once and a half, and the very largest about half. The Couzens amendment would, it is estimated, have raised the number of returns from 2,711,535 under the present law to a little more than 7,125,000.

The alignment of the Senators on the Couzens amendment was substantially that between the agrarian States and the industrial States. Of the thirty-one votes cast for it my impression is that the great bulk, more than twenty-five, came from States west of the Mississippi and south of the Potomac. There were votes cast *against* the amendment by Senators from this region, but there were not half a dozen votes cast *for* it by Senators from the industrial regions of the North and East.

How is such a vote to be interpreted? It seems to me entirely misleading to suppose that the Senators from the States where there are big manufacturing cities were concerned about whether an income of $200,000 paid $77,940 under the Committee Bill or $101,030 under the Couzens amendment. The real burden of the Couzens amendment would have fallen on incomes between $7,000 and $50,000, that is to say upon active business men, upon the white-collar employees, upon executives, and upon the professional class. These are, by and large, the same people who pay the bulk of the states' income taxes and of local taxes in cities.

The fact that the support of the Couzens amendment came almost entirely from agricultural states raises the question as to why the Senators from these regions were so ready to impose severe taxes on small and moderate earnings. The answer, it seems to me, is to be found in the difference between incomes in the form of money and incomes in kind. The farmer, on the average, has a much smaller money income than the city man. But it is by no means certain that he has a lower standard of life. For a great many of the things, including food, fresh air, recreation, which the city man has to pay for in dollars, the farmer obtains without the use of money. Now the income tax reaches only money incomes. Hence it is the city man who is the chief income tax payer, even though his real income—measured in terms of food, light, air and even security in time of depression—may be much less than if he lived on the land.

I venture to suggest that this is the real reason why Britain is almost the only country which manages to support its government out of income taxes. Britain is the most highly industrialized country in the world, and that means that the great bulk of British incomes are money incomes. No other country that I know of is able to make the income tax work as it works in Britain. Everywhere else, in France, in Canada, in Australia, the income tax has to be supplemented by consumption taxes of one kind or another. It is hard to believe that this difference between British and all other practice is due solely to the extraordinary fiscal patriotism of the British people. The Canadians are of the same stock and have the same traditions. The true reason, it seems to me, is that in countries which are agrarian, the income tax alone does not reach a sufficient part of the real income of the people.

The immediate problem, of course, is to raise money where it can most readily be found. Senator Couzens, relying on the Congressional statisticians, thinks that the 1918 rates would raise $331,000,000 more than the Committee rates. The Treasury statisticians say they would raise only $193,-000,000 more. The real point is that neither schedule of rates will raise enough money to bring the budget into balance. The inescapable fact remains that at the bottom of the depression the income tax alone is not productive enough. The money incomes of the income taxpayers have declined too drastically.

Therefore, an honest effort to balance the budget must include, unless there are economies beyond anything now discussed, a new source of taxation. Tariffs cannot provide it, for when tariffs become prohibitive they cease to yield revenues. There is nothing left to tax but consumption. The choice here is between high consumption taxes on a narrow list of articles and low consumption taxes on a broad list. If it is certainty of revenue that is most important, a low tax on a broad list clearly offers our government the best assurance of revenue.

Those who face the facts coolly and really mean to balance the budget are, it seems to me, compelled to give up the notion that the issue in Washington is between something like the war-time taxes and the sales tax. If we really mean to balance the budget, we shall unhappily need both. Even then it might be doubted whether the budget would be in exact balance. But an exact balance is not of primary importance. If all the revenues of the people are tapped by taxation the object of the whole effort to balance the budget will have been achieved. The wealth of the nation will have been pledged to maintain its credit.

May 19, 1932

VIII. A SATISFACTORY TAX BILL ENACTED

*The Senate bill meets the need; Congress proves its
good faith*

The tax bill as it comes from the Senate proposes to raise
about thirty per cent of new revenue out of income taxes and
seventy per cent out of consumption taxes. The Senate did
not accept either the general manufacturers' sales tax or the
war-time income taxes. But it has accepted the highest income taxes ever imposed in time of peace and it has imposed heavy sales taxes on a large number of articles which
are in wide use. The bill has a broad base. Everyone who
spends money will be making a substantial contribution
which can fairly be described as roughly proportionate to
his ability to pay.[1]

If the House will accept this bill promptly without destructive amendments, the country is entitled to believe that in
view of all the difficulties it has a tax bill which is about as just
and effective as could be written at this time. The only important qualification that must be made is in regard to the
tariff taxes. They cannot remotely be described as revenue
measures: all of them put together are not estimated to yield

[1] The Senate had finally, as this article indicates, brought a partially
satisfactory tax bill out of the melée in Washington. The long hearings
and the secret sessions of the Finance Committee in April had resulted only
in an impasse. But Ogden L. Mills, Secretary of the Treasury, appeared
before the committee on May 6. Shortly afterward the committee agreed
upon a compromise program and brought it before the Senate. The bill
was then held in the Senate till the end of the month. An effort to reinstate
the general sales tax in modified form was defeated, 27 to 53. Early on
the morning of June 1 the bill was passed. It went through a hasty conference between committees of the two houses of Congress, was sent to the
President, and on June 6 was signed. The best estimates were that it would
furnish an addition of about $1,120,000,000 for the Federal Treasury. But
as this article indicates, many observers still felt great skepticism of any
actual balancing of the budget.

more than 6½ million dollars, and these estimates do not
allow for the loss of trade which these tariffs will certainly
cause. It can be argued that these preposterous items will
probably diminish the revenues of the government besides
causing severe damage to American exports. But apart from
these tariffs, the bill is far from being a bad bill. It is quite
good enough to be adopted and certainly not bad enough in
important details to be haggled over any longer.

It would be idle to pretend that this bill, along with the
promised retrenchments, will actually guarantee a balanced
budget next year. It is impossible to make a positive estimate
of the yield of taxes at a time when earnings, profits, security
values, and the consumption of goods are so unstable. If
business deteriorates further, obviously the budget will not
balance; the more business improves the more nearly the
budget will be in balance. A tax bill at a time like this is
necessarily a speculation on the future. Provided the government and people show a sincere willingness to tax themselves
heavily and to retrench, no creditor of the United States has
the right to doubt the good faith of the American nation in
meeting its obligations.

The object of the whole struggle to balance the budget has
been to prove that good faith. The Senate bill achieves that
end. The pledge is given that the United States means to
pay. With that pledge firmly established in the American
mind the most immediately necessary thing has been accomplished. For if it should turn out that the estimates of
yields are too high, the next Congress, which meets in
December, can vote the higher income taxes of the Couzens
Amendment and the general manufacturers' tax. With the
Presidential election behind it, the opposition to such
measures, if they are then necessary, will be much less. In
the meantime the popular demand for economy is bound
to increase as these new taxes begin to bite. Next winter the

struggle to deflate the special subsidies, and particularly the subsidies to unwounded veterans, will become practical politics.

There is no reasonable ground for despair about the prospect of the Federal budget. The program in sight meets the emergency by measures which are sound and just in principle. The results depend now, not upon the budgetary program, but upon the course of business. A bad budgetary situation undoubtedly hurts business, and bad business throws the budget into disorder. Congress is now by way of making a budget adapted to bad business conditions. If it adopts that budget, its responsibility in this field is discharged for the time being, and attention must then be centered upon the restoration of confidence in business, the resumption of investment, the restoration of trade, and a rise in prices. It will not be fair to say that business is paralyzed because the budget is in disorder. The budget will be essentially in order provided business recovers from its paralysis.

June 2, 1932

IX. THE BRITISH TAX SYSTEM: LESSONS
TO BE LEARNED

Superior yield of British tariff, inheritance, and income taxes; the reasons

With the virtual completion of the tax bill by the House it becomes rather interesting to compare our system of raising revenue with that of the British. Sufficiently good figures are available showing how in the depths of their depression the British have managed to finish the year with a slight surplus.

For purposes of comparison I have divided sources of revenue into four classes, namely: from income taxes, from estate taxes, from customs duties, and finally from miscellaneous excise and nuisance taxes. I have calculated very roughly the percentage of the whole tax revenue which the British government has actually received in each of these four categories and also the percentage of our whole revenue which under each of these categories it is estimated that the original Crisp bill and the new Progressive bill now passed will yield. I am not sure that my figures are strictly accurate, but in the hope that my arithmetic has not failed me, I feel fairly sure that they indicate the general proportions fairly.

The British tax revenues are derived about as follows:

from income tax.....................50%
from estate tax......................10%
from customs.......................20%
from excise, etc.....................20%

Under the bill which the House rejected it was estimated that our revenues would be derived about as follows:

from income tax.....................32%
from estate tax......................1%
from customs.......................12%
from excise, etc....................55%

Under the bill as rewritten after the Progressive revolt, and allowing for certain economies of a rather doubtful nature, it is estimated that our revenues will be derived about as follows:

from income tax.....................37%
from estate tax......................1%
from customs.......................14%
from excise, etc.....................48%

Comparing first the new tax bill with the one which the House rejected, the significant thing, it seems to me, is that after all the talk about "soaking the rich," the Progressives have not radically altered the proportions. They have put their highest taxes upon incomes and they have only increased the percentage of the whole revenue from 32 per cent to 37 per cent. These figures, I think, magnify the result achieved, for they are calculated against a smaller total revenue, since I have given the Progressives the benefit of the alleged economies. Had the percentages for the original bill been calculated on the same base the actual achievement would be about 3 per cent. In short, the Progressive coalition has not made any important change in shifting the burden of taxation to the rich.

When we compare the American bill as passed by the House with the British results we find:

That the British have taken half their revenue from income taxes, while we hope to take slightly more than a third;

That the British have taken one-tenth of their revenue from inheritances, whereas we hope to take about one one-hundredth;

That the British have taken three-fifths of their revenue from incomes and inheritances, whereas we hope to take rather less than two-fifths:

That the British have taken one-fifth of their revenue from customs duties, whereas we hope to take about one-tenth.

These propositions are worth studying. Let us look first at the last one. Here, on the one hand, is a nation of forty-six million people who have a tariff but not *our* kind of tariff, and they have collected more revenue absolutely and twice as much relatively as we who have a population nearly three times as great. Does this possibly suggest that our tariff has so successfully shut off imports that it has lost a large part of its utility as a source of revenue? For, of course, no customs duties can be collected on goods that are not imported.

Let us look now at income and inheritance taxes. The British, out of a population a little more than one-third as large as ours, have actually collected more revenue than the House bill is estimated to yield. What is the explanation? Has the Progressive Coalition failed to tax the rich as boldly as the British do it? The figures show that for incomes of a million dollars and over the rates are practically the same in both countries, that at $250,000 and up the British rates are from 40 to 50 per cent higher, and that from $100,000 down to $5,000 they are from two to twenty times as great. In other words, the superior yield of the British income tax is due to the fact that small and medium incomes are so much more heavily taxed.

As to the inheritance tax, the differences would be worth study. They will be found to lie, I imagine, in two circumstances: that part of our inheritance taxes go to the states and that the British tax the large number of small inheritances more heavily than we do.

The net conclusions, it seems to me, are these: The income tax, which is the most desirable of all taxes, because it is the fairest and the most visible, is a relative failure in the United States. Compared with the British it has two great weaknesses: it has a hole at the top through which the rich can escape into tax-exempt bonds, and it has a hole at the bottom because Congress hesitates to tax small and medium incomes.

With these holes in it, the American income tax is a fair weather tax. It is very productive when profits are big. But in times like these it is ludicrously inadequate, as the House tax bill shows when, in a spirit of the utmost optimism and of giving itself the benefit of every doubt, it hopes to get from incomes only 37 per cent of our revenues.

May 2, 1932

X. CONGRESS AND SCHEMES FOR INFLATION

Prosperity cannot be won back by spending money;
national credit paramount

Congress is about to take measures against the further deflation of credit. The plan is to make about two thousand
million dollars of Federal credit available to financial institutions which have funds tied up in sound investments
that cannot now be turned into cash except at large losses.[1]
The theory of the plan is that the Federal government is rich
and strong enough to lend financial agencies the money to
hold these investments until they recover their value, and
that by helping them in this fashion, the banks will not need
to call good mortgages, cut off credit to business, and sell
bonds at cutthroat prices.

It must be obvious that the success of the scheme depends
upon maintaining an absolute confidence throughout the
world in the credit of the United States government. We
are proposing to use the national credit to stop a panicky
liquidation. We are proposing to sustain the confidence of
depositors and of bankers, of borrowers and lenders, by
bringing to their assistance the most powerful agency in the
whole world. For there is no other institution in existence
which has resources comparable with those which the United
States Government can command.

Yet at this moment the government is living beyond its
income. Is it not plain that if the government is to assist
private credit, there must be a prompt guarantee that the
government itself has ample revenues? How can the government help the banks if it has to borrow huge sums from
the banks to pay its own expenses?

[1] This two billions of available credit was of course in the hands of the
Reconstruction Finance Corporation.

It should be clearly understood by Congress that the needs of the country at this time cannot be met by voting large sums of money. We are in the midst of a crisis of confidence, that is to say, in a time when men's faith in promises to pay is at a low ebb. Unless their faith can be restored the crisis cannot be resolved. Of all promises to pay there is none in which men have such faith as in that of the United States Government. This faith is somewhat shaken by the fact that the government's promises to pay, that is its bonds, have lost up to 15 per cent of their market value. The real problem is to restore that value. If the feeling can be created that the government's bonds are secure, that money invested in them is safe, the effect should be like bringing up a new corps of picked, trained, and well-equipped troops behind a shaken army. The mere presence of the new force, the mere belief in its power, is, through its effect on morale, worth ten times its weight in numbers.

Congress can effect such a result by adopting promptly a bold and far-seeing financial policy. Congress cannot arrest the deflation simply by spending two thousand millions. It may arrest it by spending a very small part of two thousand millions if it first makes the national credit invincible. For our problem is a problem not of obtaining money but of restoring credit. Credit is faith. And faith in this emergency means faith in the financial power of the United States Government. The country may need comparatively little help from the government if it has absolute confidence that the government could give all the help that may be needed.

That faith depends on two things: on proof that Congress is prepared to deflate the cost of government in proportion to the reduction in people's incomes; and on proof that Congress has guaranteed the receipt of ample revenues for several years.

January 5, 1932

XI. CHEAPER MONEY AND THE BONUS

*Why the Thomas bonus bill creates alarm; the
Federal Reserve System alone can be trusted with
monetary inflation*

The most powerful force behind the bonus agitation is the
desire for cheaper money.[1] The matter was put very clearly
by Father Coughlin, of Detroit, when he appeared before the
Ways and Means Committee:

> The payment of the bonus would place $2,000,000,000
> in circulation. The money thus released would go to the
> grocers and those who have been rendering credit to the
> jobless veterans. It would go into channels of trade and
> commerce and help revive business.
>
> But I am in hopes that the payment of this vast sum
> will produce a more far-reaching effect, that is that it
> will compel us to revaluate the dollar to the approximate
> level it attained in 1929.

The problem posed by Father Coughlin is the central
problem of the whole crisis. Money has become too dear.
A dollar will buy too many goods. Prices have fallen too
far. On this point there is virtually unanimous agreement
by experts and practical men throughout the world. Thus,
for example, the Financial Committee of the League, on
which sit financial authorities from all the principal countries,
has just issued its report in which it points out that the crux

[1] Representative Wright Patman early in the session of Congress introduced a bill for the immediate payment in full of all adjusted service certificates, the cost being estimated at about two billion dollars. The House
Ways and Means Committee held hearings on the bill and reported it
adversely on May 6. Nevertheless, on June 15 it passed the House by a vote
of 209 to 176. It became evident that it could not pass the Senate, and on
June 17 it was defeated there by a vote of 62 to 18, while thousands of
veterans from all parts of the country were holding a demonstration about
the Capitol in its behalf.

of the crisis is the fact that whereas in 1928 it took 100 units of commodities to pay a debt of 100 gold units today it requires 170 units of commodities. It is obvious that this is an impossible burden upon producers and debtors and that there must either be extensive default or the value of gold currencies must be reduced.

Their proposal is to depreciate the currency by printing money and paying it to a great bloc of voters. If this proposal were adopted by Congress it would signify two things to the world: the first, that Congress felt itself free at any time to change the value of American money; the second, that Congress would change the value of American money whenever the political pressure made it expedient. This would mean that notice had been served upon everyone that the value of American money was to be fixed henceforth by vote of Congress, and that the vote of Congress would be determined by lobbyists and logrolling. It would mean that whenever a group of voters was strong enough to move Congress the money of the American people—their wages, their savings accounts, their life insurance policies, their mortgages and bonds—would be tampered with by the politicians.

This is no theoretical speculation. The history of currencies shows conclusively that once the sovereign, be it a king or a popular legislature, assumes the right to change the value of money to pay its bills or to endow its favorites or to accomplish any other purpose, that currency is headed to destruction. For when a people gives its government the right to manipulate the value of its money, it has given to the government an unlimited series of blank checks. Invariably those checks are drawn. France and Italy are the only two important countries which have stopped the depreciation of their money short of its absolute destruction and in both instances it was necessary to resort to a dictatorship to do it. An ordinary government cannot stop the printing presses once it starts them because the pressure to continue in this easy way of raising money is irresistible.

This is the fundamental reason for the great alarm produced throughout the world by the pending bonus bill. It is a plan to turn over the management of American money to fluctuating Congressional majorities. Now no one in his senses is willing to have the value of money altered whenever it pleases Congress to alter it. This is a power so despotic that it is intolerable. The proposal strikes, therefore, at the heart of confidence by putting every man's money at the mercy of Congressional lobbyists.

Because it strikes at the heart of confidence, the bill would defeat the very purposes which Father Coughlin and Senator Thomas have in mind. For as fast as the government could dish out printed dollars to veterans other people would hasten to change these dollars into gold or into some currency which was not subject to manipulation by blocs of voters.

Such a flight from the dollar would produce runs on banks, which in turn would force banks to call loans, which in turn would depress prices. Thus instead of helping "to revive business" the measure would prostrate it.

Perhaps the most important lesson which mankind has learned in its painful experience with money is that the power to manage money must not be confided to kings, ministers or legislatures. For governments, because they have to spend money, cannot be trusted with the power to manufacture it. That is the reason why in all advanced countries the central banks of issue—that is, the institutions which control the volume of money—are kept independent of the government. There is no other way in which an honest currency can be maintained.

For although central banks, like the Bank of England or our Federal Reserve Banks, are human and fallible, they have no bills to pay and therefore they have no interest in manufacturing money for themselves. That is why they can be trusted, not necessarily to be wise but at least to be honest, in managing the volume of money in the hands of the people.

Under the Glass-Steagall bill which Congress enacted in February, the Federal Reserve Banks now have the power to expand the credit facilities of the country. But just as a good surgeon will, if he can, choose a time for his operation when the patient's system is most ready for it, so the Federal Reserve Banks have to time their operations in accordance with their best judgment as to the conditions of the country. They could not hope to expand credit with hope of success while it was uncertain whether Congress would balance the budget. They could not hope to do it while the country was threatened with the adoption of the bonus. Even with these dangers averted, it is probable that they cannot hope to do much more than to arrest the precipitous deflations now in progress until there are signs of returning sanity on the part of governments in respect to reparations and debts, the obstructions to trade and political peace, and with these a restoration among the American people of their national morale.

But this much is certain. In so far as it is possible by monetary policy to deal with the situation, the only agency in which the American people can afford to put their trust is the Federal Reserve System.

April 14, 1932

XII. CONGRESS AND THE VETERANS

A specially privileged class of voters; the huge cost of veterans' grants; a menace to popular government as well as the Treasury

In an admirably lucid and informing article in last Sunday's New York *Times,* Mr. Charles Merz has brought forward statistics which set in high relief the real problem of economy in the Federal government. Using his figures, we can best broach the question by asking ourselves why it is that in 1932 the Federal government is spending 676 millions more than in 1922. This is a fair comparison, because the budget for 1922 contains the costs of the war. Therefore, we are dealing with an increase during a decade of peace.

As a matter of fact, a closer examination of Mr. Merz's figures shows that the increase of peace-time expenditures has really been greater than 676 millions. For in 1922 the service of the war debt cost 1,411 millions. By 1932, thanks to Mr. Mellon's policy of paying off the debt rapidly during prosperity, the service of the debt has come down to 1,017 millions. This is a saving of 394 millions. Thus, in spite of a saving of almost 400 millions on the debt, the total expenditures have increased 676 millions.

The basic question, therefore, is this: *Why, apart from the debt, has the cost of the Federal government increased more than a billion dollars in ten years?*

Again using Mr. Merz's figures, we find by comparing the main items of cost that the changes in this decade have been as follows:

National Defense	93 millions less
Veterans' Relief	329 millions more
Farm Aid	344 millions more
All Others	490 millions more

It is interesting, I think, to make certain comparisons with the position in Great Britain last year, when the British seriously faced, as we are now beginning to face, the problem of balancing the budget. I shall take the figures from the so-called May report presented to Parliament last July. They are the figures for expenditures in 1922 and the original estimate for 1931 and to make the arithmetic easier

I have converted one pound into five dollars. This does not affect comparisons.

National Defense.........	33 millions less
War Pensions..............	150 millions less
War Debt.................	40 millions more
Social Insurance...........	300 millions more

The great difference between the two countries in regard to payments to individuals is that in Britain the cost of the veterans has declined while the cost of social services to the whole population has increased, whereas in the United States the whole increase has gone to the veterans. In other words, in Britain the veterans are being re-absorbed into the civilian population, whereas in the United States they are increasingly a specially favored class apart.

But in the last analysis it is the veterans' expenditures which constitute the real difficulty of the American budgetary situation. That is the charge which is most ominous. For it amounts to a quarter of the whole budget and the rate of its increase is its particular danger. It has increased almost 50 per cent in ten years, whereas the British war pensions have decreased nearly 50 per cent in the same time. In Britain the cost of the veterans is a diminishing liability; it grows less each year as the war recedes into the past. With us the cost of the veterans is an increasing liability as the political power of the veterans advances.

Therefore, it is on this huge expenditure that the country needs to focus its attention, for it is by all odds the most important element in the problem. The cost of the national debt is arrested and will decline with a return to normal times. The cost of the national defense is almost arrested. The expansion of the social services and of public works and of subsidies presents questions of national policy about which a democracy is entitled to make its decisions. But this mounting burden of expenditures to a special privileged class of voters is a menace not only to the budget but to popular government itself.

April 26, 1932

XIII. A NEW PENSIONS GRAB

Reckless legislation for widows and children of veterans; the sale of Congressional votes

By a vote of nearly five to one and after a debate of only forty minutes the House on Monday passed a bill which would create three new classes of government dependents and obligate the taxpayers to provide something like fifteen million dollars a year for perhaps fifty or sixty years to come.[1] The three new classes are, first, widows of men who wore a uniform for ninety days, provided the widow married the veteran five years before his death and provided that in addition to her earnings she has a net income of less than $250 a year; second, the children of veterans until the age of sixteen or until they marry, provided the child does not have an actual net income of $400 a year; and third, any child of a veteran for the whole of his life if that child is permanently incapable of self-support by reason of mental or physical defect.

The actual payments provided are small: for widows the sum is only $20 a month, for a widow with children it is $6 a month additional for each child, for a child which is an orphan it is $20 a month, and $6 additional for each of his brothers and sisters. But as the committee reporting the bill pointed out: "While this measure is not what we want, it is

---

[1] The so-called widows' and orphans' bill here treated was defeated in the Senate.

the best we could do under the circumstances." It is indeed. For once the principle is established that the government must support the widows and children of veterans, the actual cash payments can be increased whenever Congressmen feel that they need to buy some more votes.

By its legislation during the last ten years Congress has created a privileged class, a class of men who have rights which no other citizens possess. All that is needed to be a member of that class is to have put on a uniform a day or two before the war ended. By this new legislation the privileges of this class would become hereditary. Our own historical experience shows that once established such privileges are never renounced and never reduced. They can only be increased.

If the country agrees to the hereditary principle, it will have created a new class of voters who will hang together because they have a common interest in appropriations from the Treasury. Because they hang together they will terrorize Congressmen. In addition to the veterans' bloc, we shall then have the widows' bloc and the guardians of orphans' bloc. That ought to constitute a large enough body of voters to make it impossible for Congress ever to resist any demand from the veterans' lobbies.

There are no doubt some Congressmen who sincerely believe that a man who once wore a uniform has done such extraordinary service to the nation that he and his widow and his children and even his parents are entitled to draw money from the Treasury for decades to come. But there are not many Congressmen who really think that. Most of them believe that the financial obligation has been discharged except to men disabled in the line of duty and to the dependents of men who died in the service. Why then do they vote these measures?

They vote them because they wish to be reëlected. Because they like to draw $10,000 a year. Because they like the perquisites. Because they like the importance which they enjoy. Because they hope to become Senators and Governors. That is the whole of it. By voting public money to the veterans and the veterans' widows they are able to buy a good many votes. It is as crude as that.

What is a nation to do when it finds itself the victim of such a traffic? Nothing, unless it has the moral strength to rise under new leaders who will lead a crusade against this utter demoralization of representative government.

May 4, 1932

XIV. THE BONUS ARMY IN WASHINGTON

The bonus marchers misled by Congress, not by Communism; a firm rejection of their demands the only course

In dealing with the bonus marchers who are converging on Washington the first thing to remember is that these veterans honestly believe that they are merely trying to collect a lawful debt.[1] They possess certificates presented to them by vote of Congress. The certificates call for the payment in 1945 of sums of money calculated on the length of

---

[1] On May 22 some 330 veterans of the World War seized a Baltimore & Ohio freight train at East St. Louis in a march upon Washington to demand bonus legislation. Other contingents supporting this demand set out from all parts of the country. By June 10 more than 9,000 men were in Washington encamped on the edge of the Potomac, living on inadequate rations and presenting a grave sanitary problem. Their numbers steadily rose. Following the defeat of the bonus bill, President Hoover early in July obtained from Congress an appropriation of $100,000 to pay for their transportation to their homes. But great numbers of the veterans remained. Finally, on July 28 President Hoover used troops, tanks, and gas bombs in ejecting the "bonus army" from Washington.

each man's service during the war. The holders of these certificates feel they need this money more today than they will ever need it again, and they cannot understand why Congress does not give it to them. Not being financiers or specialists in the operation of compound interest, it is very difficult for them to comprehend that to demand payment of the principal of a debt ten years before it is due is to demand money that is not owed at all now and to demand more money than is owed ultimately. It is not astonishing that the veterans should fail to see this, for they are encouraged in their misunderstanding by the willingness of a majority in the House and perhaps also in the Senate to vote them the money.

It is important that public opinion should be clear about the underlying facts, should realize vividly that it is Congress and not Communism which is responsible for this demonstration, and should not be diverted into wild talk or excited action by the efforts of Communist agitators to exploit the situation. The fundamental fact is that these veterans think they are asking only for what the government has contracted to pay them, and though their belief is mistaken, they are misled not by agents of Moscow but by duly elected Representatives and Senators at the Capitol.

The immediate thing to do is to explain to them in the simplest and clearest language possible why the government does not owe them the money they are asking. They are exercising their right to petition the government, and a rational, convincing answer to their petition should be given forthwith by some responsible official. When the answer has been given explaining why the government owes these veterans no money at this time, it should be followed immediately by a decisive announcement that no money will be paid. The simplest way to do this is to collect pledges from enough Senators and, if possible, from enough Repre-

sentatives to uphold a Presidential veto in the event that the
bonus bill were to pass. The more promptly and the more
conclusively it is made clear that the certificates will not be
cashed the better. The demonstration will continue and will
swell if there remains the slightest hope that it might succeed.
By settling the issue immediately and finally the authorities
in Washington will be taking the kindest, the most just, and
the most expedient course.

Once the issue has been squarely met, the problem is one of
discouraging more arrivals and of dispersing those who have
already arrived in Washington. To those who are in Washington on the day when the petition is answered the
authorities might offer free transportation to their homes.
To those who reject the offer and insist on staying afterwards
they should offer outdoor relief; that is to say, food in return
for labor on the roads, woodpiles, and the like. Those
arriving after the date when the petition is announced should
be met at the city limits and sent home on the principle that
the issue is settled and that an accumulation of masses of
men making a demand that cannot be granted is no longer
a petition and is in fact coercion of the government.

The important thing is that the authorities should not drift
along without a policy which everybody understands. They
should at once make it clear not only to the veterans in
Washington but to those who may be preparing to go there
just what they must expect. This would include an explanation as to why their petition cannot and will not be
granted, an offer of transportation home to those already
there, unattractive relief for those who stay on, and a refusal
to admit those who come after it has been made clear that
there is no lawful way in which their demands can be
satisfied.

June 9, 1932

XV. FOOLISH TARIFF LEGISLATION

*Tariffs on coal and oil; their folly; the Democratic
surrender*

Under the pretense of raising revenue the House has proposed to erect tariffs against petroleum products and coal. The Senate Finance Committee has tentatively added a copper tariff and there is a powerful agitation for additional tariffs on lumber.[1]

The insincerity of the performance is visible in the House bill. For the petroleum and coal taxes differ from all the other excise taxes, such as those laid upon toilet preparations, furs, jewelry, automobiles, in that these taxes "apply only with respect to the importation of such articles." Plainly the object is not to raise revenue but to prevent imports. Thus the coal tariff, which is at the rate of $2.00 a short ton, is estimated to yield only $1,500,000. Were the same tax applied for revenue purposes to all coal consumed in the United States in 1930 (I do not have the figures for 1931), it would yield theoretically a billion dollars. Obviously the House was not interested in revenue. It was interested in stopping the imports of Canadian and British coal. This proposal has nothing to do with the raising of revenue.

Let us look then at the meaning of this coal tariff. In 1930 the United States produced 70 million tons of anthracite. It exported 2½ million tons and imported 675 thousand. In other words, it imported less than one ton for every 100 tons produced and consumed. It exported more than four tons for every ton imported. On what theory of tariffs does an industry with a monopoly of more than 99 per cent of the

---

[1] The movements mentioned here were, by logrolling agreements, finally successful. The tax law passed by Congress and signed by Mr. Hoover carried tariffs on coal, petroleum, copper, and lumber.

domestic market and, in addition, an excess of exports, require protection?

Take next bituminous coal. In 1930 there were produced 630 million tons. There were exported nearly 16 million tons. There were imported only 241 thousand tons. What fraction of 1 per cent is 241 thousand in relation to 630 million? Can it be denied that the bituminous and coal producers of the United States have more than 99 per cent of the domestic market? At whom are they aiming the tariff?

They are aiming it at Canada. There is a trifling amount of coal produced in Nova Scotia and Alberta, in Saskatchewan and New Brunswick. A little of it finds its way into Maine and Vermont and into Washington, Montana, Idaho and Alaska because transportation conditions are favorable. This is the trade that Congress proposes to stop. But just consider the mentality of this proceeding. While we buy from Canada a microscopic fraction of 1 per cent of the coal we consume, we sell to Canada 85 per cent of our coal exports. Though we receive from Canada almost none of the coal we consume, we sell to Canada as much coal as Canada produces.

Thus in order to stop a fraction of 1 per cent of our consumption from coming in, we are proposing to endanger 85 per cent of our export trade. For it is humanly certain that Canada will not tamely submit. On July 15 an imperial conference meets at Ottawa for the purpose of uniting the empire under preferential tariffs. Could there be greater folly than to select this moment to impose a punitive tariff against a Canadian industry?

Really, when one examines the facts, when one considers what Congress is risking for an insignificant advantage to an insignificant part of the American coal trade, it is difficult to refrain from wondering whether Congress is in its right mind.

The proposed oil tariff is a little bit more complicated, but not much. The demand for this tariff comes from the so-called independent producers in Texas and Oklahoma who believe that domestic oil would replace imports and the price of oil would rise if prohibitive duties were imposed. They are supported by the coal producers, who hope by raising the price of oil to discourage the competition of oil with coal.

In 1931 the total value of our exports of petroleum products was three times as great as the value of our imports. This is fairly conclusive evidence that whatever else the industry may be suffering from it is not suffering from inability to compete in the world market. Indeed, the figures bear out this conclusion. In 1930 the United States produced 63.3 per cent of the crude oil of the world. It imported about 7 per cent of what it produced. Thus the domestic producers had 93 per cent of the domestic market. Does any one think they can monopolize the American market and hold their own in the world markets as well? Not in an era when every country in the world is under the strongest pressure, owing to our unbalanced position as a creditor nation, to buy as little as possible from the United States. The oil producers are playing with dynamite when they adopt a policy of tariff aggression. They are showing themselves to be penny wise and pound foolish.

Here then are two tariff measures which might be described as farthest north in the effort to strangle international trade. Not even the authors of the Hawley-Smoot tariff ventured to enact measures so patently indefensible. Yet the coal and oil tariffs were voted by a House controlled by the Democrats. Democratic votes are deciding the issue in the Senate Committee.

What are the Democratic leaders going to do about this scandal? It makes ridiculous their whole case against the Republican tariff policy. Is it possible that the Presidential candidates who have been criticizing the tariff in general terms, that the Democratic party which has given out tons of printed matter on the tariff, will do nothing to stop these silly tariffs which, if enacted, can only stultify the Democrats completely on one of the chief issues of the coming campaign?

If the Democratic leaders are ever going to speak out, this is the time for them to do it. Once these tariffs are made law the country will laugh at their protests.

April 5, 1932

XVI. CONGRESS AND THE DEMAND FOR LOCAL RELIEF

The Costigan and La Follette bills; difficulty of justifying local aid

There are two bills before a sub-committee of the Senate calling for Federal appropriations to relieve the unemployed. One bill, sponsored by Senator Costigan of Colorado, calls for 375 millions; the other, by Senator La Follette, of Wisconsin, calls for 250 millions. The first two witnesses called by the sub-committee were relief workers, one from New York and the other from Chicago. Both testified that the money now in sight would not be sufficient in their cities to meet the needs of this winter. If this is true, it goes without saying that all the money needed must be raised. On that point there can be no two opinions. But on the manner in which the necessary money should be raised, there can be very decided differences of opinion.

For my own part I do not see by what process of reasoning it can be held that a Senate committee should even consider Federal assistance to New York and Chicago. The estimated wealth of New York State in 1928 was about 40 thousand

million dollars—that of Wisconsin was 9; the wealth of
Illinois was 24—that of Colorado 3.5. Is it suggested that
Colorado and Wisconsin are in a position to help Illinois
and New York? Hardly. Well, then, what is the point of ·
appealing on behalf of New York or Chicago to the Senate
Committee which, in addition to Mr. Costigan and Mr.
La Follette, contains Senators from New Mexico (with an
estimated wealth less than one-fortieth of New York's),
from West Virginia (with an estimated wealth one-eighth of
New York's), from Montana (with an estimated wealth
one-sixteenth of New York's)? The resources of Illinois
alone are twice, of New York and Illinois together more than
five times, the resources of all the states represented on the
sub-committee.

I do not wish to suggest that Congress should not make a
careful examination to see whether Federal aid is necessary
in the present emergency. I do wish to suggest that the committee has started its investigation in a way that can only
cause confusion. For if it begins with the assumption that
the richest state in the Union may be unable to take care of
itself, where is the money to be found for states which are
very much less rich? The simple truth is that if Federal
aid has to be given, New York and Illinois will have to contribute not only all that is needed to take care of their own
unemployed but considerably more besides. Therefore, it
is rather a roundabout proceeding to ask social workers in
New York and Chicago whether their communities need
help from Washington.

For it must be remembered, though it is easily forgotten,
that Washington has no money for relief which it does not
take from the people who have money. Washington cannot
create money. It must get it. The only theory, therefore, on
which citizens of the richer states can be turning to Washington is that their own people need to be coerced by Congress

into doing their duty. I do not believe that a case for such coercion has been made.

The first question to inquire into is whether there are any states in the Union which lack the resources to relieve distress within their borders. There may be some states which are at the end of their taxing power and have exhausted their credit. To such states, if the need for relief is too great to be met by private contributions, Federal aid should be given.[1] But these states cannot be the great industrial states where there is the largest amount of unemployment. The industrial states are the richest states, and if Federal aid is to be extended, they must not expect to receive aid but to give it.

It seems to me that the wisest procedure for Congress would be to call Mr. Walter Gifford and ask him, not necessarily in a public session, to submit a list of states which may not be able to help themselves. The Committee might then, also not necessarily in a public session, confer with the governors, the chief financial officers, and leading social workers in these states, and make an estimate of the amount of help which may be needed. The facts having been established, Congress might then authorize the Emergency Reconstruction Corporation or some Federal commission to lend those needy states the money at a very low rate of interest, and on long terms.

It seems to me that a plan of this sort takes into account all the main elements of the problem. The money needed by communities without sufficient resources would be made available to them. On the other hand, the risks of a new porkbarrel would be reduced to a minimum, for it is one thing for a state to receive a free gift from the Treasury and another to receive an emergency loan that must be repaid.

---

[1] The principle here recommended was that upon which, after protracted wrangling, the relief legislation enacted in the summer of 1932 was finally based.

Under this plan it could not honestly be said that the nation had failed to provide relief where it may be needed. Yet under this plan the principle of centering responsibility on the states would be preserved. Congress would not be voting money to individuals, and all the problems that would arise out of trying to divide a fund by political bargaining would be eliminated. Congress would be doing what it might properly do under our Federal system of government. It would, in a time of need, be extending credit to sovereign states.

December 31, 1931

XVII. THE BEST METHOD OF PROVIDING LOCAL RELIEF

Growing volume of the need; relation to problem of local extravagance

After receiving reports from social workers in thirty-seven cities the *Survey* concludes that "with meager and uncertain funds these cities have somehow muddled through the winter keeping their people alive"; but they are "still planless, and with no sign of improved employment, with relief needs growing and with relief funds dwindling to exhaustion, they turn their blind eyes to the future, where already the spectre of another winter is rising."

The editors of the *Survey* are right in centering attention upon next winter. On the most optimistic premise of business improvement huge expenditures will be required next winter to relieve the unemployed. For even if we dared to assume that the volume of unemployment will be less than this winter the intensity of the need of the large number who will inevitably remain unemployed will be much greater.

The resources of private charity must be expected to diminish and the yield of taxes cannot be expected to have improved much.

Where then are we to look for the funds which must be found? No short and easy answer can be given to that question.

The money has to come out of the existing resources of the American people. There are only three ways in which it can come. One way is by increasing taxes. A second way is by using for relief public funds now spent upon other purposes. The third is by borrowing the money. These three methods are not mutually exclusive. It will be found necessary, I believe, to resort to all three.[1] The manner in which these three measures are employed is the essence of the problem. They must be employed in such a way as to bring the maximum relief without adding more of a new burden than is inescapable. Thus the apparently easiest way to proceed would be to raise a Federal bond issue and distribute the proceeds for relief. This would seem to cost nobody anything at the moment. But to resort to a bond issue as the first step would be the most wasteful and least effective way to begin. For that kind of easy policy would at once divert attention from the essential problem. That is the problem of Federal and local extravagance.

[1] In the relief legislation finally passed by Congress and signed by Mr. Hoover on July 18, 1932, various expedients were resorted to. The Relief and Home Loan Bank Bills passed July 16, after long travail, provided $2,122,000,000 for direct loans to States for relief, for public works, and for self-liquidating construction projects. They provided for loans by Federal Reserve Banks to individuals and industries if security was adequate and if proof were presented that loans could not be obtained from commercial banks. They provided a system of eight to twelve government-supervised banks to aid in the construction and financing of homes by individuals; each to be capitalized at $5,000,000 and to be supported by a government fund of $125,000,000. This article and those which follow treat of the struggle out of which the relief legislation was finally evolved.

The real reason why, by and large—there are no doubt important exceptions—the localities are at the end of their resources is that the politicians have not yet taken the depression seriously. They are still living as specially protected individuals in the illusions of the inflation. The most preposterous case is that of the City of New York. Here is the richest city in the world, with a total budget second only to that of the Federal government itself, and there is talk that the city cannot find money to relieve its unemployed. Why can't it find the money? It can't find it because it is run by officeholders who won't relax their grip upon the people's pocketbooks. There is not the slightest question that New York City could find all the money required for relief if its rulers were willing to do what needs to be done.

I suspect that analogous conditions prevail in most parts of the country. I do not share the views of those who think complex modern communities can get along without large expenditures for social services. But the American problem of the fantastic increase in the costs of local government does not arise primarily out of increased expenditures for social services. It arises out of privilege: the privileges of officeholders who are incredibly wasteful and are often corrupt, and out of the mania for "public improvements" inspired by contractors and real estate speculators. These are the things which have inflated the cost of government rather than the relatively trifling sums spent upon teachers' salaries, libraries or dental clinics. What has brought local government to its present pass is the combined effort of officeholders, contractors and speculators who have exploited the public's passion for new, stupendous and shiny improvements. This is what has run the localities into staggering debts, has eaten up the taxes, and has sent them to Washington for help.

This is the time to break into this problem, and among the most hopeful things in America today is the sign that the

American people are waking up to the urgency of it. The need of the unemployed for this summer and next winter can largely be met by the localities if they have to. The problem has not really been faced by the localities and it would be a great mistake to relieve them of the necessity of facing it by passing the burden to Congress. The Federal government is not so happily situated that it can easily find the money, and those who want a plan prepared for next winter should begin by educating the voters in the cities and states that the primary responsibility must be theirs to meet.

I am persuaded, however, that after as much has been done as the officeholders will permit, there will remain some communities which really cannot meet the demands upon them. I am not thinking of New York City or Chicago or Philadelphia. If rich cities like these, situated in rich states, cannot help themselves, something is more thoroughly wrong with them than anyone has yet imagined. I am thinking of communities in states where the deflation of prices has really exhausted the supplies of liquid funds. They will have to have Federal aid, and the only question is how it should be provided.

The worst way to provide it is by direct appropriations. For this method, once adopted, will by all previous American experience create a new porkbarrel which vested political interests will control and exploit. It seems to me, therefore, that the Federal aid to these exhausted communities ought to take the form of Federal loans at a nominal rate of interest. It might be well to consider the creation of some kind of emergency commission which upon proof of need would have power to grant loans to states. Some such procedure as this would make the necessary money available without all of the obvious dangers and disadvantages of direct grants out of the Federal treasury.

May 13, 1932

XVIII. THE WAGNER BILL: A NATIONAL PROGRAM FOR RELIEF

Soundness of the bill in principle; its value as a demonstration of the government's ability to act

The Wagner Bill for relief and public works provides a golden opportunity for prompt national coöperation.[1] The bill is a compromise among the various projects advanced by Mr. Young, Senator Robinson, Senator Wagner himself, ex-Governor Smith and the President. It is a self-respecting compromise which they can all accept without feeling that they have sacrificed seriously the essential principles for which they have been contending or that they have lost sight of their common aim.

On the main point at issue, the bill provides that three-quarters of the Federal credit to be pledged shall be devoted to self-liquidating projects. Of the remaining quarter, which is to be spent directly on public works, it can fairly be said that a part, such as that to be devoted to flood control and the Hoover Dam construction, represents a wise national investment, and another part, to be spent on public buildings to replace structures on which the government pays rentals, may, if properly administered, represent a real saving of public money. When it is considered also that these 500 millions for public works include 195 millions which Congress would authorize anyway, the moderation of the Wagner Bill is manifest. It is true that these public works are to be financed by borrowing, and not on the pay-as-you-go prin-

---

[1] Senator Wagner's Relief Bill, introduced May 25, provided $2,300,-000,000 for immediate State loans for unemployment relief, Federal works, and self-liquidating enterprises. A large part of the funds were to be raised and administered by the Reconstruction Finance Corporation. President Hoover at first opposed the bill, but finally accepted its main features as part of the relief legislation agreed upon in July.

ciple, but provided the budget is otherwise brought into balance, the government credit ought not to suffer at a time when the supply of liquid capital is so large.

Those who strain at this gnat will later be forced to swallow a camel.

The bill should be accepted in substance by the President for the Administration and by Speaker Garner for the Democrats in the House. It should be accepted by the financial community and by public opinion generally and Congress should enact it promptly without acrimonious debate, destructive amendments, filibustering and all the other devices of confusion and delay. Each one of us will be making some concession on his pet theories, but this is no time to be finical and stubborn.

Apart from the merits of the bill itself, it can be said, I think, that the country would benefit more at this moment by a good demonstration of its capacity to agree on something than by anything else that could happen in Washington. What has been most disturbing to confidence in the last few months has been the increasing doubt as to whether the government in Washington could govern. Here is a measure which provides relief and, in addition, honestly seeks to meet the public demand for positive action towards a resumption of work. It combines in an harmonious program the ideas of the principal leaders of both parties. If there is to be co-operation in this crisis, this is an excellent chance to coöperate; if there is to be leadership, this is an excellent opportunity to follow the leaders. In a democracy where nobody must expect to have things just as he would like them, the Wagner Bill is as statesmanlike an adjustment of conflicting opinions as we are likely to see.

A prompt agreement on the principles of this bill will facilitate the main business of Congress. That business is to balance the budget by drastic economies and adequate taxes.

If the same spirit which animates this bill could be concentrated on the budget problem, it would be an incalculable gain. The Wagner Bill represents the ideas of men who have been sponsoring large programs of Federal relief and public works and also the ideas of men who have in the past opposed such programs. The same kind of agreement by open-minded concessions is needed on retrenchment and taxes.

At the present time this main business is submerged in a welter of plans, amendments and votes. Why not lift the whole subject out of the confusion and simplify it? Let it be agreed that as to retrenchments there shall be a 15 per cent cut in all the appropriations, this saving to be made by cutting all salaries over $1,500 10 per cent and the remainder by such reorganization and economies as the President may order; that as to taxes there shall be restored the war-time rates plus the manufacturers' sales tax.

A program of this sort is not too drastic if the budget is really to be brought into balance. Its enactment would pinch and hurt everybody considerably. Nobody can possibly like the whole of it, but no program can be devised that everybody will like. The country is in a position where an adequate solution must be a painful solution. But though this program is painful, it would make the national credit secure, and the sacrifices which it would call for would help greatly to restore the national morale. To adopt it requires patriotism, a real willingness to make individual sacrifices for the common good. It would more than pay for itself, however, in the self-respect and self-confidence which the nation would feel at having confronted its great problem and mastered it.

May 27, 1932

· V ·

AMERICA, THE WAR DEBTS, AND
EUROPEAN DEPRESSION

I. ADMINISTRATION POLICY AND THE
WAR DEBTS

*A permanent settlement needed, not a moratorium;
capacity to pay a discredited theory; a good settlement will give Europe a strong impulse forward*

It is generally understood that the Administration is now
studying the problem of the war debts. Such a study is
necessary, for it is perfectly evident that full payments cannot be resumed when the moratorium expires on July 1 of
next year.

A decision cannot be put off until just before that date. All
the governments concerned are now beginning to prepare the
budgets that have to be voted before July, and none of them
can make its plans unless it knows what it is to receive or to
pay under war debts and reparations; moreover, the agreement among the private creditors of Germany expires on
February 1, and unless there is a clear settlement of these
matters before that time, the financial position of Germany,
and then that of all the world, is certain to receive another
series of blows as great or greater than those which have been
dealt this summer.

There can be no ordering of government budgets, no
stabilization of currencies, and no real beginning of a restoration of confidence, while the future course of these great pay-

ments is undetermined and at the mercy of domestic politics in all the countries. The bases of a definite policy have to be laid very soon, no later in fact than when M. Laval comes to Washington about ten days hence.

The most convenient way to deal with the matter politically would be to extend the moratorium and thus postpone a settlement of troublesome issues. There are the strongest objections to this course. For a moratorium, however necessary it may be in an emergency, has the fatal defect that in relieving the debtor it destroys his credit. It stamps him as insolvent, and puts him in a position where he is paralyzed by the uncertainty of what is to happen when the moratorium ends. Neither the debtor nor the creditor can make plans for the future. Yet the very essence of financial confidence is the willingness of men to invest capital for a long term. The revival of long term investment, which is indispensable to a recovery from present conditions, cannot take place, if war debts and reparations, with all they involve in the way of international confusion and bitterness, are left hanging unsettled over the financial markets.

It is certain, therefore, that a settlement which the nations will regard as permanent, rather than an extension of the moratorium, is what is needed.

There is every reason to suppose that the Administration takes this view. The next question, then, is to ask ourselves on what principle a settlement should be made this winter. Within the last few days the Administration has allowed its attitude to become known. It is that capacity to pay was the original basis of the debt settlements, that incapacity to pay was the basis of the moratorium, and that capacity to pay in the future should be the principle of our future policy.

In my judgment this is a discredited and a dangerous principle on which to base American policy. When I say it is discredited I mean that the experience of ten years has shown that there are no statesmen wise enough and no experts expert enough to estimate the future capacity of nations to pay. All the estimates made by all the conferences and committees have failed to provide true estimates. Germany's capacity to pay has been estimated three times: by the Peace Conference, by the Dawes Committee, by the Young Committee. The efforts of the Peace Conference to apply the principle of capacity to pay ended in the Ruhr invasion. The efforts of the Dawes Committee produced about five annual payments and ended in the conviction that a new estimate was necessary. The efforts of the Young Committee produced not quite two annual payments and ended in a moratorium. What reason is there to think that another committee can make a better estimate?

Our own application of the principle to our own debtors has been no less unsuccessful. We sat down in all our expertness to estimate each debtor's capacity. We decided that Britain could pay at the rate of three and a third per cent, Italy at less than half of one per cent, Belgium at the rate of one and four-fifths per cent, and France at the rate of one and three-fifths. In short, we estimated the British capacity at double that of France's. At this moment that looks like a profoundly silly guess. In less than five years the whole outlook has been reversed. Now who knows what it will be in another five years? What reason has Mr. Hoover to think that he can make a reliable estimate now when as a member of the Debt Funding Commission he could not make a reliable estimate a few years ago?

The trouble with the principle is that there is no such principle. These debt settlements are calculated for a period running until 1988. Is there anything in the science of economies by which anybody can know what the economic position of nations is going to be in 1938, in 1948, in 1958, and so on? The notion of national capacity to pay has no scientific basis. Nobody can know. Nobody can even guess. Yet for ten years governments, which cannot forecast the future three weeks, have been pretending to forecast it for three generations. All they have succeeded in doing is to entangle the peoples in a maze of bitter antagonism and to discredit their own sense of reality.

Not only is capacity to pay a discredited theory, it is a very dangerous one. Let us visualize the proceedings this winter were Mr. Hoover to attempt to apply it to our debtors. One by one they are invited to step up to the judgment seat and show what has happened to their capacity to pay since the last time we passed judgment on it. First come the French. It appears that their capacity to pay has improved. Do we ask them to pay more? We do not. We are compelled to admit that such things are not done, and that, therefore, in respect to our most solvent debtor we are not applying the principle at all.

Then come the British. We look solemnly at the statistics, and conclude that the British do not have all the capacity we once thought they had. So we reduce, and send the British home to contemplate the bitter fact that by an official American judgment it has been announced to the world that they are not what they used to be. To make their feelings even pleasanter we send them home with the knowledge that while France is paying less than her present capacity Britain is paying up to our notion of her capacity. What that will do to create that atmosphere of good will and fair dealing in which we like to specialize, I shall not dwell upon.

Capacity to pay may be a workable principle in dealing with individual bankrupts; it may be a workable principle for extracting tribute from a conquered enemy. But as between friendly nations over a period of three generations it is, as an economic principle, nonsense, and as a foreign policy, brutal, unjust, and highly dangerous.

The principle should be scrapped, and under no circumstances should we put ourselves in the odious position of having to pass official judgment upon the economic future of our neighbors or of having to discriminate among them. Whatever relief is accorded should apply to all debtors equally, and should aim, not at obtaining more or less money, but at liquidating all the war transactions as rapidly and completely as possible. For the financial stake of our Treasury in the war debts seems large absolutely but is relatively not large at all. What the debtors paid was a fraction of our surpluses in the good years; what they won't pay this year is less than a sixth of our impending deficit. Our overwhelming interest is not, therefore, in these payments but in the restoration of economic activity, and any settlement of them, no matter how reduced the amounts, which Europe feels it can manage with ease and tranquillity of mind, ought to be acceptable to us.

October 15, 1931

II. HOW MUCH HAVE THE DEBTS BEEN CANCELLED?

Current beliefs regarding the cancellation of pre-armistice debts; extent to which this belief is unjustified

It is widely believed in this country that the United States has cancelled the debts contracted before the armistice and that the present debts were incurred not to prosecute the war but for reconstruction afterwards. It may be interesting to inquire what authority there is for this belief and to what extent it is true.

The notion that the pre-armistice loans have been cancelled

is a garbled version of two statements made by Secretary Mellon in 1926 and in 1927. Writing to President Hibben of Princeton University on March 15, 1927, Mr. Mellon said:

> I remind you that I already had occasion to point out (in a letter to Mr. Frederick W. Peabody dated July 14, 1926) that the present value of these debt settlements at 5 per cent, a rate less than most of the other nations now pay for money, is, except, in the case of Great Britain, either less than or approximately the same as the amount borrowed after the armistice.

This is, so far as I know, the only official authority for the current notion that the pre-armistice loans have been cancelled. Let us note that Mr. Mellon expressly excepts Great Britain. Let us remember that British borrowing was a little short of half the borrowing.

In order to simplify the discussion, only three debtor countries need be considered—Britain, France and Italy. They did nine-tenths of all the borrowing. To simplify further, I shall use figures exact only to the nearest million dollars. Let us fix in mind what each debtor borrowed before and after the armistice.

GREAT BRITAIN

Before: 3,696 millions
After: 581 millions

Britain repaid 202 millions before the funding of her debt. Thus her net borrowing was:

$$4,075 \text{ millions}$$

As Britain borrowed 581 million after the armistice, her post-armistice borrowing was about 14 per cent and her pre-armistice borrowing 86 per cent of the total.

FRANCE

Before: 1,970 millions
After: 1,027 millions

France also received 407 millions worth of war materials which our army left in France. She repaid 64 millions of principal before funding her debt. Therefore, France's net principal debt was about

3,341 millions.

As France borrowed 1,434 millions after the armistice, her post-war borrowing works out at about 40 per cent and the pre-armistice at about 60 per cent of the total.

ITALY

Before: 1,051 millions
After: 617 millions

Italy's net debt after a small repayment was:

1,648 millions.

As Italy borrowed 617 millions after the armistice, her post-war borrowings were about 37 per cent and her pre-armistice borrowings about 63 per cent.

In order to prove the thesis that the debt settlements cancel the pre-armistice debts it must be shown that the British debt has been reduced 86 per cent, the French 60 per cent, and the Italian 63 per cent. Now, as we have seen, Mr. Mellon, who gave currency to the idea that the pre-armistice debts had been cancelled, expressly excepted the British. What of the others?

The French settlement was made as of June 15, 1925. France acknowledges that she then owed us 4,025 millions. This sum was arrived at by adding up the 2,997 millions cash advanced, the 407 millions for war supplies left behind by Pershing, accrued interest of about 700 millions and subtracting certain French payments. France agreed to repay the principal of 4,025 millions in sixty-two annual instalments beginning in 1926 and ending in 1987; she also agreed to pay interest annually on the unpaid principal at the average rate of 1.6 per cent.

How much cancellation was this? The question cannot be answered offhand, for the answer depends upon what we choose to regard as the rate of interest which the debtor nations ought to pay over a period of sixty-two years. There are three possible rates of interest which can reasonably be argued about.

It is possible to say that 5 per cent is the proper rate. This is the rate which the original demand notes bore when the money was advanced during the war.

It is possible to say that 4¼ per cent is the proper rate. This was the average cost of the money to the Treasury at the time the loans were made.

It is possible to say that 3 per cent is the proper rate. This was Mr. Mellon's estimate in 1926 of what money would on the average cost the United States for sixty-two years.

If you compare what France has agreed to pay with what she would have had to pay at 5 per cent, the theoretical cancellation is 60.3 per cent. This is the interest rate employed by Mr. Mellon when he set out to prove that the French pre-armistice loans had been cancelled. As we have seen, the French pre-armistice loans were 60 per cent of French borrowings. Therefore, it is true that at the highest theoretical rate the French pre-armistice loans have been cancelled.

Suppose you take a rate of 4¼ per cent—the rate Congress thought proper. Then the cancellation is only 52.8 per cent.

If you take the 3 per cent rate—Mr. Mellon's estimate of what this money will actually cost the American taxpayer—then the cancellation is only 35 per cent.

The net conclusion is that only by assuming a 5 per cent rate can it be shown that the French pre-armistice loans have been cancelled.

Applying the same yardstick to Italy, we find a very much more lenient treatment. At 5 per cent, 80.2 per cent of her debt is cancelled; at 4¼ per cent it is 75.4 per cent; at 3 per cent it is 36.4 per cent.

Italy's pre-armistice loans were 63 per cent of her borrowings. Therefore, at 5 or at 4¼ per cent her pre-armistice loans have been cancelled. At 3 per cent they have not been entirely cancelled.

By the same measures the results for Britain are these: at 5 per cent the cancellation is 30.1 per cent of the debt; at 4¼ per cent the cancellation is 19.7 per cent; at 3 per cent nothing is cancelled and, in fact, Britain pays 4.4 per cent more than her total borrowing.

Since Britain's pre-armistice debt is 86 per cent of the total, and since she has promised to pay, depending upon the rate of interest assumed, anywhere from 70 to 104 per cent of the total, no possible claim can be made that Britain's pre-armistice debt has been cancelled. Mr. Mellon, of course, never made the claim, but many persons think so who have heard from somebody who heard from somebody else who did not read carefully what Mr. Mellon said.

It may be said, therefore, of the current belief as to the cancellation of pre-armistice debts that in regard to our three principal debtors, the belief is: one, true for Italy at 5 and 4¼ but not at 3 per cent; two, true for France at 5 per cent; not true for Britain at all.

February 5, 1932

III. A CONGRESSIONAL DECLARATION OF
POLICY ON THE DEBTS

*Resolution by the House against any reduction of
debts; its expression of a dominant mood; this and
the French attitude hostile to world recovery*

The declaration by the House that it is "against the policy
of Congress that any of the indebtedness of foreign countries
should be in any manner cancelled or reduced" should be read
in the light of M. Laval's statement to the French Chamber
after his return from Washington.[1] What M. Laval said
then was this:

> For the period of the depression we shall not refuse to
> examine the bases of new agreements between debtors
> and creditors. . . . We shall accept a new modification
> only for a limited period. We shall consent to a revision
> of reparations only in so far as there is at least an equiva-
> lent reduction granted us in respect of our war debts.

Assuming that the Senate adopts the declaration made by
the House, it will mean notice that this Congress will not
now consent to that reduction of war debts which M. Laval
postulates as the condition of a reduction of German reparations. Congress has not said that it will refuse to examine
new agreements for "a limited period" after June 30. It

---

[1] Premier Pierre Laval of France, with his daughter, arrived in the
United States on October 22, 1931, and departed on October 27, having
meanwhile held two conferences, one lasting for seven hours, with President
Hoover. He and Mr. Hoover issued a joint statement. The general tenor
of their agreement was that France was to receive fuller American support
in carrying out her financial policies in Europe—that at any rate, no such
surprises as the moratorium proposal were to be unexpectedly sprung upon
her; and that she was to accept the responsibility involved.

has had the practical sense to realize that whatever its "policy" may be as to the terms of the debts, actual payment under present conditions is something that no Congressional fiat can guarantee.

Thus the upshot of the business is that while the door to temporary adjustments is still open, the two creditor nations have made declarations, which, if adhered to, must prohibit a permanent revision of the debt structure. All that the forthcoming conference in Europe can then do is to make arrangements designed to postpone and temporize for the period of the depression.

It would be folly to deny that Congress and the Chamber have accurately expressed the dominant mood of the voters in the two countries. The specific sums which would have to be sacrificed to obtain a definite settlement bulk larger in the imagination of both peoples than do the intangible benefits which would come from getting rid of the whole troublesome question. There is a reason for this. It is not merely that the two peoples feel poor and are disinclined, as they see it, to take upon themselves the burdens of foreigners. It is not merely that they object to surrendering part of the promises to pay. It is that they see no advantages to be gained by compromising.

Both peoples are unhappy about their foreign relations, the French because they have not yet found the kind of security they want, the Americans because they feel that their entanglement with Europe since April, 1917, has brought them nothing but trouble. In neither country is there a general belief that fresh sacrifices would do any good. The French do not believe they can produce a reconciled Germany by any settlement of reparations. The Americans do not believe that Europe will settle down in peace if the debts are forgiven. There is a deep conviction in both nations that the European trouble is deeper and more stubborn than debts and reparations, and until there is a radical change in the European outlook it is not likely that either people will consent, except under the compulsion of events, to make new concessions.

The question now is whether any temporary expedient, such as the combined policies of the Chamber and Congress contemplate, can meet the situation. Is it possible to avert a complete collapse in Central Europe and to proceed towards a general recovery after slamming the door against permanent revision of reparations? That is the question both the creditor nations need to ask themselves.

They can answer it optimistically only if they believe that German credit can be restored though Germany must continue to owe in full the Young payments. Does anyone believe that? Does anyone believe that Germans will keep their money in Germany if they have to face sixty years of reparations? Does anyone believe that American, French, British, Dutch and Swiss citizens will buy German bonds or that their banks will extend credits if the reparation business is to be continued in full force? Is there an American Congressman or a French Deputy who wishes to put any of *his* savings into Germany if reparations must be collected in full? It would be hard to find one.

Therefore, though expedients to relieve Germany of payments for a limited period might, perhaps, postpone or avert a complete collapse, no temporary relief can revive the flow of credit, production and trade. As long as the capitalistic classes of the world regard Germany as a bad risk, Germany must continue to exercise the same profoundly depressing effect upon trade which she has exercised on Europe since the war and on all the world for many bitter months.

December 22, 1931

IV. SELF–RIGHTEOUSNESS AND OUR OWN REPUDIATED DEBTS

*Congressional bile and its bad effects; our own bad
debt record; some $375,000,000 in principal and
interest repudiated*

The air of truculent self-righteousness with which so many
of the Congressmen are expressing themselves can perhaps
be explained as an eruption of accumulated discontent.
Congress has not been allowed to meet for nine months.
The Administration has kept it in idleness brooding impo-
tently upon the hard times and upon all manner of reasons
to explain them. The safety valve of popular government has
been fastened down, and now that it is released the pent-up
angers are exploding. The effect is disconcerting. It works
cruelly upon the President. It is greatly damaging to the
good name of the country. It is destructive to the already
weakened fabric of faith and credit among the peoples.

This venting of bad will, these discharges of malice, this
outpouring of falsehoods and half-truths, of suspicions and
rumors, this search for conspirators and scapegoats, is the
price of suspending the normal operation of popular government for so long a time during so critical a period. The
price will have to be paid. It is not possible for reason to
rule till the force of unreason has in some measure spent
itself.

There is no use in trying to shout down the orators. But
it is well to keep reminding them, for when they are tired
of shouting they may listen, that in so great a crisis of
civilization it is not possible for any man to be so absolutely
right as these orators imagine themselves to be. For all of
us are in the presence of events of such surpassing magnitude
and complexity that certainty is the trade mark of a fool.

There is nobody who knows all about the state of the world, nobody who fully understands the causes, nobody who can predict the future, nobody who can do more than to propose tentatively the next steps to be taken. Because the facts are so obscure and the best human minds so uncertain, we must for our safety depend to a very large degree upon sympathy, upon the will to coöperate, upon faith in the fairness of other men, upon a spirit of give and take, of live and let live. These are the ultimate bonds of a community, and if we can exercise enough restraint upon ourselves not to disrupt them irremediably, we shall find the way out of this crisis as men have done through worse ones many times before.

The past is often clearer than the present, and recorded history is a mirror in which we can sometimes see ourselves best. Thus it might be profitable for Congress and for the country to recall just now, as the cry resounds from Washington that we must be unrelenting creditors, that we too were once a debtor nation. It was not so long ago. Until the World War we had been for a hundred and twenty-five years of the life of the Republic the debtors of Europe. It was with the savings of Europeans that our development was in part financed. It was from Britons, from Frenchmen, from Dutchmen, and from many others, that we obtained a great part of the funds with which to conquer the wilderness and build our physical structure.

Now that the position is suddenly reversed, now that we who were the debtors of all Europe have become the creditors, ought we forget too rapidly how much more than the money itself we owe for the indispensable service Europe performed for us? Ought we forget too rapidly how it feels to be the debtor when things go badly? Above all, ought we to forget in the vehemence of our demand for the payment of just debts that there are pages of our own record which, if we now had the candor to read them, would cause us to look upon these matters in a new perspective and with a chastened spirit?

It is almost forgotten here, but it is not forgotten in Europe, that there are eight states of the American Union that have repudiated bonds, a large part of which are held in Europe. The face of this debt is about 75 million dollars of principal and about 300 million dollars of interest. Most of these debts were incurred by the carpetbag governments imposed upon the Southern states after the Civil War, though in the case of two states the bonds were issued and the proceeds spent before 1861. The bonds were repudiated by the states, and the foreigners, who were mostly British, lost the money they had lent in good faith. I think there is little doubt that the Southern states were morally justified in repudiating the debts imposed by the carpetbaggers, but how can the nation justify its refusal to make good the debts incurred by its agents?

Yet, for sixty years the nation has refused to make good, and for sixty years the foreign bondholders have sought in vain for any redress. I think this is a good moment to remember so disagreeable a page in the history of our own conduct when we were distracted debtors after a devastating war. It may help us to act and to feel somewhat more charitably. It may help us to realize that in the complication of human events things are not so simple as we are now stating them to be. It may give us the grace to understand that we are of the same common clay as the foreigners whom we somehow find it so easy to despise.

It may even give us one small touch of that humility which is the beginning of wisdom.

December 18, 1931

Exact nature of the repudiation; not Confederate war debts

The repudiated state debts are as follows, the facts being summarized from a study by Mr. Charles P. Howland and published in *Foreign Affairs* for April, 1928:

PRE-CIVIL WAR DEBTS

Florida. About $8,000,000 principal, of which $3,900,000 was to provide capital for the Union Bank of Florida. These bonds were sold in Europe between 1834 and 1839. The rest of the repudiated bonds were in aid of the railroads. I am not able to give the date of this portion, but the bonds were not Confederate bonds.

Mississippi. $2,000,000 bond issue of 1831–1833 in aid of the Planters' Bank; $5,000,000 bond issue of 1838 in payment for shares in the Union Bank. On the first issue a proposal to pay interest was defeated by popular referendum in 1852. On the second issue, though the Supreme Court of the State sustained the validity of the bonds and the legislature wished to recognize them, the Governor recommended repudiation and was supported by a popular vote. In 1875 the repudiation of these bonds was made part of the state Constitution.

POST-CIVIL WAR DEBTS

Alabama. $18,000,000 of railroad aid bonds were issued or endorsed after the war. Some of the issues were taken up by the funding act of 1876. The repudiated portion is about $13,000,000.

Arkansas. Some of the debt goes back to 1838, when the state chartered a Real Estate Bank. Most of it was created by the issue of railroad aid or levee bonds after the Civil War. The Supreme Court declared some of the railroad bonds unlawful. Mr. Howland does not give figures on this debt.

Georgia. Bonds issued chiefly for railway guarantees after the Civil War. There was corruption in the transactions. Estimates of the repudiated bonds vary from $9,863,500 to $13,500,000.

Louisiana. The state's debt was increased about $20,000,000 in 1870–1871. Bonds were issued to provide state funds, to aid railroads and banks, and to assist the City of New Orleans. In 1912 a state referendum on the repayment of some of these bonds was rejected by popular vote.

North Carolina. The bonds were post-war railroad aid and special tax issues. The principal amount is not given by Mr. Howland, but in 1870 the annual interest charges would have amounted to $2,500,000. The technical objection to payment was that the state agent exceeded his powers.

South Carolina. The repudiated issues are partly post-war refundings of pre-war issues and partly railroad aid bonds. It is not clear what is the total amount repudiated.

It should be made clear again that in respect to the debts incurred under carpetbagger rule the moral obligation rests not upon the Southern states but upon the Union. The contention of Southern spokesmen that their states should not be held liable for corrupt and wasteful debts forced on them by Federal policy is unanswerable. But from the point of view of the bondholders, many of them British, the repudiation is not excused by this fact.

It should be noted, too, that other states, namely Pennsylvania, Indiana, Illinois, Michigan, and Maryland, attempted repudiation before the Civil War, but these states made terms with their creditors. The debts which are still repudiated amount to about $75,000,000 principal and $300,000,000 interest.

The moral is that people who live in glass houses should not throw stones.

December 23, 1931

V. EUROPE'S MOVE ON DEBTS AND REPARATIONS

Germany's inability to meet the Young Plan payments; the question of dividing the consequent losses; the duty of Britain and France to agree first on a fair settlement with Germany

To anyone who has read the Wiggin Report of last August the report last week of the Young Plan Advisory Committee contained no surprises.[1] It has been demonstrated once more that Germany cannot now pay in gold the whole amount called for under the Young Plan. The whole amount due when the Hoover moratorium ends would be about 450 million dollars a year. Of this amount about 165 millions are "unconditional." The Committee was not allowed to discuss them. The remaining 285 millions cannot, in the opinion of the Committee, be paid in gold or its equivalent.

The question now being discussed with great heat on both sides of the Atlantic is how the losses resulting from Germany's failure to pay these 285 millions, are to be divided. For it happens, not by coincidence but by design, that the net debt of the European governments to the United States is almost equal to the amount which Germany will not pay

[1] The report here referred to is that of the advisory board called together at Basle by the Bank for International Settlements to report on the possibility of continuing the Young Plan payments. It asked for an immediate meeting to review the plan, and this, after a postponement in January, became the Lausanne Conference which is treated later in this chapter.

next year. The war debts are about 250 millions for next year.

The European theory, embodied in the agreements reached at the Hague on January 20, 1930, is that the war debts owing to the United States are really Germany's obligation, that the so-called "conditional payments" are required chiefly to pay the United States. It has become a European dogma that if the war debts are to be paid they are to be paid by Germany; that if Germany does not pay, the United States ought not to be paid. The comments cabled to this country from all quarters in Europe rest, I believe, without exception on the theory that virtually the whole sacrifice to relieve Germany should be borne by America.

The American dogma, as expressed by Congress, is that no part of the sacrifice should be borne by America. Thus as matters stand there is a general agreement that Germany cannot pay now, and a deadlock as to which of the creditors is to take the loss. In each creditor country the government is paralyzed into rigidity by its own previous declarations of policy and by an inflamed popular sentiment. Mr. Hoover is bound down by the declaration of Congress that nothing can be yielded. Mr. MacDonald is bound down by the Balfour Declaration, which compels him to collect from Germany and from the European debtors to Britain whatever Britain has to pay the United States. M. Laval is bound down by the formula of Poincaré that France must receive from Germany about 100 millions a year for her devastated regions and enough besides to pay all her external government debts. Belgium and Italy are operating under similar formulæ. It is not merely Congress which is rigid. All the creditor nations are rigid. All are standing where they have stood for years. None has as yet offered to revise its own dogma and to make any sacrifice.

The problem for statesmanship is how and at what point

and on whose initiative this deadlock is to be broken. The wise thing to do is for Britain and France to agree on a settlement with Germany which promises to restore German credit and the economic life of Europe. They should ignore the United States entirely and make a settlement which they honestly believe to be in the best interest of Europe. They should, in other words, apply the conclusions of the two Basle reports. This would call not only for an extension of the German moratorium but for a permanent revision of the reparation payments, and for any other measures, such as reductions of tariffs and the stabilization of currencies which a recovery implies.

Only when they have worked out an agreement which is intrinsically acceptable in Europe should they turn again to the United States. With such an agreement in existence, assuming it to have the approval of expert and disinterested opinion on both sides of the Atlantic, they can count upon one of two alternatives. Either the American people will decide that the European plan offers sufficient promise of world recovery to justify a substantial contribution, or, failing this, the European governments can default with a good conscience and with the minimum shock to the world's credit. For a default, or even a repudiation, based on a constructive agreement to liberate the world from the war entanglements, would be a very different kind of default from one based on the mere assumption that war debts should be paid either by Germany or the United States.

If the European nations default without reaching a real agreement which offers far-reaching promise of recovery, they will do a dangerous and immoral thing. They will declare that they are bankrupt not only in money but in statesmanship. And they will deepen the crisis without relieving themselves.

At the moment, they are in no position to make faces at

the United States. For their own policies are as rigid and as nationalistically selfish and benighted as our own. Before they are entitled to criticize us they need to improve their own position. The way to improve their own position is to make a good European settlement promptly.

Then, if we are still unyielding, they can cut the Gordian knot.

December 9, 1931

VI. EARLY ACTION BY EUROPE NEEDED

The European project for another moratorium; unwisdom of the plan; a European settlement imperative

A semi-official note issued in Paris on Monday says that "it seems to be agreed now in Paris and London" to offer Germany an extension of the Hoover moratorium for six months or a year and to ask the United States to grant the same relief to its debtors. If this is the agreement in London and Paris, it will compel the President to decide whether to go before Congress this spring and ask for an extension of the moratorium. It will not be an easy decision to make.

It is true, of course, that Congress has not expressly declared against an extension of the moratorium. It has declared only against a revision of the settlements. Therefore, it might be argued that the Franco-British project does not call for a reversal of the strict letter of the Congressional declaration. But, in fact, the temper of Congress is such that it is extremely improbable that a vote could now be obtained approving another moratorium. Had pledges not been obtained last June the moratorium would almost certainly have been defeated in December.

Apparently, it is not yet understood in Europe why it

is that the moratorium which was so popular in June had become so unpopular in December. The reason for this change of opinion is plain enough to Americans. They have lived through six months of moratorium in which world conditions, including American, have become seriously worse, and for them there is no longer any magic in moratoria. As to the reasons for this result, there can be much argument; as to the fact, none.

But this much may, I think, be said with fair assurance. The Hoover moratorium was like a very dangerous drug which, administered at precisely the right moment and supplemented promptly with genuinely curative measures, might have started Europe towards convalescence. Its efficacy depended upon the willingness of the European nations to seek real solutions under its temporarily stimulating effect. The drug was unskillfully administered; there was not enough statesmanship in Europe or America to carry through successfully an operation of such magnitude and delicacy. The discords in Europe grew worse. Then the moratorium, instead of promoting confidence, undermined it by advertising the fact that the obligations of contracts had been impaired. The moratorium was followed, not by the reorganizations and readjustments which the underlying situation required, but by recrimination, political paralysis and successive measures of partial or total default.

Thus today a proposal to extend the moratorium is simply an announcement of political bankruptcy. It is hard to see what attractions the proposal can have for the American people. They are asked to help the European governments dodge the responsibility of dealing with the reparation problem, and it will not be easy to convince them that this is to their advantage or to anyone else's. For it is one thing to be a lenient and generous creditor; it is quite another thing to encourage the debtor to continue doing the very things which have produced his difficulties.

For there can be no conflicting opinions about the fact that a European settlement of reparations is an indispensable condition of European recovery. Two committees of experts, representing all the European powers concerned, have made authoritative and urgent declarations to this effect.

From an economic point of view there is really nothing to be said for another six or twelve months of postponement. The condition of Central Europe is becoming worse, and another twelve months of uncertainty, of agitation, of diplomatic maneuvering, with no promise of anything better at the end of the period, can only hasten the flight of capital, deepen the distress, and intensify the agony. The situation is not one which can be frozen and held where it is. It is a situation where everything is in movement, and things must either become better or worse.

Finally, the whole plan rests upon the fatal illusion that if Europe does nothing but let matters drift, we shall all wake up some morning to find Congress and the American voters prepared to cancel the debts. It is difficult to have patience with such naïveté.

January 20, 1932

VII. THE END OF REPARATIONS: BRUENING'S WARNING

Germany announces that further payments are impossible; consequences to the creditor nations; a final solution brought nearer

Dr. Bruening has now crossed the Rubicon.[1] He has taken the decisive step which, we may assume, it will be impossible

[1] Chancellor Bruening's declaration that Germany could pay no more reparations was not intended as a public defiance of France. It was a privately-made statement of opinion which happened to leak out. But it was at once accepted by informed financial opinion as an inescapable truth.

for him or his successors to retrace. He has declared not only that Germany cannot now pay reparations but that no compromise solution for the future is any longer possible. There can be no further question that Germany has denounced the Young Plan and the reparation clauses of the Treaty of Versailles.

The situation which now exists was foreseen as a possibility when the Young Plan was finally adopted at The Hague in January, 1930. Under French pressure Germany was then compelled to declare that

> if one or more of the creditor Powers referred to the Permanent Court of International Justice the question as to *whether the German Government revealed a determination to destroy the Young Plan,* the German Government, in agreement with the creditor Powers, accepts the proposal that the Permanent Court should decide the question, and declares that it acknowledges that it is legitimate, in the event of an affirmative decision by the Court, that, in order to ensure the fulfillment of the financial obligations of the debtor Powers resulting from the Plan, the *creditor Power or Powers should resume their full liberty of action.*

Thus France has the right to ask the World Court to decide whether Germany has revealed a determination to destroy the Young Plan, and if the Court decides in the affirmative, France has the right to apply military sanctions in accordance with Annex II of Part VIII of the Treaty of Versailles. This is the legal situation resulting from Dr. Bruening's decision.

The actual situation is different. If Pertinax, who is usually so well informed as to French policy, is right, all that France now expects from Germany is that she should place "in the hands of the Bank for International Settlements obligations representing the value of the unconditional payments (about 150 million dollars), which would not pay interest until after the expiration of the moratorium." Thus France recognizes that Germany cannot now pay any reparations and acknowledges that Germany will not be able to pay for some period, as yet not fixed, in the future. The real issue between France and Germany is whether Germany will or will not keep alive the obligation to pay. The Germans have, in effect, said they will not do this and are prepared to take whatever penalties France dares to inflict.

It is unlikely that France can force Germany to pay, and while some measures of reprisal may be demanded by French public opinion, it is now well understood in informed quarters that force cannot produce payments. The question then arises as to what it means to France to have reparations come to an end. This is somewhat difficult to state exactly because the payments on various accounts differ from year to year. But taking the year 1931 as a sample, the end of reparations may mean that during a year France does not receive about 200 million dollars and continues to owe 105 millions to Britain and the United States. Thus, even if France were forgiven her debts, she would lose a net amount somewhere in the neighborhood of 100 million dollars. If France has to pay her debts, she loses twice as much.

The extent of the French loss, therefore, will now depend upon what she can extract from Germany by force and on what concessions by Britain and America she can obtain or compel. It is an awkward position for France. If, vis-à-vis Germany, France takes the position that political debts are sacred, then France cannot refuse to pay Britain and America. If, vis-à-vis her creditor, France demands forgiveness, her principle of the sanctity of contracts cannot successfully be invoked against Germany.

In dealing with Britain the French are confronted by the

Balfour principle, which is that France must pay Britain if Britain must pay the United States. The net result of the matter is that France and Britain together must now determine how much, if anything, they can extract from Germany, and how much they will pay the United States. Should Germany yield nothing, should France and Britain decide to pay nothing, the final result would be that France lost about 100 millions a year and the United States about 250 millions.

We have thus arrived at what may be the decisive stage in the liquidation of governmental claims arising out of the war. This liquidation has by various expedients been postponed for thirteen years. The Germans have continued to pay, first, under military pressure, and, secondly, because they were offered private credit which they very much desired. Today, the military pressure can no longer be exerted successfully, and German credit is in such a state that it can no longer be injured as much by repudiating reparations as by continuing them. Whatever the penalties which France may exact immediately, it is now plain that in the long run Germany's credit will be better for having repudiated reparations. For reparations have ceased to be regarded as an ordinary debt by the creditor classes of the world, and what the Germans have done has their tacit approval.

January 12, 1932

VIII. THE NEED FOR EUROPEAN UNITY

A united front in Europe required for post-war reconstruction; desirability of an early and complete Anglo-French understanding

Unless it is read with care, the summary as published in Paris of Secretary Stimson's memorandum on debts and reparations is likely to cause serious misunderstanding in

Europe. The "fourth point" says that "the United States government would look with displeasure on the formation of a united front by the debtor nations," and there is likelihood that this will be taken to mean that the United States does not wish to see Britain, France and Germany come to a common understanding on the whole debt problem.

The phrase about our displeasure at a "united front" is unfortunate, for the one thing that offers real hope in the present situation is that Europe should unite within itself. The post-war reconstruction has been bedeviled by disunity. It is the everlasting maneuvering of the British with the Germans against the French, of the French with the Poles and Czechs against the Germans, of the Italians with the Germans and the Hungarians, which has made any solution impossible. For in this maneuvering the financial and economic elements of the reparation problem have become overshadowed by the fear of political and military combinations, and a vicious circle set revolving in which France, fearing for her security because of her political isolation, has become irreconcilable on reparations. This in turn has promoted political combinations against her which in their turn have made her more irreconcilable.

The only hope of breaking through this destructive entanglement lies in united action by Britain and France. Only if British and French policy can be brought to a common basis is there a chance of orderly solution. For it is a tragic mistake to think, as so many would like to think, that France can be isolated and coerced. Even if such a policy were desirable it would be impossible, and at this point in time impossible policies are exorbitantly expensive.

The essential interest of Britain is that there should be a financial and economic settlement in Europe. The essential interest of France is that there should be political and military stability. Why is there not here the basis for agreement which takes account of the essential interests of both countries? Why is it not possible for London and Paris to strike a bargain on reparations *and* security?

There is no reason why a Franco-British entente of this sort should be in any real sense anti-German. For if it is true that French irreconcilability is the result of the French sense of insecurity, the restoration of an entente with Britain should go a very long way towards enabling Frenchmen to act with the generosity that only the strong are capable of. There is much that a France, which felt secure, could concede to Germany. It could concede a reduction of reparations to a point where the charges on the German taxpayer would be virtually invisible. It could go further. It could offer to repeal the war-guilt clauses, which, while they stand, must always be a moral barrier to good feeling across the Rhine. Finally, it could offer Germany a Locarno in the East based on the assurance that in quieter times and by pacific means the attempt would be made by negotiations with Poland and Lithuania to see whether a new solution cannot be found.

All of this is difficult. None of it is even conceivable unless London and Paris firmly decide to work together. United they can begin to clear the air in Europe; disunited, at odds, they can only injure everyone, themselves included. They need have no fear of our displeasure if they unite.

January 22, 1932

IX. TASKS OF THE LAUSANNE CONFERENCE

Necessity for restoration of confidence at the world's financial centres; opportunities at Lausanne to remove anxieties

At Lausanne the European governments have resumed the negotiations which were broken off just about a year ago.[1] They are attempting today to reach those agreements which were meant logically to follow promptly upon the announcement of the Hoover Moratorium last June. They are seeking not only to lay the foundations for a permanent settlement of inter-governmental debts but to prepare the way for other agreements which will arrest and then reverse the tremendous world-wide deflation of prices.

A year ago the intelligence and good will of the nations were not equal to constructive effort on such a scale. The question now is whether the misery of the people is great enough and the danger to the established order visible enough, to have brought men's minds to a readiness for the sacrifices which a program of recovery demands.

During this year of disaster the actions of men everywhere have been governed by a desire to save themselves—even if they have to ruin others in the attempt. Every government, every central bank, virtually every commercial bank and every producing interest, millions of individuals, have been in a panic. There has been a wild scramble for the exits, and more have been trampled than have been saved. In order to "protect" the home market and the domestic currency, each government has ruthlessly done its worst by means of tariffs, quotas, and exchange restrictions to stop the exchange of goods. Among banks and investors there has been a frantic shifting about of funds from one international center to

---

[1] The Lausanne Conference for the revision of the Young Plan of reparations payments was first scheduled for January 18, 1932. It then seemed best to postpone its work until after the French and German elections. It finally opened late in June, and was the first major economic conference of an international character to be held since the great financial crash of 1929. All the nations which had signed the Young Plan (of which the United States was not one) sent delegates. The Conference opened on June 16, after Prime Minister MacDonald and Premier Herriot had held an advance meeting in Paris, June 11 and 12, to examine the situation. Following the French swing to the Left in the recent elections, hopes for a successful scaling-down of reparations ran high.

another in an hysterical effort to find security. Bankers have
been engaged in a wild competition to make their banks
liquid, and depositors in their fright have been hoarding currency and gold. It has been a year in which on an unprecedented scale the rule has been each man for himself and
the devil take the rest.

The result of this anarchy has been the most violent contraction of credit within human memory. During the past
twelve months more than half of the short-term indebtedness
among nations has been called in and a large part of the
remainder has become frozen. Inside each nation the destruction of bank money through the calling of bank loans
has been stupendous. In the United States the destruction
was proceeding last winter at the rate of 25 per cent per
annum.

As the effective money of the world is not gold or silver
or paper currency but bank credit, this worldwide destruction of bank credit had to bring with it a catastrophic fall
in prices. The fall in prices had to bring in its train the
destruction of profits. The destruction of profits had to be
followed by bankruptcies, by wage reductions, and by increasing unemployment. These in their turn brought about
such a loss of government revenues as to throw every budget
out of balance and to compel the peoples everywhere to choose
either to tax themselves to the limit of endurance or to
plunge themselves into complete financial chaos.

The objective, therefore, of any constructive effort is to
stop this destruction of bank money and then to promote
the re-creation of some part of the bank money which has
been destroyed. This objective can be attained only by the
restoration of confidence in the financial centers of the world;
but such a restoration of confidence will not be brought unless two great things are achieved. The first is the reëstab-
lishment of enough peace among the great powers to assure

lenders and borrowers that the extension of new credit does not bear the risk of political entanglements and of eventual war. The second is the attainment of arrangements under which there will be sufficient freedom and sufficient stability of trade to make what remains of public and private indebtedness bearable, over a limited period of years, by the debtors.

The first task at Lausanne is to remove the political danger. The problem here is purely European; in fact, it is essentially Franco-German. The reparation question, since Germany cannot or will not pay much if anything, is today a political and not a financial problem. It does not involve the transfer of funds but the balance of political power in Europe. If France and Germany can reach a settlement which promises political stability as between themselves, the Lausanne Conference will have made a successful start. If they cannot reach such a settlement, the conference is a hopeless failure and the outlook in Europe is dark indeed.

The second task at Lausanne, assuming a successful political settlement between Berlin and Paris, is to make arrangements by which old debts are made bearable enough to warrant the creation of new debts. This must mean that some part of the old public and private debts will have to be reduced. It must mean, also, that all the nations must give and receive assurances that the existing impossibly high barriers to the payments of debts in goods will be reduced and that the trade war will stop. It is here that the supreme test will come as to whether the peoples have learned enough from their suffering in the last twelve months to be willing to make the sacrifices which they so unwisely rejected last summer.

June 22, 1932

X. ACHIEVEMENTS OF THE LAUSANNE CONFERENCE

The new understanding between Britain and France; America's alternative of a reasonable debt settlement or repudiation

The world has had so much bad news for so long a time that it is difficult to appreciate how great was the achievement at Lausanne. Nothing was expected except another dreary postponement which would evade every issue that disturbs the peace of Europe and paralyzes the confidence of men. Instead we find that the long servitude of reparations is ended and that Germany is once again economically free.[1] On that front the war is over. But this is not all. With the abolition of reparations as an issue in European diplomacy the great conflict between the French political interest in reparations and the British economic interest in the revival of Central Europe has been resolved. Britain and France

[1] The Lausanne Conference resulted in an agreement in the second week of June for the virtual abolition of reparations. It was agreed that for three years the existing moratorium should be continued. Germany was then to make a final settlement (if the Bank for International Settlements considered her resources equal to it) by paying over a bond issue with a face value of 3,000,000,000 marks. The capital amount of this sum was not greatly larger than the *annual* payments under the Dawes Plan. If it should turn out, when the time came to issue the bonds, that Germany was not able to make the payment, and if this situation continued for fifteen years, then the whole debt should be written off. This settlement was initialed by the representatives of the various governments gathered at Lausanne. But it was accompanied by a "gentlemen's agreement" that it was not to be ratified by the Allied Powers unless and until they had obtained a "satisfactory adjustment" of their war debts to the United States. If the United States refused such an adjustment, then the Lausanne agreement would fall through and the European Powers would take counsel again on their course. This "gentlemen's agreement" produced much excitement in certain American circles, and brought from such men as William Randolph Hearst angry denunciations of Great Britain and France.

are thus once again in a position to work as partners rather than as rivals in the settlement of other questions.

The restoration of Franco-British understanding is as great an achievement as the ending of reparations. For on no other basis can Europe hope to obtain a period of tranquillity. Rivalry between Paris and London has meant intrigue, maneuver and confusion in every European center and on every European question. It has precluded any possibility of Franco-German understanding by filling the extreme nationalists in both countries with dangerous fears and dangerous hopes. The diplomatic rivalry between Britain and France made all prospect of political appeasement and of reduction of armaments entirely vain, for unless these two countries know whether they are to be friends or opponents they cannot and will not and dare not limit their powers of offense and defense. Franco-British coöperation does not solve all European questions, but it is the indispensable preliminary to their solution. Therefore, the so-called Accord of Confidence is the most promising political event in the recent history of the world. It can do more to promote peace and restore confidence and make possible the solution of other questions than any agreement that could have been devised.

Much energy has been expended in charging and denying that the Lausanne agreements mean a united European front in relation to the debts owing the United States. Those who are nervous on this point should ask themselves whether the general interest of all nations would be advanced if Britain, in order to obtain some financial relief for herself, were to desert France and leave her angry, humiliated and alone. What chance would there be then that nationalist and monarchist Germany could be kept from attempting some new adventure? What chance would there be for an agreement on armaments? Or for financial coöperation between London and Paris to restore Central Europe? Or for a termination of the tariff war that is strangling the trade of the world? Or for the eventual solution of German-Polish problems?

Those who now think that Paris and London ought to be rivals rather than partners in dealing with the debts take a short and narrow view of the situation. It is to the interest of France and Britain, it is to the interest of all Europe, and in any long view it is to our interest that the settlements of the debts should not drive a wedge between the two European nations who alone have the power to reunite Europe and save it from overwhelming disaster.

When the smoke blows away, when the confusion arising from mere phrases is forgotten, this will become, I venture to believe, the considered view of the American people. For what have we to fear and what have we to lose if France and Great Britain take the position that they will stand together in the forthcoming debt negotiations? If Congress refuses to consider a new settlement, will the shock to the credit of the world be any greater if Europe makes a common default than if each nation defaults separately? On the contrary, separate defaults would be the greater shock, for they would signify bankruptcy and political confusion, whereas a common default would be recognized everywhere as a political act which did not really impair the validity of genuinely economic obligations. It would put political debts into a wholly different category from all others.

To say all this is not to invite a default, but to face frankly the situation which would exist if there is no change in the present temper of Congress. For, of course, if Congress is absolutely inflexible against a new settlement it will without any doubt whatever precipitate the issue of repudiation. The existing debt arrangements cannot and will not be carried out. They belong to a past which no longer exists and is now irrevocable. But it does not follow from this that the only alternatives are repudiation or cancellation.

The way is still open to a new settlement which will complete the payments by a lump sum. That is almost certainly what our debtors mean to offer us and I cannot believe we shall be so foolish as to reject it out of hand. There never was an intelligent creditor who refused a cash offer and preferred to cling to his obviously bad bonds.

When the time comes around for discussion of this question a cash offer will not be unattractive to the American people. Suppose we were offered a billion dollars in final settlement of all the debts. Would we really wish to reject that and then try to collect the payments nominated in the bond? Does anyone wish to condemn this generation and the next generation and the one after that to the task of collecting every cent of the debts?

I doubt it. Next winter when this question will confront us we shall again be facing a large deficit. We shall again be confronted with the necessity of increasing taxes. A billion dollars in hand will look a great deal better than sixty annual payments that are very legal but no good. Therefore, in spite of what the Senators are saying now, there is every reason to believe that the hard facts of the situation will be stronger than their present theories.

It is but natural that American opinion should require some time to accustom itself to the radically new state of affairs created at Lausanne. Nobody dreamed that Mr. Herriot would deal as he has dealt with Germany or that Mr. MacDonald could so swiftly and radically restore the shattered entente with France. The events have confounded all the prophets, so dramatic has been the change of mind in Europe. But now that the thing is done we can see why it has been done. The peoples of Europe have come to the edge of the precipice, have looked over, and turned around.

They had to. They have indulged their passions as long as they dared. They had finally to save themselves.

What they have learned we shall learn. The moment will come when men will say to themselves here that the war which began eighteen years ago must end, that it is time to stop waving the bloody shirt, that it is time to deal as Lincoln would have dealt, with his kind and patient strength, and to retire into the obscurity which would be their worst and sufficient punishment all that brood who inherit the implacable hatred and the evil genius of Thaddeus Stevens. We have had enough of the political terrorists who, appealing to all that is base in our natures, have brought the politicians to a point so abject they dare not call their souls their own. Let the exploiters of hatred and the makers of discord get out of our way. They have hurt and humiliated us long enough. We have other business to do. For this people will not forever allow its interests to be perverted, its policy to be distracted, its reputation to be lowered, its honor impugned, its magnanimity and greatness denied by the scratching and wailing of jingoes and ignoramuses.

June 29, 1932

XI. AMERICA AND THE SUCCESS OF THE LAUSANNE CONFERENCE

The end of the reparations system; prospects for a debt settlement

It may be said that an economic solution of the reparations problem has been reached at Lausanne and that what remains to be done is to adapt the solution to popular sentiment in the various countries. Thus it is agreed that Germany should not be asked to pay anything for at least three years. It is agreed that the payments she makes thereafter must be so small that the whole of it would not at the outside be equal to much more than two annuities out of sixty odd called for under the Young plan. It is agreed that these small payments shall be due only if or when in the judgment of a neutral body, the World Bank at Basle, Germany can borrow the money to make them.

Although there is still some dispute as to the exact amount which Germany is to promise she will try to borrow, the creditors appear to have committed themselves to three principles: no payments for three years, a small cash payment as a final settlement, and this cash settlement to be made only if German credit is good enough to permit the sale of her bonds. Once the creditors agree to these principles at Lausanne they will, of course, mark the upper limit of any demand they can ever again make upon Germany. More than this the creditors will not obtain whether or not the agreement is ratified by the various parliaments.

Henceforth, Germany's liability under reparations cannot be larger than the interest and amortization on a loan of about $750,000,000. The German taxpayer may have to find about $100,000,000 for ten years. Under the Young plan he had to find five times as much for thirty-six years and nearly four times as much for another twenty years.

The proposed settlement would bring to an end the existing reparation system. This system was arranged so that Germany should pay the whole debt owed by the Allies to the United States and a small surplus, most of which went to France. Under the Lausanne proposals Germany would at the outside pay enough to cover three European payments to the United States, and even these payments would not begin for three years and would be contingent upon Germany's ability to borrow the money. It is plain, therefore, that if the creditors make this agreement at Lausanne, they will emerge having virtually cancelled what is owed to them and still obligated to pay all that they owe to the United States.

It is easy to see why M. Herriot, who on paper at least has made the largest concessions, is standing out for an agreement that the plan should not be ratified in Europe until there is a settlement with the United States. But what, in fact, would this mean? It would mean that M. Herriot would not, on this issue, have to risk defeat in the French Chamber during the next six months. M. Herriot will have plenty of other troubles and it would be cruel to ask him to do so unpopular a thing as to forgive France's debtor while France's creditor is adamant.

Besides relieving M. Herriot of a political embarrassment, the effect of suspending ratification would be two-fold: it would delay the restoration of German credit and it would make it a little more difficult to deal with the American Congress. For as long as the plan is not legally in effect, the reparations problem will be politically alive, and while no succeeding French government could hope to obtain more money from Germany than the sum now being fixed at Lausanne, there would be a real possibility that M. Herriot's successor might try to sell ratification for political concessions. Thus the atmosphere would remain troubled, and in a troubled atmosphere the stricken credit of Germany cannot be restored.

In dealing with the United States there can be little doubt that Congress would be most firm if the impression were created that Europe had contrived a situation in which America must yield or take the blame for prolonging the financial disorder. The temper of Congress is such that it is most likely to be magnanimous if there is no moral compulsion from Europe. I do not think any competent American observer would dispute the statement that the most promising way to deal with America is for Europe to make the settlement now contemplated at Lausanne, and then to open negotiations here.

This procedure involves no financial risk. For the European creditors cannot get any more out of Germany just because they fail to get complete relief from America. On the other hand, if they arrive to negotiate, having burned their bridges and solved the problem in Europe, their moral position here will be invincible. They will have testified to their conviction that the prompt liquidation of the war debts is desirable, and that the whole agitation does not conceal hidden political maneuvers. It will cost them nothing to do what is right and most expedient.

No American is in a position to say what kind of settlement can be made here, just as no Frenchman was in a position thirty days ago to say that France would be as generous and as farsighted as France has shown herself to be. It should be noted, however, that the Republican platform is silent on the subject of debts, and this silence signifies a realization that a new deal is necessary. No responsible Republican official at Chicago had any doubt on that point.[1]

The Democratic platform has a direct statement opposing "cancellation" of debts. But this sentence did not appear in the original draft as it came from Governor Roosevelt's advisers. Their view is to be found a few sentences earlier, where there is a declaration for "the maintenance of good faith and of *good will* in financial obligations." The anticancellation clause was forced into the platform by Mr.

[1] President Hoover, in his speech of acceptance on August 11, 1932, opposed the cancellation of war debts, but declared he might favor an arrangement by which "some other tangible form of compensation, such as the expansion of markets for American agriculture and labor and the restoration and maintenance of our prosperity," might be substituted for any particular annual payment.

McAdoo and the Hearst influence; it was accepted regretfully but on the understanding that a debt can be radically readjusted without being cancelled. Events at Lausanne show how far it is possible to go without "cancelling" a debt.

There is thus every reason to believe that, if matters are conducted with tact and consideration, the American people will be just about as reasonable, though they are as reluctant to be reasonable, as their European neighbors. But even if this prophesy should prove to be untrue, there is nothing that Europe can gain by keeping itself embroiled over reparations because it fears that the American Congress is irreconcilable.

July 7, 1932

He makes out the Bureau conference. It was supposed right-
fully but not the trading venture that a wary out we redeeming
common wisdom some contract
a new chance or transfer to protest
these
enable.

· VI ·

THE CRISIS IN THE FAR EAST: AMERICAN POLICY

I. THE MANCHURIAN PROBLEM: A TEST AND A DEMONSTRATION

Difficulty of the Manchurian question; our consultation with the League

In many ways Manchuria presents the most difficult international question in the world.[1] No other question which troubles mankind—the relations between France and Germany, or between Europe and Russia, or our present economic confusion—is so intractable as the underlying conflict in Manchuria. Here in literal truth there is a conflict of vital interests which may be delayed and postponed but cannot be resolved by any peace-making device now in existence.

The question is whether Manchuria, which is a land as great as France and Germany combined and physically richer, is to become part of the Chinese Republic or of the Japanese Empire. That question is not going to be settled this week or this year or perhaps in this generation. It is not going to be decided by the League of Nations, by the signers of the Kellogg Pact, or by any set of living diplomats. It could not be decided by war, though three wars, the

---

[1] For a long period there had existed in Manchuria a tense situation between the Chinese, who had been emigrating to the province in enormous numbers, and the Japanese, who had large investments there. The Japanese

187

Chinese-Japanese, the Russo-Japanese, and the German-Japanese part of the World War indirectly, have been fought over it, and others may be. Peace treaties and diplomatic adjustments merely arrest for a little while the irresistible movement of conflicting forces. For the Chinese are colonizing Manchuria at the rate of about a million Chinamen a year, and the Japanese have for a generation been establishing a structure of vested rights in Manchuria. There is thus on the one side the superior organized force of the Japanese Empire, and on the other the irresistible pressure of Chinese numbers.

Recent events, such as the killing of Japanese and Chinese and the military coup, are incidents of the perpetual tension which must prevail where interests so vital as these are in real conflict. There is no more possibility of investigating each particular incident to determine "the aggressor" than it would be to determine who first jostled the other man in a crowded subway train. There is here no such thing as

---

in 1931 complained of three main grievances in Manchuria. These were (1) the opposition of the Chinese government at Mukden to all Japanese requests for business concessions, and particularly to Japanese ambitions in the field of railway construction; (2) disputes over the land question, and especially the Japanese demand that the Koreans in Manchuria, who were Japanese subjects and numbered more than half a million, should have the privilege of leasing land; and (3) the growing evils of brigandage, disorder, and local governmental corruption and oppression in much of Manchuria. The Chinese for their part complained of Japanese aggressions. The importance of Manchurian coal and iron to Japan was patent. Repeated "incidents" occurred early in 1931. In August the Japanese consul-general in Mukden demanded an apology and an indemnity from the Chinese authorities for the killing of a Japanese army captain. On September 18 Japanese troops in force seized Mukden. It soon became evident that, in the face of the world's disapproval, they intended to make themselves masters of all Manchuria. Large military forces were landed; the occupation was steadily extended; on February 5, 1932, the Japanese entered Harbin, and within a short time the whole province, to the Great Wall, was under Japanese control. The Japanese erected a new state under the name of Manchukuo, nominally independent but virtually a fief of Japan.

an "aggressor" and a "non-aggressor." There are, if any-thing, two aggressors, the Chinese pushed into Manchuria by the pressure of their conditions and the Japanese pushed by the pressure of theirs. For these fundamental reasons diplomacy cannot be expected to intervene with a clear-cut solution. In the nature of things it must work for time and for a localization of conflicts, looking for an ultimate solu-tion, not to formal agreements, but to an historic decision as to whether Chinese numbers, inspired by Chinese nation-alism, will in the long run prove stronger than Japanese mili-tary and economic force.

It is in this light that we must, I think, look at the present efforts of the League, and of the signatories of the Kellogg Pact and Nine-Power Treaty. There is no real doubt that the Japanese army has violated the spirit, and probably the letter too, of all these treaties. Theoretically, all the machin-ery of moral and political coercion ought, therefore, to be set in motion. But it will almost certainly not be set in motion because the Powers cannot afford to do it, being too weak, and because it would not be wise to do it if they could. For a serious intervention to compel Japan to surrender im-mediately the advantages gained by the coup would morally oblige the Powers to guarantee Japan against Chinese re-prisals, and also against the continuation of Chinese aggres-sion upon Japan's position. The Powers would thus be faced squarely with the problem of the future of Manchuria. But that is a problem they cannot solve.

They are compelled, therefore, to evade the issue and to rely upon what little delicate pressure they can exert, hoping that the civilian and commercial classes of Japan will keep the army within bounds. It is disheartening to have to con-fess that the Powers are not in a position to do more, to vindi-cate law and order majestically and set justice upon her throne. They are not. The Manchurian issues lie beyond the present resources of our civilization, and the fact that the League, under the guidance of Secretary Stimson, has recognized this limitation is not a sign that diplomats lack good will, but that they are capable of acknowledging an unpleasant truth.

As a matter of fact, the Manchurian affair has marked a definite step forward in the organization of international relations. For while nothing effective has been done, or is likely to be done now, to establish permanent peace in Manchuria, the action of our government, if properly understood in Europe, ought to help in the European situation. For ten years Europe has been asking us what we would do if the League were confronted with a great issue in Europe. For four years Europe has been asking us how we would reconcile our obligations under the Kellogg Pact with our supposed hostility to the League.

We have steadfastly refused to answer either question, and our refusal has contributed to the uncertainties of Europe. Secretary Stimson has now given a demonstration which answers these questions. He has shown by his action that in a crisis we shall consult with the League, and formulate a common policy with it. We have done this for two weeks as to Manchuria, and we should do it again elsewhere.

It is to be hoped that M. Briand and the French public will study this aspect of American policy. It is to be hoped that Congress and the American public will study it. For if actions speak louder than words we have gone a very long way toward answering the questions as to how the United States would conduct itself if the peace of Europe were threatened. We have shown that though we have signed no treaty which commits us to consult with a view to common action, we are, and know ourselves to be, committed by the logic of events.

September 29, 1931

II. JAPAN VIOLATES THE NINE–POWER TREATY

Japan's intention of creating her own government in Manchuria; unwillingness of the Powers to consent

Within the last few days, the behavior of the Japanese diplomats in Paris has greatly aggravated the situation in the Far East. With the seizure of Tsitsihar, the army has in its possession the capitals of the three Manchurian provinces. It had already seized all the railways in which Japan has any financial interest. The grand strategy of the action is now plain. Japan is uprooting and destroying the local Chinese authority in Manchuria in order to substitute for it Chinese puppet governments which will do her will. The object of this strategy is to create a government in Manchuria which will accept without question Japan's interpretation of all her claims.

The position taken by Japan at Paris unfortunately leaves no doubt upon this point. A month ago the world was being told that Japan would withdraw her troops when the safety of her nationals was assured. With this argument, though it involved a breach of the letter of the treaties, it was possible to have sympathy. But now the world is told that Japan will withdraw only when China has given evidence that she will acknowledge the whole body of Japanese treaty claims. Moreover, the Japanese position now is that these claims cannot even be stated or defined publicly, that the other powers have no right to know what the claims are that Japan insists China must respect. How can the conclusion be avoided that what we are witnessing is not a mere police action to put down local disorders, but the execution of a carefully prepared and far-reaching plan to give Japan undisputed control of the economic, political and administrative life of South Manchuria?

This unveiling of the Japanese plan brings her policy directly within the purview of the Nine Power Treaty.[1] That Treaty was drawn up and signed at Washington in 1922. It provides in Article I that the Contracting Powers agree "to respect the . . . *administrative integrity* of China." The Manchurian provinces are indisputably a part of China. The setting up of puppet governments controlled by Japan is unmistakably a violation of the administrative integrity of China. It is not a petty violation. For there are some twenty-eight million Chinese in Manchuria. It is not an inadvertent violation. For the destruction of Chinese authority has been systematic and comprehensive.

The Nine Power Treaty was signed for Japan by the present Foreign Minister, Baron Shidehara. It was signed for the United States by Charles Evans Hughes, Henry Cabot Lodge, Oscar W. Underwood and Elihu Root. It was signed by the plenipotentiaries of seven other powers—Britain, France, Italy, Belgium, The Netherlands, Portugal and China. This treaty antedates the Kellogg Pact. It was made by a Republican administration which had just come into office after a campaign to repudiate the League of Nations, and the treaty is signed by the arch-enemy of American participation in the League, the late Senator Henry Cabot Lodge. It is well to recall this now, for in certain quarters there is a disposition to talk as if the United States were gravely concerned about Manchuria today because the Administration has been seduced by the idealists of the Kellogg Pact and the League. The truth is that the issue raised by

[1] The Japanese operations in Manchuria were never a direct violation of the Kellogg Pact, for there was never open and declared war; but as is here explained, the effort to set up a virtual Japanese government in the province was a violation of the Nine Power Treaty. The first article of this treaty, as signed in Washington in 1922, bound Japan and the eight other signatories "to respect the sovereignty, the independence, and the territorial and administrative integrity of China."

Japan today is one with which American diplomacy has been actively concerned for more than thirty years. Had the League never been created and were there no Kellogg Pact, the State Department would nevertheless be consulting today with the same Powers it is now consulting with at Paris.

For Japan's fundamental thesis that what goes on in Manchuria is a matter entirely between herself and China is a thesis to which none of the great powers has ever subscribed. The Chinese question is an international question. That is why nine Powers signed treaties at Washington about it. Japan herself has recognized that it is an international question by ratifying these treaties, and her present demand that she be allowed a free hand is a breach of the letter and of the spirit of the treaties. Her present position refutes the assertions made by her spokesmen that Japan is seeking no new rights in Manchuria. Japan is insisting upon a wholly new right, and that the greatest of diplomatic rights, the right to a free hand in dealing with another nation's property.

In asserting this claim Japan has placed the seven Western Powers who signed the treaty in a position where they cannot acquiesce. The foreign offices may be cynical about the League covenant and the Kellogg Pact, but they cannot fail to realize that if they allow Japan to tear up the Nine Power Treaty they will undermine their own influence in the whole Oriental world. It will have been demonstrated to the East that the West is too feeble to exert its authority, and the process initiated by Japan in this instance will become a provocative and revolutionary precedent. The Powers cannot, as a matter of self-respect and self-interest, yield to Japan. They cannot do what Japan demands of them, which is that they tell China to surrender.

Nor are they so weak as they seem. They cannot and need

not make any threats. They have only to be patient and let public opinion become informed. For the Japanese objective is one which cannot be attained without their help. Japan seeks a recognition of her treaty claims in Manchuria. She cannot get that recognition by occupying Manchurian cities. She cannot get it from puppet governments. She can get it only by an internationally recognized legal procedure, from some kind of international conference in which the other Powers are represented.

In this respect her position is worse after the coup than it was previously. For up to September 19, an interpretation of her confused and often dubious treaty rights was being worked out by usage and precedent. Now, in demanding a summary acknowledgment of all her claims, Japan has made it necessary for the Powers to examine those claims, to see just what they really are and how they fit with the interests of others.

November 20, 1931

III. THE MANCHURIAN AFFAIR AS A TEST OF THE KELLOGG PACT

Japan conducting not a war but an intervention; the League and America might have pronounced it outside the scope of the Kellogg Pact; now they must see it through

The outstanding fact in the Far East today is that neither the government at the Chinese capital in Nanking nor the government at the Japanese capital in Tokio has effective control over the forces operating in Manchuria. There are Chinese armies and Chinese officials of various kinds, but in no true sense can they be said to be accountable to the

Chinese Government more than a thousand miles distant, and there is no good reason to suppose that Nanking could commit them, even if it wished to do so, to the observance of definite agreements. The Japanese army in Manchuria, though more disciplined than the Chinese forces, is not under full civilian control, and it is pursuing a policy which the diplomats in Tokio do not initiate but are nevertheless compelled to justify.

The lack of a central authority in China has produced a situation not unlike that of Europe in the Middle Ages. Independent and generally corrupt local chieftains hold portions of territory which they exploit. They are not amenable to public law and international agreements. These chaotic conditions, which prevail over so large a portion of China proper, have now spread to Manchuria. As a result the great Japanese investments in that land, and the whole strategic position of Japan on the Asiatic mainland, are jeopardized. They are threatened by the depredations of the Chinese feudal lords who are in turn encouraged by the intrigues of aspiring but impotent patriots a thousand miles away.

The Chinese Nationalists do not, of course, acknowledge that Japan has any moral right to be in Manchuria at all. But Japan is there; her right is merely the right of conquest, but it is established by treaties. That these treaties have been violated continually there can be no doubt, and among Chinese Nationalists treaty breaking by local generals and officials, usually for their own corrupt purposes, has acquired a kind of moral sanction. The Nationalists look on the business of sabotage as part of their campaign to drive Japan out of all Chinese territories. The Japanese have been confronted, therefore, with local corruption and disorder promoted from China proper and exploited as a method of disguised warfare.

It is only fair to the Japanese to say that by ordinary international standards they have been extremely patient under great provocation. The civil government was apparently willing to continue to be patient, for it was aware of the change in world opinion since Austria and Germany under analogous circumstances lost their patience with Serbia. The Japanese civilian government has, in fact, been a conspicuously loyal supporter of the whole post-war effort to organize peace. But in the face of increasing Chinese provocation, it was not strong enough to control the army and the patriotic sentiment of the Japanese people. On September 19 the Militarist party took matters into its own hands by seizing Mukden. In that action the civilians, however much they may have regretted the manner of it, have felt it necessary to concur.

The Japanese military policy has been, it appears, to occupy, up to the Russian sphere of influence in Northern Manchuria, all the railroads built by Japanese capital. By controlling the railroads Japan has control of commerce and of the centers of government; it has been employing this power to set up local Chinese governments which are dependent upon Japan. The procedure is a familiar one, and all the Powers have in the past followed it at one place and another, ourselves included, as in Nicaragua, Haiti and elsewhere. The Japanese army is, in a word, carrying on not "a war" but "an intervention."

The problem which confronts the League and us is whether in outlawing war we intend to outlaw not merely formally declared wars but any use of armed force to settle political questions. Unfortunately the Japanese seizure of Mukden took the world by surprise at a moment when its statesmen were distracted by the economic crisis and were unable to think very clearly. Tired, confused, and not well informed, conscious of the fact that the Western World sorely needed the assurance that peace would be preserved by common action, they plumped for an interpretation which brought Japan's intervention within the scope of the Kellogg-Briand pact renouncing war.[1]

Once this was done, the Manchurian affair assumed world-wide significance. It was made the test of whether the new institutions of peace were strong enough to control the actions of a great Power, and the outcome of that test may very well decide how far the nations of Europe and the Western World will be willing in this coming winter to stabilize their relations and substitute faith in treaties for competitive armaments.

A different decision might have been taken. Instead of challenging Japan's action under the Kellogg pact, the Powers might have devoted themselves to facilitating nego-tiations between China and Japan, recognizing that the Manchurian problem is infinitely complex, seeking by pa-tient conciliation to work out some sort of working ar-rangement. Such a course might, to be sure, have multi-plied the cynicism of mankind and might have been highly demoralizing to European hopes for a European peace. The course taken has been bold. It is a gamble with the prestige of the whole post-war machinery of peace which, if it is successful, should bring untold benefits in the way of in-creased human faith and confidence, but which, if it fails, cannot but be a disastrous disillusionment to all the peoples.

The decision to make the gamble having been taken, there

[1] On September 19, 1931, the Chinese first brought the Japanese mili-tary operations in Manchuria to the attention of the League of Nations. The League Council, after hurried consideration, decided—as it is stated here—that the acts of Japan fell within the scope of the Kellogg-Briand pact. The Council also acted under Article XI of the League Covenant. Under this article it appointed a commission of inquiry, headed by Lord Lytton, to go to the Far East and investigate the troubles there. This com-mission, proceeding by way of New York, reached Tokyo on February 29, 1932. Meanwhile, the conflict in Shanghai had broken out.

is no other course open but to see it through. That does not mean that it is necessary even to consider the coercion of Japan. On the contrary, it is still possible, and more necessary than ever, to recognize the merits of the Japanese case and to repudiate firmly all Chinese efforts to exploit the situation. But it does mean that the nations of the world must stand together presenting a common front, and that they must not relax their moral pressure.

What they have to prove is not that they can at once push the Japanese soldiers back to the railway zone, but that in the end a militarist coup of this sort is unprofitable to the nation which attempts it. That alone will enable civilian Japan to regain control of the army. The way to deliver the proof that the coup is unprofitable is to continue unremittingly to seek a settlement by negotiation which will give Japan her full rights, but no new advantages as a result of the adventure,[1] and to accompany these efforts at conciliation by repeated evidence that the outer world is morally united in a determination to support its covenants.

December 10, 1931

IV. THE ATTACK ON SHANGHAI: AMERICAN POLICY

Our sole object to protect American lives and interests; Secretary Stimson's note of January 7

The most important thing to fix in mind about the present situation at Shanghai is that the United States is not engaged

[1] The idea here stated found later embodiment in Secretary Stimson's identic notes of January 7, 1932, to Japan and China, notifying them that the United States would not recognize any situation, treaty, or agreement entered into by the Japanese and Chinese Governments in violation of the Nine Power Treaty or the Kellogg-Briand pact, and affecting American rights in China.

in trying to enforce the Kellogg Pact or the Nine Power Treaty.[1] Its sole objective is to protect American lives and interests without becoming embroiled in a war with Japan.

The objective implies three main lines of action. The first is to act in concert with Great Britain, France and Italy to put enough ships and troops into Shanghai to defend the International Settlement and if necessary to evacuate Europeans and Americans who may be in danger. The second is by concerted diplomatic action to persuade Japan to cease using the International Settlement and Chinese territory contiguous to it as a base of operation. Further than that it is impossible to see ahead at this time.

The first phase of our disinterested intervention to obtain respect for the Kellogg Pact and the Nine Power Treaty ended with Secretary Stimson's note of January 7. The League and the United States had failed to check the Japanese advance over the whole of South Manchuria, and the Japanese army was in possession of the territory. The position taken by the American Government then became substantially the same as that which it took in 1915, when Japan

[1] Even before the Japanese began occupying Manchuria a boycott of their manufactures had developed in the Shanghai region. It was resented by the Japanese Government, and this resentment was increased by various fresh "incidents" in which Japanese citizens suffered. During the autumn of 1931 Japanese warships were ordered to Shanghai. By January, 1932, a large force of marines was in readiness. The Japanese consul-general addressed an ultimatum to the mayor of Greater Shanghai calling for the suppression of anti-Japanese associations and for other measures. The mayor returned a reply which the consul-general called satisfactory. But the Japanese admiral commanding there took the situation into his own hands, issued a proclamation stating that he was taking steps for the enforcement of law and order, and on January 28, 1932, launched a combined land and air attack on the Chapei district of Shanghai. Fighting rapidly developed on a large scale, and the Chinese 19th Army made a surprisingly effective resistance. On January 29 the Chinese representative on the League Council invoked Articles X and XV of the League Covenant. The Council made strenuous efforts to bring about a cessation of the fighting, and set on foot efforts at mediation between the local Chinese and Japanese commanders.

presented China with the Twenty-one Demands. That position is that while it will take no positive action to oppose whatever designs Japan may have, it reserves the right not to recognize as legal any treaties and agreements which may result from Japan's military seizure of South Manchuria.

That declaration was meant to end what had become an intensely humiliating chapter in the history of western diplomacy. For three months the Western world had sought to make its post-war peace machinery effective in the Orient. It had failed for the simple reason that the Western nations were too distracted and too divided to bring the pressure of their collective power to bear upon the situation. Moral force was shown to be no force at all to achieve immediate results. Mr. Stimson's note of January 7 was a recognition that since physical force is ruled out, and moral force has no present effect, it was time to stop humiliating ourselves by making further protests, and to leave the whole business in such a way that perhaps in time Japan will find it wise to square her position with the treaties she has violated.

Such as it is, that was the end of our present efforts to check the Japanese military party.

The affair at Shanghai arises out of Chinese resistance to Japan's conquest of Manchuria. The boycott has quite evidently been so effective that Japan has felt impelled to invade China proper in order to destroy the organization of the boycott. Once again it appears that the Japanese commander has outrun his instructions: in this instance his haste resulted in a severe defeat, followed by Japanese retaliation upon the defenseless civilian population. The bombing of Chapei was an act that will long be remembered, and if the civilized world were not paralyzed by its stupid internal quarrels, that bloody business at Chapei would evoke such a thunder of condemnation as to shake even the most arrogant of militarists.

As it is, the West is in a position where it must concentrate upon the task of seeing that the conflagration does not spread. It must send ships and troops to Shanghai, not to threaten Japan, but to guard and, if necessary, remove the large colony of foreigners who are there and in the interior cities. At the same time, ignoring all sentimental considerations, it must seek by diplomacy to remove the zone of the fighting from the vicinity of the International Settlement. If this means backing up the Japanese demand that the Chinese troops should be asked to retreat, there should be no hesitation about asking the Chinese to retreat. Then the Japanese can be asked, and perhaps persuaded, to remove their base from the International Settlement and the vicinity.

No one will pretend that such action by the Western powers is noble or calculated to enhance their prestige. It is merely cold-blooded prudence, aimed to achieve the supremely important object of not embroiling the United States and other powers in a desperately destructive war. It is to be hoped that Japan too will have the cold-blooded prudence to do her part in averting such a war.

February 2, 1932

V. EUROPE ENDORSES THE AMERICAN POLICY IN THE EAST

Mr. Stimson's note of January 7 endorsed by League Council; can its principle be made good?

Geneva, February 23

Last week the twelve governments represented on the Council of the League subscribed to the principle laid down in the American note of January 7. They declared that they will not recognize as valid new titles and new treaties brought into existence by violation of existing treaties, such as the Pact of Paris, the Covenant of the League and the Nine-Power Treaty.[1] These declarations may conceivably amount to nothing. But it is just possible that they may mark one of the great moments in the evolution of international law.

The position in which we find ourselves is this: It has been demonstrated that as the world is now organized the power does not exist to prevent or restrain a determined aggression like that of Japan in Manchuria. The Far East is a peculiarly difficult case. The lack of a strong government in China, the power of the military caste in Japan, the isolation of the Orient from the influences of Western conceptions of law, the lack of effective coöperation by Russia and the United States with organized international society, combine to make ineffective in the Orient the ideal of the prevention of war. Thus there has been war in the Orient, and in respect to Manchuria the Japanese are completely victorious. There is no possibility of denying it.

Nevertheless the Western nations, while admitting that they cannot halt the Japanese army, have now declared that

[1] On February 16, 1932, the League Council handed a forcible note to the Japanese representative at Geneva. It was signed by the twelve members of the Council other than Japan and China. These twelve signatories declared that it was "their friendly right to direct attention to this provision [Article X of the Covenant], particularly as it appears to them to follow that no infringement of the territorial integrity and no change in the political independence of any member of the League brought about in disregard of this article ought to be recognized as valid and effectual by the members of the League of Nations." The twelve members of the Council thus supported the position which Secretary Stimson had taken in his note of January 7. Mr. Stimson on February 24 underlined this position by publishing an open letter to Senator Borah. He declared again that the United States would not recognize any situation in violation of the Nine-Power Treaty or Kellogg-Briand pact, and remarked: "If a similar decision should be reached and a similar position taken by the other governments of the world, a caveat will be placed upon such action which, we believe, will effectually bar the legality hereafter of any title or right sought to be obtained by pressure or treaty violation. . . ."

they will not recognize its achievements. Is this important or is it not? No one can say with certainty. But if the principle we have announced is firmly adhered to, much might come of it. For when the fighting is over there must be a treaty, and if this treaty is not recognized as valid by the world, it will be from the Japanese point of view a rather useless treaty. The acts of the puppet government in Manchuria will be invalid. Its laws will have no force. Any titles to property which it may grant will be tainted. Investments in Manchuria will have no standing in any court of law and no one who buys bonds or sells or buys goods will have any rights which any Western government will uphold. The Manchurian empire of Japan will have to depend upon Japan's own resources for its developments. Moreover, the stability of that empire will continually be threatened. For even if a Chinese government now surrendered and signed what Japan demands, its signature would be valueless and succeeding Chinese governments would be entitled to repudiate it.

Thus if the objective of the Japanese is to impose peace and order on Manchuria, they will fail if the world adheres to the principle it has announced. They can conquer Manchuria; indeed they have conquered it, but what they hold is something which they cannot consolidate. They are condemned to uncertainty and to turbulence as long as they remain in Manchuria in defiance of their unquestioned treaty obligations.

It will require determination by the Powers to uphold their principle. It will require disinterestedness, for Japan will offer temptations to investors and traders. It will require unity among the Powers and a very well informed public opinion. But if the principle is upheld, the world may yet make a victory out of its present humiliation and defeat. It will have gone a long way towards making aggression unprofitable, and as against the immediate triumph of military force it will have vindicated the efficacy of law.

The principle of the note of January 7 is that illegal force can no longer establish legal rights. In the past the use of force has been legal and its results have been recognized. In the post-war world military force used as an instrument of national policy is illegal and its results are therefore invalid. That is where we stand today, we and all the Powers excepting Japan. The event will show whether we can make good our declaration, whether in the long run law can be vindicated against force.

February 24, 1932

VI. AMERICAN POLICY AND THE LEAGUE ASSEMBLY

Importance of a firm American position when the League Assembly considers Far Eastern affairs; opposition to interventionist steps the truest wisdom

Geneva, February 25

When the Assembly of the League of Nations meets next week it will be highly important that Geneva and Washington should understand each other well. Otherwise there are many possibilities of serious confusion. For there will be many nations represented in the Assembly who will wish to have the League vindicate itself as an agency for enforcing peace, and the United States must beware of letting itself be maneuvered into a position where it is said that but for the United States the League would have intervened firmly and successfully. The temptation to lay the blame for the disappointment on the United States will be tremendous. On the other hand, there is danger also that the Assembly will be swept by a demand for some sort of action—short of war, but on the road to war—like the withdrawal of ambassadors from Tokio, which would cost no nation except Britain, France and the United States anything. In that event there is danger either that we might join in a move which is a first step in a direction we should not wish to go, or that we should find ourselves morally isolated and in opposition to the opinion of the civilized world.

It is therefore of the utmost importance that the principles of the American policy should be made quite clear at Geneva. What needs to be made clear particularly is that in the whole Sino-Japanese affair the United States has not left itself committed to nor has it sought to pursue a policy of enforcing peace. This is not clearly understood at Geneva. Although as a matter of fact the League has done no more than attempt mediation now and, following the American leadership, has declared against recognizing as legal the results of Japan's aggression, the notion persists in Geneva that the League ought in fact to be used with force to deal with the Japanese. This notion, combined with the fact that the League has no force, is the reason why the League's action has been vacillating and confused.

The nations represented on the Council undoubtedly realize by this time that the situation is one in which threats of force are empty and therefore dangerous. They realize it because they are as little willing as is the United States to take the risks of enlarging the Sino-Japanese war into a general war. But the nations of the Assembly may not realize it. They have a strong interest in proving that the League is really a league to enforce peace. It is therefore desirable that it should be made quite plain to them why the United States would not associate itself with a movement to apply force against Japan.

There is much to be said in favor of the conception of a league to enforce peace. It is likely that in no other way could an action like Japan's have been prevented. But if a league to enforce peace is to work it must exist before hostilities begin; it must be known to exist and must be believed to be effective. At this stage it would be sheer folly, it would be unutterably tragic, to improvise a league to enforce peace and take measures which might lead to war with Japan. For Japan is now so deeply involved in China that the threat of force would no longer be effective; at this point it would be necessary to use force—that is, to go to war. The military caste in Japan has by this time staked its existence upon the Chinese adventure, and it is as certain as anything can be that it would rather go down to defeat by dragging in the world than go down to defeat by surrendering to threats from Geneva, London and Washington.

A war with Japan would create stupendous misery and vindicate no principle whatsoever. The idea of war should, therefore, be renounced clearly and decisively, even to the point of evacuating American citizens from the theater of war if that is deemed necessary. It should be made as clearly known in Tokio and Nanking as in Geneva that in respect to the war now in progress the United States will confine itself to mediation, and that in respect to the ultimate settlement it will stand on the principle of its note of January 7; that is to say, that it will not recognize as valid any new rights created by illegal force.

Having made its position clear, the United States should oppose measures in the nature of an intervention. It should oppose further denunciations of Japan on the ground that the paper record is already complete and more rhetoric can only be provocative and irritating. It should oppose the withdrawal of ambassadors from Tokio on the ground that this is a measure implying the ultimate use of force. It should oppose a one-sided embargo on munitions as inconsistent with the general policy of non-intervention by force.

In taking this line it will be severely criticized by many friends of the League. But it is the only logical and coherent line to take, in view of the fact that the United States has deliberately decided against the theory of a league to enforce peace. Incidentally, it will be expressing the real intentions of the principal Powers of the League. The United States will be doing openly and sincerely what the other great Powers, because of their commitments, are not able quite candidly to admit they intend to do.

February 26, 1932

VII. A WORLD POLICY IN THE ORIENT

The Western nations now a unit in declaring they will not recognize the fruit of Japanese aggression; a possible means of triumphing over military force

Geneva, March 10

In adopting as their own the principles laid down in the Stimson-Borah letter the nations of the Assembly have modified radically the nature of the League of Nations. It might almost be said that they have suspended the covenant and have reconstituted themselves as an association of nations acting under the Kellogg-Briand pact.

The principle of the Covenant is that the nations of the League are pledged to maintain peace, by force if necessary. It is obviously the intent of the Covenant that in the Manchurian case the members of the League should have instituted a boycott if Japan did not withdraw her troops and agree to a pacific solution of the dispute. That is the plain meaning of Articles X to XVI. What has happened is that the League got about as far as paragraph III of Article XV and could go no further. For just ahead loomed Article XVI, which calls for war. The Covenant simply failed to work because the great Powers, which would have had to pay the costs of making it work, flatly refused.

It is only fair to realize that the authors of the Covenant did not contemplate a situation like that in the Far East, where among the five powers most concerned, China, Japan, Britain, Russia and the United States, two are not members of the League. But this explanation does not alter the fact that the system of peace-making laid down in the covenant has failed totally in Manchuria.

At this point the American principle has provided the means of saving all our faces and conceivably even of saving ultimately the situation itself. The American principle of not recognizing the results of aggression, though the act of aggression cannot be prevented, is the direct opposite of the procedure of the Covenant. It is in its implications the most absolutely pacifist principle imaginable; it carries into international law something of the philosophy of Mahatma Gandhi. In place of a superstate maintaining international order the nations are to ignore and ostracize the consequences of law-breaking. The principle is novel and far-reaching; its effects in their application to the real world are very difficult to foresee. But the principle is the logical outcome of our American opposition to anything in the nature of a superstate and it is practically convenient in that it rather grandly reserves all our rights for the future without requiring the expenditure of more than words in the present.

This combination of principle and expediency also suits exactly the members of the League in their present predicament. They are enabled to keep alive all of Japan's obligations not to resort to aggression without being compelled to act upon their own obligations under the Covenant to protect China against Japan's aggression. Yet this is the best possible outcome given all the circumstances. It does not obtain the immediate evacuation of Manchuria; it does not preserve China's territorial integrity and existing political independence as against external aggression. But it does outlaw the fruits of conquest. It does encourage China to continue to refuse to sign new treaties dictated by the Japanese military. It does subject Japan to a legal blockade which should have very great financial consequences. For it is hardly thinkable that any bank in London, Paris or New York would dare to extend credits to Japan while the whole legal relationship of Japan to the Asiatic mainland is under the taint of world-wide outlawry.

The world has in effect announced a campaign of passive resistance against the Japanese aggression. Such a campaign requires a higher morale, more understanding and more enlightened patience than the application of sanctions. But if it succeeds it will have greatly advanced the development of international society by arming it with weapons which the small nations as well as the great powers can employ.

The world has entered upon a fascinating and perhaps a momentous experiment. This experiment has for the moment the moral support of all the governments, including, one may assume, the Russian. There is thus a unanimity which probably has no precedent, and if the peoples understand what their governments have agreed to, they can determine the result. For the Japanese cannot exploit the results of their aggression if the governments and peoples of the world really adhere to and resolutely practice the principles they have proclaimed.

March 11, 1932

THE POLITICAL SCENE IN EUROPE

I. THE BRITISH CRISIS: RAMSAY MACDONALD'S BRAVE COURSE

MacDonald's courage in breaking with his own party; currency collapse and human suffering; the cut in the dole as a symbol of the determination to restore national solvency

In St. Michael's churchyard in Charleston there is an engraved tablet to the memory of James Louis Petigru, a Unionist who died in that city during the Civil War. The inscription is one of the glories of American literature as well as one one of the very finest expressions of civic virtue. It was a great favorite of Woodrow Wilson's, and, if I am not mistaken, he cabled from Paris to the postmaster of Charleston during one of the dark periods of the Peace Conference asking him to send him the full text. Someone ought now to send it to Ramsay MacDonald, for he has twice shown that he is of the breed of Petigru.

The inscription declares that

Unawed by Opinion
Unseduced by Flattery
Undismayed by Disaster
He confronted life with antique Courage
And Death with Christian Hope

It then goes on to say that:

> *In the great Civil War*
> *He withstood his People for his Country*
> *But his People did homage to the Man*
> *Who held his conscience higher than*
> *their praise*
> *And his Country*
> *Heaped her honours on the grave of*
> *the Patriot*
> *To whom living*
> *His own righteous self-respect sufficed*
> *Alike for Motive and Reward*

Patriotism of this order is the rarest kind of patriotism. In a thousand men who will face physical danger there is scarcely one who will face the contempt of his own friends, and sacrifice his career to his conscience. For the applause of the Conservatives is no compensation to a man in Mr. MacDonald's position, who must face the accusations of his own kind that he has betrayed them.[1] There is no shamming in such courage, and in a world where human motives are very mixed, his motives at this juncture can be held to be as noble as they are unusual.

It has often been said in the last few days that Mr. Mac-Donald's decision to head the new government was the act of a Socialist who at the critical moment lost his nerve. Those who believe this hold that if Ramsay MacDonald had been true to his socialist faith he would have let the crisis break, and would then have proceeded to establish a socialist commonwealth on the ruins of capitalism. The answer to

[1] On August 24, 1931, the Labor Government headed by Ramsay Mac-Donald resigned following a bitter internal dispute over budget policy. The King at once asked Mr. MacDonald to resume the place of Prime Minister and to form a National Government to deal with the financial crisis. Mr. MacDonald did so, and amid the attacks of most of his former followers prepared for a general election.

this argument is that Ramsay MacDonald never has been that kind of socialist. He is, therefore, no renegade. The socialism of Ramsay MacDonald has always been democratic and evolutionary: the new order of things was to be created by the consent of majorities as a progressive development of a highly advanced capitalistic system.

Had he deliberately allowed the existing order to collapse he would have been false to the real convictions of his whole life. As a matter of fact, the charge that Mr. MacDonald flunked the chance to establish socialism is not the official view of Mr. Arthur Henderson and the Labor Party. Most of his former followers have as little desire as he had for a revolutionary gamble on a national catastrophe. What they charge is either that Mr. MacDonald was fooled into thinking the crisis was greater than it really was, or that in meeting it by agreeing among other things to a reduction of payments to the unemployed, he has adopted a principle which opens the way to a general movement for the reduction of British wages.

In one sense these charges cannot be absolutely disproved. If I see a man teetering on a window ledge and pull him back into safety, there is no way I can prove that he would certainly have fallen into the street. I may say he had the look of being about to fall, and he can retort that he didn't fall and wouldn't have.

But by all the probabilities based on the experiences of other countries it is certain that at the beginning of August, Britain was sliding down the steep incline towards national bankruptcy. All the important symptoms had appeared: a large deficit in the budget, decreasing revenues, mounting expenditures, an increase in the burden of the debt as a consequence of falling prices, and behind these a growing deficit not merely in the government's budget but in the nation's balance of payments to the outside world. These conditions being known to business men, bankers, and investors all over the world, there resulted, in the atmosphere a panic brought on by Germany's troubles, a run on London like, though on a much greater scale, a run on a bank of which the assets are known to be frozen and the liabilities over-expanded.

Almost all over South America, in Germany, Austria and elsewhere, these conditions have led to insolvency. It is no use saying that British credit is the best in the world. A man's credit is no better than his creditors think it is, and at the beginning of August, British credit was dangerously shaken. Steps had to be taken to restore it. Before the British could borrow money in any market, before any foreign bank could in justice to its own depositors put any of their money into England, the financial opinion of the world had to be satisfied that the British Government would take immediate steps to live within its revenues.

That this was a real and not an imaginary crisis there can really be no doubt at all. The most difficult aspect of it from Mr. MacDonald's point of view is to make his own followers understand what it would have meant to them personally if the British currency had been allowed to lose its value. The currency is a mysterious thing to most of us, and unless we have lived in a country which was undergoing the ordeal of falling money it is almost impossible to imagine how terrible it is.

The worst effects are suffered by those who can bear them least: by old people with little pensions or little savings, by wage-earners and salaried people. A collapse of money means that prices go sky-high in terms of that money. And as a result, unless everybody can jack up his income not merely from year to year but literally from hour to hour, he finds that his week's wages in his pay envelope may not buy a loaf of bread. I was in Germany some years ago when money was moving to the point where it was not worth the paper it was printed on. It is impossible to describe what this meant in suffering to housewives who had to stand in line half the day waiting for a chance to buy food which had gone up so far in price before they had a chance to buy it that they could not afford it. What it meant in suffering to those who carried on the cultural interests of the German people, to schoolteachers, to professors, to technical men, to musicians, actors, writers, all of them dependent on fixed salaries or royalties, was heartrending.

I can well understand that when Ramsay MacDonald looked into such an abyss of agony opening up before his people, he knew that he must act first, and explain afterwards.

There remains the question of whether it was absolutely necessary to cut the unemployment benefit in order to restore confidence. Could the money which is to be raised by cutting the dole have been raised by other economies or by still heavier taxation than is about to be imposed? At this distance no one can, I think, speak with certainty on this point.

But I suspect that what really happened was something like this: the British dole has been growing larger in terms of money, and owing to the fall in prices, larger still in terms of purchasing power. In other words, its real cost grows steadily greater. Now rightly or wrongly the conviction has gained ground in England and on the Continent that Britain cannot recover her export trade in world markets unless she reduces her costs of production. The conviction has also spread that England will not be able to do this directly because her trade-union movement is too strong.

When the crisis broke at the end of July there was no time to solve the knotty problem presented by Britain's declining position as an exporting nation. But it was necessary to take some steps which would demonstrate that a British government could move in the direction of a reduction of costs. The mind of the world had fastened on "the dole" as a symbol of the causes of British difficulties, and it was as a symbol of its determination, in addition to the necessities of the budget, that the new Cabinet, I think, committed itself to a ten per cent reduction in unemployment benefit. It took the most dramatic way of convincing the creditor classes of the world that it was moving, not merely toward governmental, but toward national solvency.

The conflict over this decision will not end with the balancing of the budget. For the greater problem, to which Mr. MacDonald alluded, of balancing Britain's economic payments as a nation remains, and it will bring to a head some of the sharpest issues in British history.

September 10, 1931

II. THE CAUSES BEHIND THE BRITISH CRISIS

The fundamental causes of Britain's difficulties; necessity of either buying less abroad or selling more; industry caught between the demands of the trade unions and the financial interest

It is a grave misunderstanding of the British crisis to charge it up entirely to the dole and other social services. These expenditures are one cause, but by no means the only cause, of the events we are now witnessing.

The fundamental cause of England's difficulties lies in the economic system which she has inherited from the nineteenth century. This system required her to buy abroad and to import about 60 per cent of her food, as well as great quantities of raw materials. In order to pay for these imports England had to export coal and manufactured goods,

had to draw an income from the rest of the world in shipping freights, banking, insurance and other commissions,
and had to rely upon dividends and interest on her past
savings invested in foreign countries. It followed that if for
some reason Britain could not sell enough of her own exports, or if her foreign income from the other sources declined, it would become increasingly difficult for her to pay
for her imports.

Long before the war there were already signs that England
was losing her relative position as an exporter in the world's
markets. In other words, she was being forced increasingly
to pay for her food and other imports out of the income from
her huge investments rather than from the sale of goods.
The war greatly increased this tendency. For among the consequences of the war was the development of manufacturing
industries in countries which had formerly bought English
goods; another consequence was the raising of tariffs everywhere which cut down British trade.

A recent official report from England, made by the so-
called MacMillan Committee, shows that between 1913
and 1930 the volume of imports into Great Britain and
Northern Ireland increased by 18 per cent, or nearly one-
fifth, whereas the volume of British exports has decreased
by 32 per cent, or nearly one-third. As other sources of income have not increased in this period, Britain has had to pay
for larger imports with smaller exports. She has done it by
drawing upon the income of her foreign investments.

This could not go on forever. A point had to come where
England had to buy less abroad or to sell more. She could
not keep on buying more and selling less. With the world-
wide depression this point has been reached. For the last two
years she has been selling still less, and the income of her
foreign investments has, of course, fallen off. But she continued to buy. The result was that the money markets of the

world began to ask themselves how England was going to pay for her imports. When finally it became clear this summer that world trade was not due for a quick revival, when in addition it was seen that British investments in Germany, in South America, in Australia, and the Orient were badly frozen, the belief spread that since England could not pay for her purchases abroad in goods, and could not pay for them out of her foreign investments, she would have to pay in gold. There was not enough gold in England to do that. So the money markets began to withdraw their own gold deposits from London, and precipitated the financial crisis which culminated yesterday in the decision of the government and of the Bank of England not to sell gold for British paper currency.

The crux of the difficulty is in the British export trades. For the last ten years they have not been able to sell enough goods abroad at a profit. This is the immediate cause of British unemployment, not of the extra unemployment which the world depression has produced but of the permanent unemployment which Britain has had for at least ten years, and perhaps for more than a generation. The figures show that unemployment is and has been most severe in her great exporting industries.

Since this was the fact even before the world depression, it is plain that there is some radical trouble in the British economic system. This trouble has been traced to several causes. One is the rise of competing industries in other parts of the world and the closing of many markets by means of tariffs. That is important, but it does not tell the whole story. For the evidence shows that British manufacturers have been finding it increasingly difficult to compete in markets where they had an even chance. This may be due in part to the high cost of somewhat obsolete plants, but it is due also to high wages, taxes and overhead.

Since the war British manufacturing for export has had to face an actual increase in wages, maintained by the strength of the trade-union movement, an enormous increase in taxes to meet the interest on the national debt and the cost of social legislation, an increase in the cost of capital, and a decline in the prices received for goods sold. Business has been unprofitable because the costs have been rising and the returns diminishing.

It is here that political factors enter the problem. In the last ten years the two strongest interests in the British nation have been the City, that is to say, the creditor classes, and the trades-unions. The City, in its insistence on restoring the pound to parity, added about 30 per cent to the cost of all private and public debts, which industry has had to pay in terms of interest or taxes, and it has added a very considerable percentage to the cost of all pensions, fixed salaries, and contractual wages. The trades-unions, on the other hand, in refusing to let wages fall as prices fell, have added 15 or 20 per cent to the wages bill, and, in extending and enlarging the dole and other social services, have added still more to the cost of manufacturing. Caught between rising expenditures for wages and the rising cost of debts, manufacturers for export could not make profits. They have had to lay off men and create unemployment.

The recent political crisis which ended in the fall of the Labor government was at bottom a struggle between the City and Labor as to which would give way next. For ten years industry had given way to both. It is prostrated and could give way no more. The question then was whether wage standards should be reduced or whether fixed incomes should be reduced. It was evident that at least one or the other had to go down if industry was to proceed. The outcome seems to be that both wages and fixed incomes will be reduced.

For that is what a reduction in the gold value of the pound will mean. It will mean an automatic scaling down of wages, salaries, insurance benefits, doles, taxes, debt charges, of every kind of fixed income expressed in money, except, it should be clearly noted, foreign obligations payable in gold. The events of yesterday may be regarded, therefore, as the beginning of a desperate surgical operation to release British manufacturing from an unbearable burden of fixed charges.

In retrospect it will appear, I believe, that no other solution was possible. The orthodox financial view would have called for a reduction of wages and social services while the yield of debts was maintained. This view has a kind of Spartan integrity about it and the justification that it would serve Britain's interest as the world's banker. But it defies human nature. It leaves out of account the fact that in these times wage-earners will not bear the whole burden of deflation, and that a deflation of their wages without some corresponding deflation of income from capital outrages their sense of justice. The last few weeks in England, with the mutiny in the fleet as the warning sign, have shown that even British solidarity could not stand the strain of reducing wages directly without touching other forms of income.

If the orthodox financial view was impossible, so also was the unorthodox financial view, as represented by the majority of the MacMillan Committee. This would have called for concerted international action to inflate the price level. The remaining creditor nations, France and the United States, would have none of that for the present. No less impossible was the orthodox Labor view, which is that wage standards could be maintained by drawing upon the accumulated capital of England. This theory failed to take into account how quickly even a large fund of capital can be exhausted.

So events, rather than the will of any party in England, have decided the issue. For it was impossible to agree on a solution, and one has therefore been forced upon the people.

December 22, 1931

III. THE BRITISH ELECTIONS: THE CONSERVATIVE LANDSLIDE

British willingness to experiment with tariffs does not alone account for the huge Conservative majority; what the election really means

In interpreting an election like that in Great Britain it is generally safe to assume that the margin between a normal victory and a landslide is due not to the positive strength of the winners but to the collapse of their opponents. The evidence has been clear enough for some time that in Britain a conservative protectionist victory was in the making. But no reasonable person can suppose that so extravagant a victory actually represents a wholesale conversion of the British people to Tory doctrine. The extravagance of the victory must be due to a wholesale loss of confidence in the distracted personnel and policies of Liberalism and Labor.[1]

The progress of the protectionist theory has been steady since the war. Beginning in 1915 with the McKenna duties on motor cars, films and a few other objects, there has gone on ever since a gradual abandonment of free trade. Although no general tariff was imposed, by one measure after another, sometimes legislative and often merely administrative, and usually under disguises meant to conceal the fact, Britain has

---

[1] The general elections of October 27, 1931, in Great Britain, resulted in an overwhelming triumph for the National Government, and a disastrous defeat for the Labor Party. In the House of Commons the National Government had more than 550 seats to about 60 for the Opposition. Ramsay MacDonald at once formed a new National Ministry.

been sidling towards protection. Opinion has been moving rapidly in this direction. Last year the Trade Union Congress took a vote which showed that it had really abandoned free trade; the Chamber of Commerce in Manchester, that citadel of free trade, voted for protection; and even the City, the center of British finance, backslid.

This would account for a Conservative victory. But it does not account for the landslide. For in spite of the evidences of conversion to protection there are profound reasons why British opinion must be reluctant and skeptical about protection. Britain is not a self-contained nation. It must import food and raw materials, and a large part of its income is derived from foreign investments, from shipping and banking. The British know in their bones what we are just beginning to learn rather painfully, that monopolizing the home market is no way to expand exports or play the part of banker to the world. To go in wholeheartedly for high protection is for Britain tantamount to surrendering hope of maintaining her world-wide economic and financial position. It is a policy of defense, like an army retreating to a shorter line, and if it were to be regarded as permanent and as thoroughgoing, it would be something like the liquidation of British power and influence as we have known it.

I do not believe the British people mean that, or that the world in its soberest thought can desire it. For British international experience and the British institutional equipment, both in diplomacy and in finance, are things which cannot be improvised by any other nation in one generation, much less in a few years. They are indispensable to the reconstruction of the world. Therefore, it seems to me probable that a protectionist Britain will use her influence and her increased bargaining power to lead the world out of the protectionist jungle into which it has strayed. Because her deepest interests are bound up with free international trade, I believe, in spite of the election returns, that Britain is not protectionist at heart.

Certainly she is not protectionist by any such margin as these returns indicate. For besides tariffs there were at stake the much more immediate issues arising out of the abandonment of the gold standard. At this distance it has been impossible to obtain any definite idea as to what the National Government or the Conservatives who dominate it mean to do about stabilizing sterling. Yet this is the great question which has to be faced, and on the wisdom with which it is decided may depend not only the character of the recovery throughout the world, but the existing social order in Britain itself.

The victors seem to have made no commitments, but the voters, realizing the tremendous things involved, appear to have decided that they could not entrust their destiny to the Labor leaders, who are so palpably inexperienced and confused in these matters. They have turned in mass from the prophets of a new order to the high priests who are supposed to understand the mysteries of present-day currency and finance.

For Britain's sake, and for all our sakes, it is to be hoped that this time the high priests will achieve a greater wisdom than they had in 1925 when they stabilized the pound sterling. For if they attempt once again to sacrifice British industry and the British taxpayer in the effort to reëstablish the prestige of British international finance, they will fail, as they failed then, but more quickly, since the whole world now understands the impracticability of the attempt. What is more, they will set the stage at home for a landslide even more drastic than this one, but to the left and towards revolutionary change.

September 29, 1931

IV. SUCCESS OF THE NATIONAL GOVERN-MENT: BRITISH CONFIDENCE

The psychological change; general attitude toward protection and tariff policy; greater strength in European affairs

London, March 16

To come to London today after visiting the Continent is to find oneself in a different mental world. The mood of the Continent, it has seemed to me, was essentially fatalistic; men feel themselves in the grip of forces that are beyond their control. That does not mean that they despair. On the contrary, I was astonished to find how generally the people in each country think they are weathering the storm rather better than their neighbors. But the mood of the Continent, whether it be gloomy or cheerful or resigned, is passive. Public men do not expect to do more than ride out the storm. But in Great Britain there is a different feeling. These islanders have worked themselves up to a pitch of high confidence in their power to manage events. They are, I imagine, the only people in the capitalist world who actually feel that they can make large plans and carry them out; that they are the masters to some degree of their own destiny.

In seeking explanations for this great psychological change in Great Britain two main causes seem to stand out. The British people feel that they took an exceptionally heroic course in the way they taxed themselves to balance their budget. The fact that their sacrifices have been followed by some real improvement in trade has seemed to give the whole nation the kind of exhilaration which comes not only from doing a good deed but from being loudly applauded and well paid for it at the same time.

Psychologically, it does not matter whether the economic improvement is due only in part to the fiscal heroism of the people and in large measure to the depreciation of sterling, the continuing deflation of gold prices, the miraculous outpouring of the Indian gold hoards and the Chinese boycott of Japanese textiles. In the sequence of events things took a decided turn for the better immediately after the British people decided for orthodox financial righteousness. The effect has been to make them feel that their own courage is the cause of their own success. That is naturally immensely stimulating to their confidence.

The other great cause of hopefulness is that the British people are enchanted by the untried possibilities of protection. One of the great advantages of their change from free trade to protection has been that it was a radical change. Any one is, therefore, entitled to believe it is a change for the better. But it is not only the change which is exhilarating. There is also the feeling that at last Britain is armed to make herself felt in the economic war which is waging in the world.

My own impression is that Britain is not yet a really protectionist country. It will come to that later when protection has created vested interests. Today Britain is a country which is really aiming at two things: at forcing other countries to lower their tariffs on a basis of reciprocity, and at creating a sheltered market within the empire. I don't suppose that the policy is as yet fully formulated. But it looks very much as if Britain might turn to the idea of establishing tariffs at three levels: a moderate tariff, say 10 per cent, for any nation agreeing not to make a higher tariff against British goods; less than 10 per cent as an imperial preference for the dominions if they give equal advantages; and, finally, really high tariffs on the American or French pattern for nations which do not agree to the reciprocal low tariff standard.

This general scheme is not that of the government, but it represents the point of view of what might fairly be called center opinion, and it might prevail if the ultra-protectionists in the Tory party do not get out of hand. At any rate, whether or not the general scheme I have sketched is adopted as British policy, of this much we may be sure: it is now the intention of the British people to use their economic power as they have not used it for a century. They are exhilarated at the prospect. They greatly enjoy the idea of making protectionist countries realize what tariffs feel like to the outsider. They like the new power they exercise in Europe. And so they feel quite sure of themselves.

Their internal confidence is reflected back to them from the Continent. Not only is there a return of funds into sterling and a general bullishness about Britain, but also there is unmistakable evidence of an enormous recovery of political prestige. One must not be misled by the apparent weakness of Sir John Simon's diplomacy in dealing with Japan. This is a Tory imperialist government, which at bottom sympathizes with Japanese action in Manchuria. The real measure of British prestige is that on the Continent all the Scandinavian countries, Italy and Germany, are moving within the ambit of British economic and financial action. There can be no question whatever as to the reality of the British influence in Europe.

The position of last summer, when it almost seemed as if London had ceased to command, that Paris was supreme, no longer holds. Paris is still very powerful and it would be egregious folly to underestimate its strength. But Great Britain has resumed its ancient position among the powers of Europe.

March 17, 1932

V. THE PROBLEM OF SECURITY IN EUROPE

The French anxiety on the subject; the Polish Corridor the supreme difficulty; not an insoluble problem

In his address on landing in New York, M. Laval pointed out the central problem toward which France and America have to work out a common attitude if "in a world torn with doubt" they are to restore "calm and reëstablish equilibrium." That problem is how they "can agree and unite" in organizing security. For, said M. Laval,

> Our only desire is peace. But we set great store by our security. Governments and peoples should understand that security cannot be expressed merely in words of hope; it should be organized.

If understanding between the two peoples is to be promoted, it is necessary to discuss frankly and sympathetically what it is that divides them in their search for security, though both desire it. It may then be possible to see how a bridge could be built over which they could walk together.

In frankness it might as well be said that American opinion is substantially convinced that the supreme difficulty lies in the Polish Corridor as now established. It is satisfied that the Corridor is the insuperable obstacle to a European understanding, and that European security cannot be organized without evidence of a willingness on the part of Poland, Germany and France to modify the arrangement so as to end serious agitation of the issue.

I do not know whether an American can hope to state fairly the French view of these matters. But I believe the essence of it to be about as follows: Rightly or wrongly the Allies imbedded the Corridor in the peace treaties. These treaties were based on the assumption that America would take a leading part in the League of Nations and that French security would be guaranteed still further by a special treaty with Great Britain and the United States. When America withdrew from Europe in 1920, the system of security promised to France collapsed. France had, therefore, to find a substitute against the possibility of German revenge; the substitute was a series of military alliances with Belgium, Czechoslovakia and Poland, three neighbors of Germany who shared with France a vital interest in maintaining the peace settlement. France cannot, therefore, fail to support the Poles in the Corridor without endangering her whole system of alliances, and leaving herself alone in Europe next to Germany, a larger and industrially more powerful nation. France must keep faith with the Poles if she is to expect her allies to keep faith with her.

The situation, therefore, is one in which the United States will not and could not participate in maintaining the Corridor, while France cannot propose that the Corridor be modified. This is the deadlock at the bottom of the whole matter, and the statesmen who can resolve it successfully will earn the lasting gratitude of men. For if the problem of the Corridor could be conquered, the whole atmosphere of Europe would change. There would be a wholly new spirit in Germany, a possibility of understanding with Poland, a disappearance of the great fear which divides the French and Germans. Western Europe could settle down to some kind of natural equilibrium, and to such a Europe both Great Britain and America could well lend support.

Is the Corridor an insoluble problem? I think not. In the last analysis the problem of the Corridor is whether Poland's access to the sea can be guaranteed in no other way but by cutting German territory in two parts. Nobody can question for a minute that a large and growing nation like Poland must be certain of access to salt water. But Poland is not the only landlocked nation in Europe. Czechoslovakia also lacks a sea coast. Yet Czechoslovakia has done excellently well without a Czechoslovakian corridor by exercising the rights in German ports guaranteed her by the treaties. Switzerland has no corridor. Yet it thrives. Therefore, it is not necessary to have a corridor in order to have access to the sea. As for the supposed military advantages of the Corridor, they are rather a military liability. A thin stem of Polish territory thrust up through Germany is in a military sense the worst kind of exposed salient.

The real difficulty about the Corridor is not that it is an economic or a military necessity, but simply that Poland has possession of it, and no way of letting go of any part of it has been suggested which Poland can accept with dignity. The Germans are not making it easier to find an orderly and self-respecting way, what with their Hitlerite demonstrations and their incredible arrogance toward the Poles. The time is probably not ripe, therefore, for a solution of the question, but it may not be too early to go to the Poles and ask them to begin considering whether the unmodified Corridor is not an unmistakable example of one of those "international conditions," referred to in Article XIX of the Covenant of the League of Nations, "whose continuance might endanger the peace of the world." To say that to Poland would be no infringement of her dignity. It would, on the contrary, be a recognition of her importance and her responsibility in the affairs of the world.

It goes without saying that if a move of this sort were to be made it would have to be left to France to decide how it should be done. France, being the dominant power in Europe, the proved friend of Poland and the chief guardian of order, is the only nation which could hope to act effectively. But such an effort would have the blessing of all of France's former allies, of all the European neutrals, and in the United States it would most certainly break down the real obstacles to Franco-American coöperation.

October 24, 1931

VI. THE FRENCH POLICY ON REPARATIONS

The three principal objects sought by French policy; determination of the French not to pay unless paid; a compromise essential

Paris, February 17

The month of June lies between the French elections, which must be held not later than May,[1] and the expiration of the Hoover moratorium, which would call for a German payment on July 15. That is why June has been selected as the time for the meeting at Lausanne of the proposed conference on reparations. It is acknowledged that politicians facing an election cannot deal intelligently with the problem of intergovernmental debts, a sentiment that Hoover will appreciate. The intention is to effect a three months' truce on oratorical declarations by heads of governments and to employ the time to negotiate what would be essentially a Franco-British understanding.

The French government has rejected the British proposal, made last December, calling either for direct and immediate cancellations of reparations or for indirect cancellation by means of a five-year moratorium. The French counter proposal, which has not been accepted, embodies what might be

[1] The French Parliamentary elections (two ballots) were held on May 1 and May 8, 1932. They revealed a marked swing to the Left and to the leadership of Herriot, whose Radical Socialist party obtained 156 seats. As a result, Premier Tardieu, who had succeeded Laval on February 23, resigned on May 10. Herriot came in as the new Premier, and the path to a satisfactory understanding at Lausanne was greatly smoothed.

called the latest phase of the French official philosophy on the subject. It needs to be understood if the French position is to be appreciated. It may be said, and I think, that the French government no longer counts upon the receipt of substantial payments from Germany. It is concerned with these things: first, that the legal basis of the peace settlement shall not be destroyed; second, that Germany shall not emerge from the crisis with special economic advantages; third, that the French taxpayer shall not have to pay the war debts.

Their first point, about the maintenance of the sanctity of the treaty, can best be discussed in relation to French general foreign policy, and I am reserving it until tomorrow's dispatch. The second point, that Germany should be handicapped economically, is one that much more is likely to be heard about in the months to come. The French argue that if reparations are abolished the German exporting industry will have acquired a decisive advantage as against all of their competitors. For the state railways of Germany are, owing to the inflation, practically free of debt. In 1930 their fixed charges absorbed only 2.5 per cent of their revenues, whereas in both Britain and France the percentage was 33 per cent. If therefore, say the French, the 660,000,000 reichsmarks chargeable against them under the Young Plan are cancelled the Germans would be in a position to cut railway rates more than 20 per cent. This would be equivalent to an enormous subsidy to German industry, and the differential would be insurmountable. The situation in Europe would be like that which would exist in America if railroad rates for producers in, say Pennsylvania and Ohio, were 20 per cent lower than in the rest of the country.

It is to eliminate this kind of special advantage that the French government is proposing that Germany be asked to bond her railways to an amount which will produce an annuity of 660,000,000 reichsmarks. They are willing to have these bonds pay no interest for two years. They do not insist upon any particular division of the proceeds among Germany's creditors. They do insist that the fixed charges be continued so that in a general recovery Germany shall not have acquired advantages by the process of bankruptcy.

It is believed in Paris that this point of view will gradually impress British industrialists.

The French attitude toward the debt to America is accompanied by a feeling of deep embarrassment. On the one hand, there is the solid determination of the French people not to pay if they are not paid. On the other hand, there is the principle of the sanctity of contracts, which is the basis of all French dealings with Germany. This moral defect in their position is quite plain to French logic.

For the moment one can hear in Paris any number of arguments to explain away the dilemma. The most effective, to my mind, is that when President Hoover imposed the moratorium in June he ruptured the Young Plan, of which the United States is not a signatory, and associated reparations and war debts under the single category of intergovernmental debts. The French say that President Hoover destroyed Germany's will to pay reparations and that the United States is morally bound to acknowledge the consequences to France. Why, they ask, should the United States presume, even without consulting Germany's chief creditor, to suspend Germany's payment unless the United States recognizes that all the debts are really one great transaction?

That some such argument as this will be used if Congress refuses to reconsider the French debt is certain. It is a powerful argument in morals if not in law. But actually the effort will be made to settle the problem rather than to debate principles. That is the reserved purpose of the proposal to bond the German railways. These bonds would provide a fund quite insufficient to pay all the claims of all the creditors, but still something substantial on which the governments might by scaling down reach a compromise.

A compromise involving substantial sacrifices by every country is the only possible solution which can avert repudiations or defaults and all that they imply in the way of a brutalization of international intercourse. Public men have a very grave responsibility and any man who commits himself against the possibility of a compromise is causing a deep injury to the whole world.

February 18, 1932

VII. THE FRENCH POLICY ON TREATY MAINTENANCE

Difficulty of revising frontiers without war; French belief that such revision is possible only under an organized superstate

Paris, February 18

Underlying all other problems in Western Europe there is the question of the maintenance or the revision of the frontiers fixed in the peace treaties. This is the irreducible core of the argument. It is the essential meaning of the French insistence upon the sanctity of treaties. It is the fundamental cause of the division between France and Germany, between France and Britain, between France and Italy, between French opinion and American on all matters connected with peace and disarmament. It is the root of unrest in Europe, with all that it entails by way of armaments, diplomatic rivalries, extreme nationalism, and economic distrust.

It is mere confusion of the argument to talk as if there were militarist nations and pacifist nations. The real alignment is between the nations headed by France, who stand for the maintenance of the existing frontiers, and the nations which, like Germany, passionately desire to revise the frontiers, or like Britain and the United States, would look with favor upon revision. It is no less misleading to suppose that the French stand for maintenance of all the existing frontiers because they regard them as inherently just and strong. The real difference between French opinion on the one hand and British and American on the other is that the French deeply believe that under present conditions no territorial revision is possible which would not provoke armed conflict. At bottom it is the French desire to avoid war which causes the government to oppose all discussion of frontiers.

It is admitted in France that an irritating frontier like that of the Polish Corridor might provoke a war some day. But the French insist that as matters now stand an attempt to open a territorial question of that kind would provoke violence almost immediately. Thus the French pacifist is rigidly conservative. The French say that history shows that mankind has not yet found a way of altering important frontiers by peaceable methods and that, therefore, any one who wishes to avoid war here and now must set his face against proposals to revise them. They do not like the situation by which they find themselves the only great power committed to the upholding of all the existing frontiers. They realize the costs and the dangers and they are deeply disturbed at the extent to which their guardianship of the status quo has isolated France in Europe and in the world. Yet they are paying the price because they do not see a practicable alternative. They insist that British and American opinion is unrealistic and wishful in thinking that revision is possible without violence.

This is to understand the actuating purpose behind the elaborate and grandiose French schemes for European union and for arming the League of Nations. The outer world, seeing France so hard and realistic about the status quo, has been at a loss to understand why France should at the same time be so extremely idealistic in her plans for organizing peace. The explanation, I think, is that France is seeking to teach the world what sacrifices of national sovereignty are necessary if mankind is to arrive at the point where issues hitherto always decided by war, that is to say, great territorial issues, are to be decided by pacific means. There is a passage in the propositions submitted by M. Tardieu at Geneva which is the key to the matter: "He who desires the end [that is, reduction of armaments] must desire the means." In substance the French position is that he who desires a peaceable evolution of territorial disputes must advocate a superstate. Only under the guardianship of superior international force is it safe to attempt revision of frontiers.

That such a superstate is not within the realm of practicable politics the French know quite well. They are declaring the principle that in the existing anarchy of sovereign states there is no security except by the maintenance of the status quo. Because of this principle they feel compelled to insist upon the letter of contracts, for outside of written engagements they see at present no principle of order in Europe.

The practical problem is to find a substitute for the armed superstate which will provide a sufficient sense of security to justify a French government in consenting to some amendment of the status quo. The only conceivable substitute is a renewal of the Franco-British entente. That alone could relax the rigidity of the French position. Hand in hand with Great Britain the French would feel safe enough to be liberal.

It may be said, therefore, that the fate of Europe depends upon the prospects of understanding between London and Paris.

February 19, 1932

VIII. THE GERMAN ELECTIONS AND THE RISE OF HITLER

Hindenburg victorious, but the growth of Hitlerism menacing; result simply a reprieve to liberalism

London, March 14

While Hitler did not make good his claims, he has made spectacular gains since the elections of 1930.[1] He has nearly doubled the absolute number of Nazi voters, and he has increased their percentage of the total vote cast from eighteen and a half to thirty. The Communists show a slight loss since 1930 and so do the Nationalists, but their combined loss is not nearly enough to account for Hitler's gains. He has clearly made his gains at the expense of the Socialists and of the other Republican parties. In the net result the Weimar republic, aided by Hindenburg's almost legendary prestige, has mustered the support of only half the German people.

There are two ways of interpreting this result. If the present moment is to be regarded as the bottom of Germany's depression, if we may believe that Europe is setting itself toward reconstruction at Lausanne and elsewhere, then one may say it is immensely reassuring that after eighteen months of the deepest despair and suffering the intransigent vote has increased only from 39 to 49 per cent. This is evidence of the deep resistance of the German people to policies of desperation. On the other hand, if no improvement is in sight, if the governments and their public opinion are going to con-

---

[1] The German Presidential election occurred on March 13, 1932. Out of some 37,660,000 votes cast, Von Hindenburg received 18,662,000; Hitler 11,328,000; Thaelmann, 4,971,000; and Dusterberg, 2,517,000. President von Hindenburg failed by a narrow margin to gain the required majority, and a second election was necessary on April 10. In this he achieved an easy victory over Hitler, but the latter made impressive gains.

tinue in a deadlock over reparations and debts, if the economic war of tariffs, embargoes, quotas, exchange-controls, is to go right on, then this vote is ominous. If in the next year Hitler gains followers at the rate which he has been gaining them in the last year, the German republic is doomed. For when Hitler's following approaches 50 per cent of the voters he will not hesitate to seize power by force.

There are still the Prussian elections ahead [1] as well as the second ballot of the Presidential election. But assuming the present alignment of the voters holds, it may be said that the German elections provide another and perhaps a last opportunity for solutions by reason and conciliation. It would be too much to say that liberal ideals are victorious or that reaction has been defeated. Rather one must say that liberalism in central Europe has been granted a reprieve.

March 15, 1932

IX. THE RESIGNATION OF CHANCELLOR BRUENING

Bruening's fall a heavy blow; traceable to failure of France, Britain, and the United States to offer a reasonable settlement; outlook for the future

Now that he has fallen, tributes will be paid to Dr. Bruening all over the world, and everywhere there will be great regret that so experienced and upright a statesman is no longer the German spokesman. [2] He is the best liked

[1] In the elections of April 24, 1932, the Hitlerites obtained 38 per cent of the votes in Prussia and 30 per cent in Bavaria.

[2] President von Hindenburg on May 30, 1932, required the resignation of the German Chancellor, Heinrich Bruening, although only three weeks earlier Bruening had received a vote of confidence in the Reichstag. The President's action was taken as a result of Nationalist pressure; and it immediately followed a proposal by the Bruening Cabinet to break up the great

and most trusted man in Europe. No one else who has been in power has displayed such courage, such mastery in political maneuver, such intellectual grasp and clean devotion. Every personal quality necessary to guide Germany and to bind Europe together again has been his. He has lacked only men of equal stature in other countries with whom he could work.

For though it appears that he has fallen because of intrigue by the Nationalists—the generals, the old junkers and perhaps the heavy industrialists—what undermined him and thus made the intrigue possible was the failure of France, Britain and the United States to take a single constructive step toward the restoration of international confidence and of the trade and credit which depend upon it. Eleven months have passed since the moratorium was proclaimed and in those eleven months the politicians, particularly in France and the United States, have delayed and protested and have dug themselves into a pit of illusions. As time dragged on the chances of a reasonable solution diminished, and the position of Dr. Bruening grew steadily weaker. Eleven months ago a workable adjustment with the forces he represented was possible. But the politicians in Paris and Washington, playing upon the suspicions of their bamboozled constituents, would concede nothing. They gave Dr. Bruening no support, and now that he is gone, they will have to deal with men with whom it will be much less easy to deal.

The Bruening Government was a dictatorship which rested upon the army, but enjoyed the consent of moderate German opinion. Although it was a dictatorship, it was republican in spirit and pacifist in principle. It aimed at the consolidation of Germany during the economic crisis and at

Junker estates of East Prussia in order to settle the unemployed as farmers. Bruening was succeeded on May 31 by Franz von Papen, and a general election was set for July 31. This resulted in an extension of the tenure of the Von Papen Ministry.

the gradual revision of the Treaty of Versailles by international consent. But in recent months, under the pressure
of economic misery and of the disappointment resulting from
the wooden policies of Paris and Washington, the moderate
opinion which tempered the underlying military dictatorship
has been whittled away. Of late, it has been evident that Dr.
Bruening was rapidly losing the civilian support which he
had used so skillfully to hold the army in line.

At the time of the elections it was already beginning to
be clear that only the personality of President von Hindenburg remained to moderate the force of nationalist sentiment.
The situation was very unstable. For one old man, however
great his prestige, could hardly be counted upon artificially
to hold up a government which had ceased to represent either
the dominant sentiment of the nation or the real concentration of force within it. That Von Hindenburg has now re-
verted to the views of the class from which he sprang is not
astonishing. That is where, for the moment at least, the real
power in Germany resides.

It would be idle just now to attempt to forecast the consequences for Europe and the world. There is this much,
however, that can be said which is reassuring. It is always
an advantage, especially in critical times, to deal with men
who are principals, with men who wield the actual power.
Dr. Bruening had ceased to be a principal. He had become
weakened to a point where, in order to remain in office, he
was being compelled to carry out the will of the hidden
powers. Now those powers must come forward and plainly
reveal their purposes.

What those purposes are the world does not clearly know,
but it is a reasonable surmise that they will usher in a period
of reaction within the Reich. Whether this reaction will be as
black as the Hitlerites would make it, or whether there im-
pends a more moderate type of reaction which will be strong

enough to rob the Nazis of their thunder but not so strong as to throw opinion violently to the extreme Left—these are questions which no one can answer now.

In the field of foreign affairs it is, however, plain that Germany will not agree to pay any more reparations. It has been evident enough for a long time that Germany would not actually pay. The only real question has been whether her non-payment would be temporarily disguised by some new formula which the politicians could use to delude their peoples a little longer. It now looks as if there would be no new formula, and that the time for amiable pretenses has passed.

What else the Nationalists have up their sleeves there is no way of telling. But this much is as clear as anything can be. The one single check that can be applied to their ambitions is a solid coöperation between Paris and London. The German Nationalists will understand and respect that. The question, therefore, is whether London and Paris will have the good sense to see that the stability of Europe depends upon their willingness to scrap the issues which divide them. For if each continues to play its own game, if M. Herriot keeps his mind fixed upon proving what a strong man he is, if the British government lets itself be directed in part by the anti-French prejudices of the City and in part by its traditional theory of a balance of power in Europe, there will be no Franco-British coöperation; and the German Nationalists will have a free hand at keeping everyone's nerves on edge.

June 1, 1932

· VIII ·

TAMMANY, MR. SEABURY, AND
NEW YORK CITY

I. THE FORCE OF A BAD EXAMPLE

*Low condition of public morals in New York and
outside; complacency of national leaders over the
Harding scandals as one cause*

THE political campaign now being conducted in New York
is proceeding in an atmosphere of listless degradation. Both
party organizations are compromised by corruption, favorit-
ism, and shady bargains; the voters are either indifferent or
cynical; there is not a single leader on either side who has
ventured to make himself the outspoken champion of decent
standards in public life.

On the Republican side the leading candidate for municipal office turns out to have sought Tammany influence when
he needed it in his private business; the Republican State
Chairman, who is full of wrath against Tammany, turns out
to have participated in an odious bi-partisan arrangement
to share judicial offices; the eminent Republicans of the
State are absorbed in national affairs and are taking no public
part in local politics.

On the Democratic side the Tammany candidates are
defiant in the face of the Seabury exposures; former Governor Smith has given his formal support to the machine, and
Governor Roosevelt pursues his carefully calculated course of

doing just precisely as much as he has to, and not one bit more than he has to, toward facilitating the exposure of corruption in New York. Thus with ex-Governor Smith silent and regular, and with Governor Roosevelt silent and aloof, the awakening of an honest impulse to clean house is effectively discouraged.

This low condition of the public morals is not confined to New York, nor are its originating causes in New York alone. In the last ten years there has been generally in the United States a remarkable indifference to the maintenance of public standards, a dying down of the old popular fervor in attacking corruption. The sins of Tammany happen to be nationally advertised, but there is no other large city which does not live in a glass house.

The immediate causes of our post-war demoralization are obvious enough and have often been described. War itself is an intensely demoralizing experience which over-stimulates the grosser passions and instincts, while it weakens and even discredits the fragile, lately acquired, and unstable habits of civilized life. The aftermath of war is invariably a period of inflation, of false values, and therefore of frantic greed. We have passed through a war and two booms. Besides these, we have had the prohibition experiment, in which systematic law-breaking has become so respectable that indignation about law-breaking has come to seem hypocritical.

Yet when these major causes of our political demoraliza-tion are set down, and to them are added the perplexities, the worries, the preoccupations of an era of stupendous change in the manner of our life and in the relations of classes, nations and continents, we have still omitted, I believe, the final and decisive cause of the low state of public morals. For a vigorous people which is properly led does not become the passive victim of conditions; it resists them and overcomes them. My belief is that the American people in the post-war era have been so much the victims of post-war conditions because from the highest places they have been set such bad examples.

I refer to the example set in dealing with the scandals of the Harding Administration. The responsible and personally honest leaders of the Republican Party eight or nine years ago were confronted with the worst corruption which had disgraced the national government for fifty years. I do not say that they failed to prosecute the guilty. I do say that they exerted the whole force of their well-disciplined partisan power to smother an awakening of the public conscience and to escape the retribution which their party had earned. In this they succeeded, and the effects of their success continue to demoralize our public life. Their success was based on the discovery that if the party under attack does not reply, the attackers soon exhaust their ammunition, bore the voters and lose heart themselves.

This discovery has been appropriated by the Democrats in New York. Mr. Smith and Mr. Roosevelt, in dealing with the Tammany scandals today, are following the same pattern of conduct which Mr. Coolidge, Mr. Hoover and Mr. Hughes followed in dealing with the Harding scandals. In the Harding era the initiative in exposing corruption came from Senator La Follette, an independent Republican, and from Senator Walsh, a Democrat. In New York today the initiative comes from the Republican State Chairman, Mr. Macy, and an independent Democrat, Mr. Seabury. Then, as now, the honest men in high places were willing to assist the processes of the law when specific assistance was needed. But now, as then, those in high places do nothing to stimulate the exposure. Now, as then, they refrain from employing their extra-official knowledge and power as party leaders to make the exposure thorough. Privately they deplore the corruption, and publicly they are wet blankets to damp down popular indignation.

What makes this kind of political conduct so demoralizing is its success. Two men who adopted this pattern have been triumphantly elected President. With these examples before them is it surprising that young men entering public life should feel that the rewards go to the cautious, the calculating and the complacent, or that the people at large grow cynical and listless about their public affairs?

October 28, 1931

II. THE SEABURY INVESTIGATION

Effectiveness of its early revelations; Mayor Walker and his missing agent

In his admirable story of Tammany Hall, Mr. Werner quotes a remark of E. L. Godkin's that Mr. Seabury should find pleasure in remembering as he watches the spokesmen of Tammany writhe and whine and howl. It is that "the three things a Tammany leader most dreaded were, in the ascending order of repulsiveness, the penitentiary, honest industry, and biography." Mr. Seabury has no power to prosecute. The prosecuting agencies are controlled by Tammany. He has no power to remove from office. That, in most cases, is within the province of the Governor. But he is the most terrifying biographer that Tammany has had in modern times.[1]

[1] The Republican legislature of New York in the spring of 1931 authorized an investigation into the government of New York, to be conducted by a legislative committee. The Hofstadter Committee obtained for counsel a prominent Democratic attorney and former judge, Samuel Seabury, who proved able to uncover a mass of governmental corruption and irregularity. His work culminated in proceedings for the removal of Mayor Walker on charges, open hearings by Governor Roosevelt on these charges in August, 1932, and the resignation of Mayor Walker on September 1, 1932.

The best evidence of what he has thus far achieved is to be found in the dissenting report filed by Assemblyman Cuvillier, a Tammany member of the legislative investigating committee. Mr. Cuvillier writes that

> The investigation so far has only shown the acquiring of wealth by certain public officials outside of their public official duties. . . .

If this means that it has not been shown that public funds have been embezzled, that is, with some possible exceptions, true. What has been shown is that a great deal of wealth has been acquired by Tammany officials for which they are unable to give any reasonable public explanation. It has thus far been shown, for example, that fourteen scattered politicians, one Tammany law firm, and one corporation "ostensibly engaged in the sale of electric bulbs and other electrical equipment," have in the last few years, banked over $16,000,000. This money did not all come out of the city treasury. It did not come from ordinary private activities. It came from transactions which Tammany has made every possible effort to conceal.

The modern investigation of corruption rarely results in catching a thief red-handed. The modern grafter is not so crude as to steal. He sells influence and capitalizes his inside knowledge. Thus the process of exposure, which Mr. Seabury has followed, consists typically of listing the politician's funds, subtracting his salary and all open and above-board sources of income, and then asking him to explain the remainder. The reply in nearly every case is silence or an explanation so absurd that morally the politician is convicted out of his own mouth.

Assemblyman Cuvillier in his reply to Mr. Seabury complains that the investigation has not been "scientific." It has dealt thus far only with certain phases of the work of a few departments and has not yet come around to a great many other departments. That is true. It takes time to search so many records and overcome the continual obstruction of so powerful an organization. Mr. Cuvillier lists the departments that "are yet to be investigated," and first among them is the office of the Mayor. That brings up the most disgraceful episode in the whole disgraceful record of concealment and obstruction.

Mr. Seabury has been investigating the office of Mayor Walker. In the course of it he discovered that a certain Russell T. Sherwood was closely associated with Mr. Walker, so closely, in fact, that since 1924 they have been the joint proprietors of a safe deposit box. Mr. Seabury desired to examine Mr. Sherwood. Promptly Sherwood fled the jurisdiction of the committee and has ever since been a fugitive. The Mayor, who knows what Sherwood knows, has made no effort to have Sherwood return and testify. Thus the city of New York enjoys the spectacle of a Mayor whose financial agent is a fugitive from investigation.

Tammany complains that Mr. Seabury has discredited the city government "from the top down." That is true. The city government is discredited from the top down. But until Sherwood is produced by Mayor Walker nothing else is possible but to regard the Mayor as discredited. Would any man of honor allow his agent to be a fugitive?

The Tammany organization is large, powerful and far-reaching. The municipal government of New York is incredibly complicated, and next to the Federal government it is the largest spending agency in the United States. The citizens of New York are cynical about politics and at the present time preoccupied with the hard times. It is, therefore, too early to expect a thoroughgoing reform of the conditions which Mr. Seabury is revealing. The investigation, which has thus far cost somewhere in the neighborhood of

$500,000, is inexpensive. Mr. Seabury has by this time saved the people of New York at least that much merely by throwing a little of the fear of God into Tammany officials.

In any event the time is not ripe to discuss remedies. There is needed a lot more biography, a lot of prosecution and a lot of removing from office. In a year or so, when the picture of graft has been more nearly completed, and New York can put its mind on municipal government, the time will have arrived for a new charter and a new deal. At this time those who are pressing for "reforms" are unconsciously obstructing real reforms.

January 26, 1932

III. MAYOR WALKER'S EASY MONEY

The mayor's quarter of a million; evils of the gambling spirit

In his testimony last week, Mayor Walker acknowledged that without any investment on his part he had, in eighteen months, made a quarter of a million dollars in the stock market. After paying taxes it is estimated that he had left about $170,000, which was about five times the salary paid him by the city during the same period. Assuming no risk, performing no service, taking no trouble of any kind, he obtained a claim on the national wealth which it would (before he raised his own salary) have required seven years' work as Mayor to earn.

Is it any wonder that the American people are bewildered and angry about stock market speculation?

The Mayor's good fortune [1] was the result, it appears, of

[1] In this article no effort was made to discuss Mayor Walker's sorry record, or the shocking facts proved as to his loose acceptance of money from others, for at the time it was written he was *sub judice*.

his friendship with a gentleman who knew how to profit in a bull market. Many other men were equally lucky in those days. But there are a few things about this transaction which stick in one's mind. The first is whether a public man in office or out of it can decently accept a fortune from anybody as a gift. The second is whether a system in which there is so much easy money available for favored insiders is in the long run compatible with any acceptable ideal of social justice. The third is whether it is, in the long run, compatible with the maintenance of public order.

To be sure, such spectacular opportunities to acquire unearned fortunes come only once in a great while. The Mayor, as to this transaction, merely participated in the effects of the great inflation. Nevertheless, the question must and will be asked whether the madness of the inflation was not greatly aggravated by the fact that the American people relaxed their moral standards and let acquisitiveness run wild. There has been speculation all through American history; the opening up of a new country is a speculative enterprise and it is not surprising that the speculative spirit, manifested equally in the excessive hopes of the boom and the excessive despondency today, should pervade our life.

But whatever may be done to explain historically our love of speculation, it is clear that among an established people who have reached maturity in their mode of life, the greed and acquisitiveness of the speculative spirit are highly dangerous. A man cannot do the public business of the city of New York as it needs to be done if his mind is on the getting and spending of huge sums of easy money. A man cannot administer great corporations which employ armies of men and serve large communities if his judgment is diluted and distracted by huge speculative transactions. A man cannot be a good banker and get himself all mixed up with intricate speculations. A man cannot be a good doctor and keep telephoning his broker between visits to his patients, nor a good lawyer with one eye on the ticker.

The popular feeling against the stock market will be a good thing for this country if, instead of producing silly laws to protect fools, it engenders a general revulsion against gambling for easy money. The mischief is not curable by laws. The mischief is in the realm of the spirit, in the loss of restraints against the lust for profit, in the submergence of all other conceptions of what life means by the greedy desire to get rich quickly. It would be priggish to single out Mayor Walker for special odium because he forgot as if he had never known what is required in the way of private morality from a public servant. While the boom was on almost everyone who had the opportunity forgot to be restrained and civilized. So as these revelations come along they call not so much for self-righteous denunciation, particularly from those who are moved by envy or disappointment, but for self-examination and a sincere attempt to reappraise our own motives and our own ideals. In such an examination we shall need to inquire most searchingly what it is that we mean by the Success which we have worshipped, what it is that we mean by the Prosperity that we have craved.

For these are the two sirens that enchant and seduce us and make us forget the things that count and must be done.

May 31, 1932

IV. GOVERNOR ROOSEVELT AND MAYOR WALKER

The Governor's temporizing policy; his resulting lack of moral freedom

Ever since the Seabury investigation has been under way Governor Roosevelt's friends have been explaining his aloofness on the ground that he had a judicial duty to perform. Under the law the Governor has the power to remove the officials who are being investigated by Mr. Seabury, and it would, therefore, have been improper, they say, for Mr. Roosevelt to lend his support to a crusade against corruption.

Apparently, however, it is proper for the Governor to denounce those who are crusading against corruption, and to impugn their motives. Thus when Dr. Holmes and Rabbi Wise asked for the removal of officials who had made a very bad showing in the Seabury investigation, the Governor savagely attacked not the discredited officials but Messrs. Holmes and Wise.[1] Now he is attacking Mr. Seabury. The attack is slightly veiled. It does not come from the Governor himself. It comes from some anonymous person who has issued a written statement from the Governor's home. In this statement the charge is made that Mr. Seabury is a Presidential candidate, that he set a political trap for Mr. Roosevelt, and that he is hurting good government.

This disposes rather thoroughly of the pretense that Governor Roosevelt's actions in the face of corruption in New York have been governed solely by a calm judicial spirit. There is nothing calm about a man who loses his temper so promptly, so completely and so often. There is nothing judicial about a man who lets it be known that he distrusts the investigator of corruption as a possible rival for the Presidential nomination.

There has been something distinctly queer in Franklin D. Roosevelt's mental processes throughout this affair. He seems to be most deeply irritated at the fact that the Seabury

[1] Early in April, 1932, John Haynes Holmes and Rabbi Stephen S. Wise, as officers of the City Affairs Committee, wrote Governor Roosevelt asking him to remove two local officials—the sheriff of Kings County and the clerk of the Surrogate's Court in Queens County. Governor Roosevelt refused in a letter in which he said little regarding the proved corruption in New York City, but in which he sharply attacked Dr. Holmes and Rabbi Wise.

investigation has been producing testimony which compels him to choose between condoning corruption and striking it. He has displayed a singular petulance towards everybody who has had any part in putting him in a position where he might have to make a decisive choice between breaking with Tammany and surrendering to it.

It is, of course, an unpleasant thing to have to consider the removal of Mayor Walker just before the Convention meets. If he removes the Mayor, Mr. Roosevelt will be accused of playing politics. If he does not remove him, he will also be accused of playing politics. It is a perplexing problem. But the problem is entirely the consequence of Governor Roosevelt's indecision during the last year.

For clearly the proper course of action would be to postpone the filing of charges, the hearing, and the decision at least until after the National Convention. It is a very serious matter to remove the Mayor of a great city, and it is of the utmost importance that it be done in such a way as to remove all suspicion that the Governor is swayed by personal ambitions. In the next three weeks Mr. Roosevelt's personal ambitions will be intensely strong, and if the Mayor is removed now, it will be impossible to persuade Mr. Walker's very large following that the Governor was disinterested.

This squalid mess is due to nothing but Governor Roosevelt's own weakness and timidity. If months ago he had done what he should have done, if he had broken with Tammany and put himself unequivocally at the head of the forces struggling for good government, there would be no dilemma today. He could postpone the Walker hearing as justice demands and nobody would question him. He elected, instead, to play an intricate game with Tammany, to act against corruption only when he was forced to do so, to feed Tammany patronage, to consort with the Tammany bosses, and to go along with Tammany in trying to discredit

Mr. Seabury and the active forces fighting Tammany corruption. Tammany and its allies will have a large vote at Chicago.

Thus Governor Roosevelt has lost his moral freedom. He is so heavily mortgaged to Tammany that he must prove his independence of it. Yet at this late date there is no way of proving his independence except by a procedure which must outrage everyone's sense of justice. For to try James J. Walker before a man who stands to profit enormously by convicting him is a revolting spectacle.

The trouble with Franklin D. Roosevelt is that his mind is not very clear, his purposes are not simple, and his methods are not direct. A clear-headed, simple, and direct man would not have landed himself in the confusion which now prevails as between Albany and City Hall. He would have made a decisive choice at the outset, have convinced the country of his independence, and because he had won the confidence of the people, he could have afforded to proceed now with scrupulous justice. But because he wanted Tammany to support him, he got himself suspected, and now he cannot afford to proceed with scrupulous justice. He himself has had to drag the question of Mayor Walker's removal into the Presidential campaign.

June 7, 1932

V. THE QUESTION OF MR. WALKER'S REMOVAL

Removal of the Mayor equivalent to his resubmission to the electorate; responsibility of Governor for seeing that the electors accept the removal

While there is no doubt that the Governor of New York has the power to remove the Mayor of New York City, the case of Mayor Walker is really unprecedented. In the past Governors have removed elected officials. Mr. Roosevelt removed Sheriff Farley. But the truth is that Sheriff Farley and the others were only nominally elected. Their names appeared on the ballot and they were voted in with the ticket; most of the voters were unconscious of the fact that they were electing them. Mayor Walker, on the other hand, was really elected by the will of the people. He obtained his nomination in an open primary, and he has twice been victorious by enormous pluralities. The difference between his position and that of Sheriff Farley is not a mere difference of degree. It is a difference in kind which is as great as it would be to fish for cod and hook a whale.

Were Mayor Walker an appointee of the Governor's there would be no doubt whatever that on the record as it stands he should be removed. The transactions about which there is no dispute, which the Mayor himself admits, would require his immediate dismissal. For it is not denied that he accepted money from private interests at a time when as a public official he was considering legislation affecting them. This may not be corruption under the law, but it is conduct unbecoming a public officer and a gentleman, and a member of the President's Cabinet or of the Governor's would be out of office twenty-four hours after the facts had been published.

It is plain, therefore, that the complicating factor in this case is that the Mayor was elected by the people, and the question to be determined is whether the Governor, having the power to remove him as though he were an appointee, should exercise that power or should apply some other standard to Mayor Walker. In other words, how bad does the Mayor have to be to warrant us in saying that he should be dismissed by the Governor rather than by the voters who elected him?

The answer to this perplexing question may be found, I

think, by remembering that if the Governor removes the Mayor it is possible for the Mayor to run again in November, 1933. It follows from this that his removal would not in fact be an undemocratic interference with the right of the voters of New York City to choose their Mayor. Since the transactions exposed by Judge Seabury have all come to light after the Mayor was elected, the Governor by removing him would actually be giving the people of the city a chance to pass upon the record. Removal would be, in the jargon of the day, a resubmission of the Mayor to the voters. No one need have any qualms, therefore, arising out of the principles of democracy and home rule. In this respect all that the Governor needs to decide is whether the record that has been exposed is one which would have changed the verdict of the voters had they known it. And he is entitled to assume that the voters are intelligent enough and disinterested enough to understand the evidence and to care about it.

But the obligation of the Governor does not end at this point. If he decides that the Mayor should be removed, he will in effect be creating a situation in which the voters of New York City will have a chance to uphold or reverse his decision. It is a matter of the utmost civic importance that a Mayor, once removed on the evidence which the Seabury record discloses, should not be reëlected. Such an outcome would be infinitely destructive of the public morale; it would be a genuine catastrophe in popular government.

It is the Governor's duty to take every possible step to avert it. The responsibility is his. On the wisdom, the courage and the leadership he displays much depends. If it is his duty to remove the Mayor, it is his duty to see that his judgment is upheld. He is not, therefore, a mere judge in a law case. He is a judge and something else. That something else has to do with convincing the people, who are the court of last appeal, that the verdict is just.

In view of Governor Roosevelt's tortuous course throughout this affair, it will not be easy, if he is nominated at Chicago, to convince the public of his disinterestedness. Political expediency has dictated so many of his actions that it is rather late in the day to remove all suspicion. It is hard to see how Mr. Roosevelt, as a nominee, can sit as judge in this case and persuade both Mayor Walker's friends and his opponents that the matter is being decided on the evidence and on principle. For the Governor, by being complicated and indecisive, has already done irreparable damage by putting himself in a position where, if he removes the Mayor now after having accepted the Mayor's support when he needed it, Mr. Walker can go up and down the city crying that he has been sacrificed to Franklin Roosevelt's Presidential ambitions.

Should the Governor, therefore, decide for removal there is great danger of a complete fiasco in the form of the Mayor's reëlection, unless the Governor does what he has never yet done, unless he stops denouncing those who are fighting corruption and puts himself at the head of the forces fighting corruption.

June 10, 1932

· IX ·

THE APPROACH OF THE NATIONAL CONVENTIONS

I. THE PERILOUS DEMOCRATIC CONTROL OF THE HOUSE

Nominal control means much responsibility and little actual powers; what the Democrats must do to succeed

It now seems very probable that the Democrats will have to organize the House of Representatives, elect Mr. Garner the Speaker, and take control of the committees. From a partisan point of view this prospect is far from alluring. For in obtaining nominal control of one branch of Congress, the Democratic Party is compelled to assume a degree of responsibility out of all proportion to its actual power. With a majority of one or two members it will not have a working majority and will not really control the House. Yet it will be on trial before the country and subject to a very severe double test: it must, on the one hand, show that it can formulate national policies of its own, and on the other hand, it must avoid action which interferes with the efforts of the Administration to deal with the world crisis.

If the Democrats in the House fail to develop distinct and definite measures to meet all the principal problems which are up for solution, their criticism of the Hoover Administration will become greatly deflated during the course of the

winter. If they press their program to the point where deadlock and confusion ensue, if they give the appearance of
practicing sabotage on vital matters, they will most certainly
provoke a violent reaction of sentiment.

If the Democrats are to succeed in their difficult task,
they need above all to have a clear conception of the position
in which they find themselves. They are members of a party
which, in the course of seventy years, has won only three
Presidential elections against undivided Republicans. In
all those seventy years the only time in which the Democrats have controlled both Houses and the Presidency was
for two years in the nineties and for six years of Wilson's
Administration. Normally they are the minority party in
national affairs.

Yet their normal weakness in national affairs is balanced
by an extraordinary vitality in local affairs. When it comes
to electing Governors, Senators, Congressmen, Mayors and
the like, the Democrats are very much stronger than they
are in Presidential elections. The record shows clearly that
only rarely do the Democrats succeed in making a national
showing equal to the sum of their local victories. They are
a party which is much stronger in its parts than as a whole,
whereas the Republicans are almost always stronger
nationally than they are locally. The effect of this has been
to produce Democratic leaders who have their minds
primarily upon issues which will win in their localities, and
to produce Republican leaders who are adepts at the compromise, discipline, and smothering of issues required to
hold together voters in different sections of the country.

That is why the Democrats appear so much more idealistic
and the Republicans so much more worldly, why, for example, the wet Democrats are the wettest wets and the dry
Democrats the driest drys, why, for fifty years every
question which has excited popular interest, sound money,

prohibition, imperialism, the League of Nations, religious toleration, has been fought out bitterly in Democratic conventions. The strength of the Democratic leaders lies in the fact that they are close to the feelings and prejudices and interests of local constituencies. That is also their weakness in just such a situation as will confront them when they organize the House in December.

November 6, 1931

II. MR. RASKOB AND THE LACK OF DEMOCRATIC LEADERSHIP

Mr. Raskob's political naïveté; the lack of clear ideas and policies among party leaders

I do not know Mr. Raskob personally, but from watching his brief political career I have the impression that in politics he is an innocent lamb. To Alfred E. Smith he seems to have an utterly genuine personal devotion. On the issues of the day he seems to have one profoundly sincere conviction, namely that prohibition is an evil, and on other matters a naïveté which is simply appalling. What, for example, could be more politically naïve than his proposal to ask the contributors to Smith's campaign fund what they think of prohibition? It is not merely that the result of the poll is a foregone conclusion, nor that the poll is by definition unrepresentative. The supreme naïveté of the thing lies in the assumption that those who contributed money to a campaign have a special right to be consulted about the party's policies. Only a man without political instinct would have lent himself to an enterprise based on the premise that the campaign contributors are a species of preferred stockholders. Only a man without political imagination, without the necessary tact and sensibility for political life, would have done this when he himself is by all odds the largest of the contributors.

Yet I have no doubt that Mr. Raskob would indignantly deny that he was trying to use the pressure of money to force the party to accept his views on prohibition. I do not suppose he means to notify the politicians that Democratic money is wet money, but in politics appearances are often decisive, and a chairman ought to have some understanding of their importance.

The chief reason why Mr. Raskob's spectacular amateurishness occupies the center of the stage so continually is that nobody else is ready to occupy it. A lot is said by the Roosevelt faction about "economic issues" being "paramount." But what these paramount issues are they are careful not to say. Governor Roosevelt belongs to the new postwar school of politicians who do not believe in stating their views unless and until there is no avoiding it. Nobody, except perhaps his circle of intimate advisers, has the least idea where he stands on any of the great economic issues that are said to be paramount. Where, for example, does he stand on the tariff, on reparations and debts, on farm relief, on taxation, on banking reform, on the railroad problem? I do not know. There is a vacuum where the paramount economic issues are supposed to be, and into that vacuum, where the angels, as it were, fear to tread, Mr. Raskob is continually rushing with his anti-prohibition schemes.

There is only one way to sidetrack Mr. Raskob and put prohibition in the perspective where, in the crisis of the world's affairs, it properly belongs. That is for Democratic leaders to come forward and formulate party policies on the great questions confronting the country. This they have not yet done. Thus far they have been living on the unpopularity of the Hoover Administration and the inevitable discontent with hard times. They cannot do that much longer. Unless they have coherent policies of their own, they will drift into confusion this winter and will find themselves quarrelling once more about the prejudices of 1928.

I can remember the time—it was 1912—when Democratic candidates for President asked for delegates by making speeches to the voters. In those speeches they stated their views. They played the game as the game has to be played if popular government is to work. But this new game, which consists in gathering delegates first and adopting policies afterward to hold them together, is ignoble in itself, and from the point of view of party action deeply confusing. Mr. Raskob's performances are the direct result of it.

December 26, 1931

III. GOVERNOR ROOSEVELT'S CANDIDACY

His failure to offer national leadership

It is now plain that sooner or later some of Governor Roosevelt's supporters are going to feel badly let down. For it is impossible that he can continue to be such different things to such different men. He is, at the moment, the highly preferred candidate of left-wing progressives like Senator Wheeler of Montana, and of Bryan's former secretary, Representative Howard of Nebraska. He is, at the same time, receiving the enthusiastic support of the New York *Times.*

Senator Wheeler, who would like to cure the depression by debasing the currency, is Mr. Roosevelt's most conspicuous supporter in the West, and Representative Howard has this week hailed the Governor as "the most courageous enemy of the evil influences" emanating from the international bankers. The New York *Times,* on the other hand, assures its readers that "no upsetting plans, no Socialistic

proposals, however mild and winning in form," could appeal
to the Governor.

The Roosevelt bandwagon would seem to be moving in
two opposite directions.

There are two questions raised by this curious situation.
The first is why Senator Wheeler and the *Times* should
have such contradictory impressions of their common
candidate. The second, which is also the more important
question, is which has guessed rightly.

The art of carrying water on both shoulders is highly
developed in American politics, and Mr. Roosevelt has
learned it. His message to the Legislature, or at least that
part of it devoted to his Presidential candidacy, is an almost
perfect specimen of the balanced antithesis. Thus at one
place we learn that the public demands "plans for the reconstruction of a better ordered civilization" and in another place
that "the American system of economics and government is
everlasting." The first sentence is meant for Senator Wheeler
and the second for the New York *Times*.

The message is so constructed that a left-wing progressive can read it and find just enough of his own phrases
in it to satisfy himself that Franklin D. Roosevelt's heart
is in the right place. He will find an echo of Governor La
Follette's recent remarks about the loss of "economic liberty."
He will find an echo of Governor La Follette's impressive
discussion about the increasing concentration of wealth and
how it does not guarantee an intelligent or a fair use of that
wealth. He will find references to "plans." On the other
hand, there are all necessary assurances to the conservatives.
"We should not seek in any way to destroy or to tear down";
our system is "everlasting"; we must insist "on the per-
manence of our fundamental institutions."

That this is a studied attempt to straddle the whole country
I have no doubt whatever. Every newspaper man knows

the whole bag of tricks by heart. He knows too that the practical politician supplements these two-faced platitudes by what are called private assurances, in which he tells his different supporters what he knows they would like to hear. Then, when they read the balanced antithesis, each believes the half that he has been reassured about privately and dismisses the rest as not significant. That, ladies and gentlemen, is how the rabbit comes out of the hat, that is how it is possible to persuade Senator Wheeler and the New York *Times* that you are their man.

In the case of Mr. Roosevelt, it is not easy to say with certainty whether his left-wing or his right-wing supporters are the more deceived. The reason is that Franklin D. Roosevelt is a highly impressionable person, without a firm grasp of public affairs and without very strong convictions. He might plump for something which would shock the conservatives. There is no telling. Yet when Representative Howard of Nebraska says that he is "the most dangerous enemy of evil influences," New Yorkers who know the Governor know that Mr. Howard does not know the Governor. For Franklin D. Roosevelt is an amiable man with many philanthropic impulses, but he is not the dangerous enemy of anything. He is too eager to please. The notion, which seems to prevail in the West and South, that Wall Street fears him, is preposterous. Wall Street thinks he is too dry, not that he is too radical. Wall Street does not like some of his supporters. Wall Street does not like his vagueness, and the uncertainty as to what he does think, but if any Western Progressive thinks that the Governor has challenged directly or indirectly the wealth concentrated in New York City, he is mightily mistaken.

Mr. Roosevelt is, as a matter of fact, an excessively cautious politician. He has been Governor for three years, and I doubt whether anyone can point to a single act of his which involved any political risk. Certainly his water power policy has cost him nothing, for the old interests who fought Smith have been displaced by more enlightened capitalists quite content to let the state finance the development. I can think of nothing else that could be described as evidence of his willingness to attack vested interests, and I can think of one outstanding case in which he has shown the utmost reluctance to attack them. I refer to his relations with Tammany.

It is well known in New York, though apparently not in the West, that Governor Roosevelt had to be forced into assisting the exposure of corruption in New York City. It is well known in New York that, through his patronage, he has supported the present powers in Tammany Hall. It is well known that his policy has been to offend Tammany just as little as he dared in the face of the fact that an investigation of Tammany had finally to be undertaken. It is true that he is not popular in Tammany Hall, but, though they do not like him, they vote for him. For there is a working arrangement between him and Tammany. That was proved last November when the Tammany organization went to the polls for the amendment which Smith opposed and Roosevelt sponsored. Tammany had no interest in that amendment. It dealt with reforestation hundreds of miles from the sidewalks of New York. Yet it was the Tammany machine which gave the Governor his victory.

I do not say that Mr. Roosevelt might not at some time in the next few months fight Tammany. I do say that on his record these last three years he will fight Tammany only if and when he decides it is safe and profitable to do so. For Franklin D. Roosevelt is no crusader. He is no tribune of the people. He is no enemy of entrenched privilege. He is a pleasant man who, without any important qualifications for the office, would very much like to be President.

It is meaningless for him to talk about "leadership practical, sound, courageous and alert." He has been Governor in the community which has been the financial center of the world during the last year of the boom and the two years of the depression. The Governor of New York is listened to when he speaks. Can anyone point to anything Mr. Roosevelt has said or done in those three years to provide the leadership we should all so much like to have had? I do not think anyone can. He has carefully refrained during these years from exerting any kind of leadership on any national question which was controversial. That was probably shrewd politics. It has helped his candidacy. But as a result of his strategic silence nobody knows where he stands on any of the great questions which require practical, sound, courageous and alert leadership.

January 8, 1932

IV. THE DEMOCRATIC OPPORTUNITY AND ITS CHALLENGE

A golden chance of success; but can the party remain uncommitted on basic issues?

The year 1932 presents the Democrats with a golden opportunity and a difficult choice. They have reason to believe that this is one of those infrequent occasions—perhaps the fourth in seventy years—when they may elect a President in a straight party contest. The prospect would be excellent did they not have reason to dread the necessity of making up their minds on the principal issues before the country.

It is evident that the bright prospects of the Democrats do not represent any conviction on the part of the country that the party knows how to lead the country out of its troubles.

It can hardly be pretended that the Democrats have as yet come together on anything that can be called a coherent program of their own. They are strong because the Republicans are weak. Their credit has been rising because the Republican credit has been falling. Their chief asset at the moment is a popular desire for change. How a change for the better is to be effected, in what direction the party would proceed if it were intrusted with power, are questions which the active politicians will put off trying to answer just as long as they possibly can.

As long as they do not have to do more than complain about the results of the Republican Administrations they can have their cake and eat it, too. They can damn the tariff for being exorbitant and for not protecting oil and copper and other products enough. They can damn the debt settlements and the moratorium for unsettling the world and for surrendering the taxpayers' money. They can damn Mr. Hoover's foreign policy for entangling us with Europe and for not having brought about peace and disarmament. As long as they have only to capitalize discontent they can talk like Mr. Hearst and Mr. Garner, and also like Mr. John W. Davis and Mr. Owen D. Young, and they can hope to nominate a candidate who, as a confused orator once put it, is like Caesar's wife, above suspicion and capable of being all things to all men.

It may be that they can put off indefinitely the horrid necessity of committing the party on important issues. Certainly, if the elections were held this month they would need little more than a respectable candidate and a troupe of orators to remind the country how unhappy it is. But it is hard to believe that in the next nine months the party can drift into a triumph. In a world crisis of this magnitude events come rapidly and choices have to be made, and it would be foolish to suppose that the Republicans outside, or the rank and file of Democrats within, will consent to a strategy of loud criticism and resounding emptiness.

February 9, 1932

V. THE DEMOCRATIC PARTY: THE CHOICE CONFRONTING IT

The Republican theory of self-containment; the Democratic choice of a new policy of world-adjustment or the old policy of alleviation

The negative character of Democratic campaigning reflects the difficulty of the choice which a positive policy involves. There are two positive directions in which the party can go: one is to accept the premises of post-war Republicanism and to propose remedies for its disagreeable consequences; the other is to attack the premises and to propose a different set of national policies. Both courses are politically expensive: the first will lead the party into a kind of new Bryanism, which will be attacked as unsound and destructive, and the second into a new Wilsonism, which will be attacked as internationalist and not quite patriotic.

This choice is inherent in the situation resulting from the conduct of American affairs since the war. The three successive Republican administrations have proceeded on the theory that in no essential respect had the war altered the American position, and they have tried for nearly twelve years to run the United States according to the theories which had on the whole worked so well up to 1917. They refused to admit that the war wrought a fundamental change in American national interests, and that a failure to adapt government policies to this change would lead to grave trouble.

The basic Republican doctrine is expressed in President Hoover's theory that the United States is a self-contained nation capable of prospering regardless of the condition of the outer world. This theory is a recent addition to the stock of half-truths, and it is a highly misleading description both of pre-war and post-war America. For had it been necessary to consider the question in 1913, no informed person would have thought of saying that the United States was organized to prosper within its frontiers. Though there was a high tariff on manufactures, the country exported vast quantities of food and raw materials, it borrowed capital from Europe, it paid large shipping freights, and it sent large funds abroad in the form of tourist expenditures and immigrant expenditures. This system of international payments worked so smoothly that the American people took it for granted, and had little incentive to realize how greatly their well-being was founded upon a complicated exchange of goods, services and capital funds. American public men who served their apprenticeship in this pre-war world— and most of the men now old enough for high public office did—instinctively believe that the pre-war economy is the normal American economy, and that somehow sooner or later our business system will settle back into the old familiar grooves.

Among the great changes brought about by the war none entails greater consequences for this country than in its transformation from a debtor to a creditor nation and the simultaneous expansion of its productive power in both agriculture and manufacture. During the last twelve years the country has been trying unsuccessfully to adjust itself to these new conditions. Since about 1925, when the actual physical damage done by the war had been repaired, the country has proceeded under the guidance of the Republican party to expand its plant, to collect huge debts, to resist imports, and to sell great surpluses of food, raw materials and manufactured articles.

From 1925 to about the middle of 1929 these surpluses were sold by the flotation of great masses of foreign loans and by a tremendous inflation of credit at home. By lending money all over the world there were created markets for the surplus products; by inflating credit at home a fictitious domestic market was created in which the American consumer, either as an individual or through governmental and corporate agencies, bought vast quantities of goods with promises to pay.

Along about 1928 the foreign lending stopped because the inflation created speculative opportunities at home which were more alluring than the yield on foreign bonds. When the foreign lending stopped, the world crisis began. For the rest of the world, in order to pay its debts to us and in order to pay for our wheat, cotton, copper and other exports, had to pay in gold. With France pursuing a policy similar to ours, three-quarters of the gold of the world was sucked into Paris and New York. The world was forced to bid higher and higher prices for gold, which is another way of saying that it was forced to contract credit and bring down prices. Under the pressure of this world-wide liquidation our own domestic credit inflation collapsed.

Then the naked fact was revealed that basic agriculture and large-scale industry had been geared to produce for, and were capitalized on the basis of, a world demand and a world price level which no longer existed. It can be seen now, much more clearly than many of us could see it when we were in the midst of it, that the post-war reconstruction had been founded not upon a healthy exchange of goods, but upon a frenzied credit inflation.

It was the credit inflation at home and abroad that enabled Mr. Coolidge and Mr. Hoover to point with such pride

—back in 1928—to the amazing spectacle of expanding exports, full employment, rising wages and profits, accumulating gold, and the successful collection of great foreign debts —all under a régime of prohibitive tariffs. When the bubble burst, the Republican party through its official voices refused to acknowledge that what had made its post-war policies temporarily workable was the foreign lending and the domestic inflation. It committed itself more deeply than ever to the notion that the country is self-sufficient and self-contained.

But the fact is that though the country might, in theory, become much more nearly self-contained, it is not so now. More than half the cotton, more than a third of the copper and tobacco, a fifth of the wheat and flour, an eighth of the refined oil, a quarter of the agricultural machinery, a tenth of the automobiles produced in the United States, were exported in 1929. How can the producers of these commodities hope to prosper without a restoration of their foreign markets? How can foreign markets pay gold dollars for American exports if Americans will neither lend gold dollars abroad nor buy foreign goods? How under our tariffs can our best customers buy gold dollars with their goods? How can gold dollars be lent to them while the world is in an upheaval? Yet if the producers of wheat, cotton, copper, tobacco, oil, agricultural machinery and automobiles are not prosperous, how can other producers in this country hope to have a profitable domestic market for their goods?

The United States is not self-contained. If it is to become self-contained, it must make up its mind to the fact that a considerable part of its capital investment has been misdirected, and it must prepare to write it off, to alter the occupations of millions of its inhabitants, and to face a long period of extreme tension, while losses are being liquidated and new jobs are being created for the displaced farmers and industrial workers.

The fundamental choice before the Democrats is whether they will make themselves the party of adjustment to world conditions or a party trying to alleviate the consequences of the present maladjustment. If they are frightened into an isolationist policy, it is plain that they must take the path of Bryanism, the path of cheap money and state capitalism. Only with cheap money can they hope, without intolerable suffering, to liquidate capital investment which must be scrapped if the United States is to be brought down to the low level of economic self-sufficiency; only by elaborate schemes for subsidizing prices, for artificially creating jobs, for paying the unemployed, can they hope to reduce the misery which a contraction of the American economy to a self-sufficient basis would involve.

This is the general direction in which men like Senator Wheeler, of Montana, are proceeding. It is the logical and inevitable direction of the isolationist policy, and the only difference between a man like Senator Wheeler and a conservative like Senator Reed, of Pennsylvania, is that Senator Wheeler would like to alleviate the human misery which Senator Reed's policies entail.

The other course for the Democrats to take is to resume— let us hope with greater realism and resourcefulness—their interrupted task of adjusting American commercial and political policy toward an effort to restore and stabilize a world economy. They would then set their faces toward a settlement of the war, toward making the peace which, after an armistice of thirteen years, has not been achieved. They would become the party of freer trade, of political and financial coöperation to settle debts and reparations, to restore the currencies, to reëstablish investments and to revive the world markets.

Politically, this is the more difficult program with which to enter a Presidential campaign. For the isolationist and protectionist feeling runs deep. But from the point of view of a successful administration, it is the only course which does not present insuperable difficulties. For while the isolationist mood is the popular one, the consequences of isolation are of a kind that the Democratic party is quite unequipped to handle. As it is now constituted, the party is not capable of carrying through a major re-arrangement of the American economic system. The Democratic leaders know this. Yet they do not now know whether they dare to come out into the open and challenge the isolationist policies which, if they are continued, make a new Bryanism inevitable.

February 10, 1932

VI. THE DEMOCRATIC PARTY AND THE POSITION OF ROOSEVELT

Roosevelt brought to the front by Democratic uncertainty; his strength and weakness

The uncertainty among Democrats as to the direction in which they intend to go is reflected in the position of their leading candidates.

It is the uncertainty which has brought Governor Roosevelt to the front. He has a pleasant personality, a vote-getting record in New York, a sentimental attachment in the South, a name potent in the West, a conservative background, a reputation for progressive sympathies. He is an ideal candidate of an undecided party and the more the party hesitates the greater will be his strength. His availability, as the politicians call it, is of the highest just so long as the component elements of the Democratic party are willing to do nothing more than blame Mr. Hoover for the depression.

If the negative attitude persists, it is difficult to see why Governor Roosevelt should be denied the nomination. But if the situation should change, owing to a turn of events or to the rise of positive leadership within the party or to a forcing of issues by the Republicans, the delicate equilibrium of his candidacy would be seriously upset. Governor Roosevelt does not have a wide national popularity. He does not have the affection of the masses in the pivotal sections of the country. He does not have the confidence of the national Democratic leaders. He has a sectional popularity, he has the support of many local politicians looking for an available candidate and a likely winner. He appears to be strong because at the moment he has only a hesitant, though potentially formidable, opposition to overcome.

Both in its strength and its weakness Governor Roosevelt's candidacy follows the pattern of Bryan's and McAdoo's. It is strong outside of the thickly-settled region lying north of the Potomac and Ohio and east of the Mississippi. In the states from Massachusetts to Illinois, which contain about half the electoral votes and the bulk of the organized Democratic party outside of the South, Governor Roosevelt commands no general enthusiasm and is threatened with serious disaffection. It is in this region that the electoral battle is almost certain to be decided.

The political plan on which the carefully managed Roosevelt candidacy has been based was to assume the delivery of Smith's strength in the Northern cities, and to concentrate on developing independent strength in the region which rejected Smith. The second part of the plan has worked. Governor Roosevelt has developed real strength in the South, in the Northwest and on the Pacific Coast. He has succeeded in placating the drys while remaining nominally opposed to prohibition. He is, of course, completely clear of the prejudices which worked against Smith. He has benefited greatly by the Eastern opposition, which is supposed to originate in the power trust and among the international bankers. He has flourished on Mr. Raskob's ineptitudes. Largely through the magic of his name he has managed, in spite of a working alliance with Tammany, to dissociate himself from it.

Finally, he has adopted enough of the key phrases of the progressives, without committing himself to their programs, to achieve the reputation of being a great reformer. He has adopted a sufficiently vague and woolly attitude on the tariff to sound like an advocate of freer trade without giving any protectionist cause for concern. He has talked about the debts in an obviously popular way, and in his anxiety to dissociate himself from the League, he has landed himself in a position of such complete isolation that his position is quite indistinguishable from that of Mr. Hearst.

February 11, 1932

VII. SMITH AND THE OPPOSITION TO GOVERNOR ROOSEVELT

Distrust of Roosevelt by Democratic leaders; the causes of Smith's antagonism

Among the national Democrats, that is to say, among the men who have held high office or have been influential in the councils of their party, the belief is widespread and strong that the election of Franklin D. Roosevelt would bring to the office of President a man of only moderate capacity. The impressive thing about this judgment is that it emanates from men who supported him for Governor and placed high hopes upon him.

It would not be denied that men less fitted than he have served acceptably as Presidents of the United States. Nevertheless, the judgment exists, and has grown more firm, that he has not the grasp of the issues or the disinterestedness or the resolution that a President must have in time of great emergency. No mathematical proof in support of such a judgment can be offered. But that it is the judgment of observers who have no axes to grind, that it is the judgment of men who have very considerable personal liking for him, is certain. All the appearances of the fit candidate he possesses. All the instinctive prejudices run in his favor. It is in spite of his attractiveness, in spite of his unquestioned personal integrity, in spite of his generous sympathies, that this judgment has formed itself among large numbers of discerning people that here is a man who has made a good Governor, who might make a good Cabinet officer, but who simply does not measure up to the tremendous demands of the office of President.

It is this judgment which is cutting deeply into his candidacy, for it is the judgment held by men and women whose opinion carries great weight throughout the nation.

The disaffection among the masses of the people in the North is influenced in part by this opinion of Governor Roosevelt's qualifications. But it is actuated also by emotions that lie in the dark realm of political feeling, and are hard to describe in words. It will perhaps come nearest to the truth to say that Governor Roosevelt has absent-mindedly hurt the feelings of a large mass of people whose feelings were already very much hurt by the character and by the outcome of the 1928 campaign.

If Governor Roosevelt had been a wiser man, had he had better advisers, he would have realized that the enormous vote for Smith was of a different quality from that of the ordinary vote for a popular Democrat. That vote in the

Northern States represented the coming of age in American politics of a part of the population which had not, until then, thought of itself as entitled to the full rights of American citizenship. The fervor which surrounded Smith's candidacy expressed the hope and pride of men and women who felt that his nomination by a national party was in a sense their emancipation. Their candidate was defeated. He was defeated even in New York, where he was supposed to be strongest, and almost certainly he was defeated primarily because he was a Democrat running during a Republican boom. But his defeat carried with it a sting because of the terrific outpouring of religious prejudice, racial intolerance and social snobbery that was let loose against him.

The sting is still felt. Although Smith's devoted followers have on the whole been extraordinarily sporting and discreet, they have not forgotten the outrages which accompanied his defeat. They are naturally supersensitive about anything which touches the recognition of Smith. They do not quarrel with Smith's opponents on public matters. They do not quarrel with his defeat. What they are on the alert to resent are actions which touch his pride and their pride in him.

Now the fact is that from the day Governor Roosevelt was inaugurated in Albany, he began to dissociate himself from Smith. There has not been, I believe, any quarrel about policies or patronage. There has just been an increasing tension as Smith and his followers saw themselves unceremoniously pushed aside. Their injured feelings have not been soothed by the repeated declarations of Governor Roosevelt's followers that Al Smith ought to be eternally grateful for the privilege of having been nominated by Franklin D. Roosevelt. They feel, and rightly, that if there is to be any discussion of gratitude, the debt owed by Roosevelt to Smith is a considerable one. For it was the impetus of

Smith's popularity that brought Roosevelt, a badly defeated Vice-Presidential candidate, back into active politics.

What there is to the Smith candidacy today is nothing more, I think, than the natural feeling of men that a candidate who polled fifteen million votes in 1928 is entitled in 1932 to a voice in the party's affairs. It is impossible to believe that Smith, who is a great realist and very honest with himself, expects to be nominated. He had no illusions about his election in 1928, and he can hardly have any now about the party's willingness to go again through an ordeal by fire. But that he does not wish to be ignored, that he believes he represents a real political force, that he intends to be consulted on the candidate and platform, is now evident.

February 12, 1932

VIII. GOVERNOR ROOSEVELT AT ST. PAUL

A chastened and thoughtful speech; sound doctrine on the tariff and the power question

Governor Roosevelt's reply to Al Smith's warning that he would "fight to the end against any candidate who persists in any demagogic appeal" is a speech which is about as free from demagogic appeal as any speech that any candidate is likely to make. Mr. Roosevelt has not persisted. He has desisted.

What made the original radio speech of a fortnight ago definitely "demagogic" was not the fact that Mr. Roosevelt expressed his sympathies for the "forgotten man." The vice of that speech was, first, that it promised the forgotten man something—namely, the improvement of his purchasing power—without offering even a hint as to how so desirable a thing is to be brought about, and, second, that it played upon his suspicions by a sheer misrepresentation of the facts as to the work of the Reconstruction Finance Corporation. To make empty promises and to arouse suspicion by misrepresentation is the essence of demagogy, and former Governor Smith was clearly warranted in issuing his challenge and his warning.

The orator at St. Paul was a chastened and a better man. Both in his general sentiments and in the two specific problems which he discussed Governor Roosevelt not only made honorable amends for his blunder, but went on to exhibit a breadth of vision and an understanding of principles which are entitled to ungrudging praise.

The generalities of the speech in which he asked for "a true concert of interest" as against sectional and class feeling are, of course, the commonplaces of political oratory. Yet I think no one can read the full text of this portion of the speech without feeling that Mr. Roosevelt is genuinely conscious of the size and of the variety of the American nation and that he is sincerely on his guard against letting his sympathies become narrowed and his understanding localized.

There was a note of autobiography behind these generalities and these quotations from all the glorious dead. For about eight years Franklin Roosevelt has been carrying on a huge correspondence with influential Democrats in all parts of the Union. It is this wide personal acquaintance which is now yielding him such excellent returns in the form of delegates. It has encouraged him to believe that he knows the American people rather better than most candidates and that therefore he is entitled to identify himself with the greatest, and in speaking of Jefferson to allude indirectly to himself saying that: "he was no local American; he was no little American."

When he passed from generalities to particulars he passed over entirely the whole of the present emergency. His only allusion to the immediate problems confronting the American people was to say that "the plans we make for this emergency, if we plan wisely and rest our structure upon a base sufficiently broad, will show the way to a more permanent safeguarding of our social and economic life." It is hard to believe that this means anything. The plans being used in the emergency are concerned with such thorny questions as central banking policy, taxation, budgets, the mobilization of credit and the relief of the unemployed. On all such matters Governor Roosevelt was entirely silent. He refrained from offering even a suggestion as to how he would deal with them "upon a base sufficiently broad." The conclusion is unavoidable that either he has no emergency plans which differ essentially from those of the Administration or that he thinks it inexpedient to announce them.

This vacuum of policy in the present emergency is easy to understand when one remembers that Governor Roosevelt could only divide his own friends if he had a policy. Senator Wheeler is an out and out inflationist, a position which Mr. Roosevelt is almost certainly unable to take. Another large group of his supporters are committed to the doctrine that the government should borrow and spend. Mr. Roosevelt rejected that two weeks ago. There remains in the field of discussion only the general program which the Administration has been gradually, reluctantly and half-heartedly been working itself towards. It would have been excessively dangerous to say how he would amend this program and very inconvenient to approve it. So after his unhappy experience in the radio speech he has apparently decided that for the present time discretion is the better part of valor.

On long-range policy designed for "the more permanent safeguarding" of the public interest, the Governor dealt with two great questions, with the public utilities and with the tariff. On both he exhibited, it seems to me, an exceptional grasp of the main principles.

What he said about the electrical utilities had four main points: the first was that the ownership of power sites should not be alienated from public possession; the second was that the effective way to insure public regulation of rates is to have governmental authority empowered and ready to undertake the transmission and distribution of power if the function cannot be performed on satisfactory terms by private initiative; the third was that utilities doing an interstate business should be subjected to Federal control; the fourth was that the development of the holding companies to an inconceivable degree of complexity and of capital inflation has made it necessary to bring these institutions under national control. The affairs of the Insull contraption, which are now being aired, adequately point the moral.

On the tariff Governor Roosevelt was equally effective. His criticism of the Hawley-Smoot tariff, of the President's action in approving it and of the world-wide consequences in tariff wars, was just and true. Even more important, however, was Mr. Roosevelt's recognition that a wholly new conception of the tariff is now needed, and that existing conditions in the world will make it necessary henceforth to deal with the tariff not simply by Congressional log rolling or even by supposedly scientific inquiries, but by the negotiation of tariff agreements. That is the practical wisdom of the matter at a time when protection has gone to such lengths as to reduce itself to an absurdity.

In a human sense this speech is extraordinarily interesting. It shows how valuable it is in public life for men to speak frankly. For so good a speech would hardly have been delivered in St. Paul had Al Smith not spoken so boldly the week before.

April 4, 1932

IX. THE JEFFERSON DAY RALLY

Governor Roosevelt's absence; a world outlook

Governor Roosevelt's decision to absent himself from the Jefferson Day rally of the Democrats showed how well he recognizes that his own candidacy tends to divide rather than to unite the party. Governor Roosevelt would not have been at ease in the gathering at Washington on Wednesday night. He would have found himself in a company of seasoned Democratic leaders who may have to accept him as their candidate but certainly would rather not have him if they could unite on someone else. Governor Roosevelt's absence was an acknowledgment of the division which ex-Governor Smith's challenge to him emphasized so sharply.[1]

When one turns from personalities to issues there was much that was genuinely encouraging in the Jefferson Day speeches. Although it could hardly be said that a coherent program was made visible, it is fair to say that in all the main speeches, in Mr. Baker's fine address at the tomb of Wilson, in Al Smith's own speech, in Mr. Cox's and Mr. Ritchie's and Senator Robinson's speeches, there was a common note of understanding that recovery here cannot be brought about by local magic.

If these speeches represent the real drift of Democratic opinion the party is headed toward a policy of seeking to

[1] The contest in the Democratic party between Governor Roosevelt and Alfred E. Smith was thrown into the open early in April, 1932. On April 7 Governor Roosevelt made a radio address in which he charged the Hoover Administration with neglecting the ordinary American citizen—"the little fellow"—in favor of big business. A week later, in the widely-advertised Jefferson Day dinner of April 13, Mr. Smith made a speech attacking Governor Roosevelt. He declared that he would "take his coat off" and fight any candidate for the Presidency who "persists in a demagogic appeal to the working classes."

revive trade by the only method by which it can be revived: by negotiations as to debts and tariffs and commercial policy. The interesting aspect of ex-Governor Smith's proposal on the debts lies in the fact that he recognizes in a true perspective how much more important it is to have international trade than to preserve the intergovernmental debts. An even more considered view of the matter was presented by Senator Robinson, who made the very important point that we are failing to see that "any readjustments which can be acceptable to the United States must fairly take into account and safeguard the interests of our people, both as taxpayers and as participants in world commerce."

An intelligible and feasible policy can be worked out on that premise. For it is now clear that we have arrived at the point where the destruction of our exporting industries and of our creditor position has gone so far that if the torn fabric is to be restored, the United States will have to undertake international negotiations looking toward far-reaching reciprocal agreements on tariffs, and credits, and debts and gold.

It is genuinely encouraging to learn that the minds of Democratic leaders are turned in this direction.

April 15, 1932

X. CONGRESSIONAL MISBEHAVIOR STRENGTH-ENING MR. HOOVER

The coal and oil tariffs; Congress as a representative of local interests, the President of national interests

In the voting on the oil and coal tariffs the Senators cast aside all pretense that there is any essential difference of principle between Republicans and Democrats or between progressives and conservatives. Eighteen Democrats voted for the oil tariff and twenty against it. So it has become rather ridiculous for the Democratic party to declaim against the Republican tariff policy. Among those Democrats voting for this tariff were to be found Mr. Barkley, who has been selected by Governor Roosevelt's friends to sound the progressive Democratic key at Chicago, Messrs. Dill, Walsh and Wheeler, the three eminent opponents of special privilege. Mr. Couzens walked arm in arm with Mr. Reed, Mr. Long with Mr. Smoot. It has, therefore, become equally ridiculous to assert that there is a progressive bloc which represents the common man against private interests. The forgotten man was completely forgotten by every Senator whose constituents desired a special privilege.

The action of the Senate in voting these tariffs will be interpreted in the outer world as another extreme example of economic nationalism. But to Americans who look closely at the manner in which the votes were assembled the really significant thing about this affair is the lack of national feeling and national responsibility which the Senators displayed. Senator Reed of Pennsylvania voted for an oil tariff because he wants a coal tariff. Senator Ashurst voted for it because he wants a copper tariff. Senator Dill voted for it because he wants a lumber tariff. As a matter of fact, the decisive reasons were even more particular. Senator Reed was not voting for the coal industry. He was voting for a small section of it which produces anthracite. He was voting against the larger interest of the bituminous miners. Senator Thomas was not voting for the oil industry, but for a section of it which preponderates in his state. These Senators could not have been less concerned for the American interest as a whole if they had been the ambassadors of separate nations.

That, indeed, is what most of them feel themselves to be.

Occasionally one of them will break out, as Senator Tydings of Maryland did, to protest against the everlasting concentration on purely local concerns. But most of the time in respect to important issues there are not ten Senators who try to represent the United States. The majority are broadminded if they try to represent their states; the most of them are content to represent a collection of special interests within their states.

This is the reason why the President is almost invariably driven into conflict with Congress. It is a rare moment in our political history when, as in the first term of Woodrow Wilson, there is coöperation between the Capitol and the White House. The normal relationship is one of conflict. This, too, is the reason why the President almost always gains in popular favor the longer Congress sits. For the President does represent a national interest, and the people are compelled to turn to him as Congress reveals itself to be a mere assembly of delegates from particular groups.

Even Mr. Hoover, who has few gifts as a popular leader, is steadily recovering prestige by the mere fact that he does strive to represent the national against the special interests. Congress has almost achieved the political miracle of restoring Mr. Hoover's shattered influence. The Democrats in Congress have proved to be the one best bit of luck which has befallen him. Mr. Garner has done more to make possible Mr. Hoover's reëlection than the whole Republican National Committee. For Mr. Garner has devoted his energies to showing how unprepared to govern are the Democrats in Congress. Senator Barkley, of Kentucky, the impending keynoter, has been a godsend; he has succeeded in robbing his party of its chief issue. Messrs. Dill, Walsh and Wheeler have been a priceless boon to Mr. Hoover; they have shown how quickly a little special advantage can blot out their sympathies with the forgotten man.

Forgotten man indeed! What has been remembered in Congress is the interest of a few localities. What has been forgotten is the Nation.

May 24, 1932

THE CONVENTIONS AND THEIR WORK

On the other hand, repeal would serve no practical purpose, injure, which do not enter today. To this, which has appeared or appear that it ....

· X ·

THE TWO NATIONAL CONVENTIONS AND THEIR WORK

I. THE PRE-CONVENTION DEBATE ON REPEAL

The demand for an alternative; repeal itself is constructive

THE most effective argument against the repeal of the Eighteenth Amendment is that employed by Senator Borah when he asks what "constructive alternatives" the repealers have to offer. Mrs. Boole of the W. C. T. U. and Bishop Cannon make the same point, and it is obvious from Mr. Rockefeller's letter to President Butler that he is somewhat troubled too.

In examining the consequences of repeal the first question to ask ourselves is what power to regulate would be left if the Eighteenth Amendment were removed. There would remain twenty states which have prohibition by their own constitutions. There would remain in every state the power to prohibit by constitution or by statute. The Webb-Kenyon Law, adopted by Congress in 1913, would remain, compelling the Federal government to prohibit shipments of liquor into a state if such a shipment violates the state laws. Congress would have the power to prohibit or regulate the importation of liquor from abroad. These two objectives—to prevent interstate traffic and to prevent importations—are just about all that Federal enforcement aims at today. They do not depend upon the maintenance of the Eighteenth Amendment.

On the other hand, repeal would revive powers to regulate liquor which do not exist today. In states which are opposed to prohibition, it is impossible, under the Eighteenth Amendment, to have temperance legislation of any kind whatever. Laws to regulate the liquor traffic are unconstitutional under the Eighteenth Amendment. The consequence is that in states where the majority is anti-prohibition, there is no effective prohibition and there can be no alternative. It is no play on words, it is not mere repartee in debate, to say to Senator Borah that only by the repeal of the Eighteenth Amendment is it possible in wet territory to have a constructive alternative to the bootleg liquor industry.

Thus the repeal of the Eighteenth Amendment will not deprive the states of any power to prohibit or regulate that they now have; it will not deprive the Federal government of any power which it effectively exercises; but repeal will empower states to regulate the traffic. It can be said in all sincerity and in all literalness that repeal of the Eighteenth Amendment will augment the total power of the people to deal with intoxicants. From the governmental point of view the essence of repeal is not the restoration of liquor but the restoration of a suppressed power to regulate liquor. For in its effect upon New York or any other predominantly wet state, the Eighteenth Amendment is simply a constitutional veto on temperance legislation.

Ever since 1913 the great argument for national prohibition has been that the states which wished to do so could not make their own prohibition effective if liquor was being sold freely on the other side of their borders. This, I take it, is Senator Borah's position. What he needs to consider now is whether dry states would not be better protected against invasion if in the wet states liquor were legal and regulated rather than illegal and unregulated.

Unless he can convince himself that the Federal Government can and will suppress the bootleg liquor industry, he must, if he is realistic, see that the practical choice is between a controlled and an uncontrolled liquor traffic. Can it be seriously denied that a legal and regulated liquor industry in the wet States can be more effectively prevented from invading the dry States than a bootleg industry run by outlaws and racketeers? I doubt that it can be denied, and, therefore, repeal would in fact aid those States which desire prohibition within their borders. By reviving the Webb-Kenyon Act they would enjoy all the Federal protection they now have under the Eighteenth Amendment and besides they would have the additional protection which would come from driving the bootleggers out of business and substituting a controlled industry.

It is fair to say that repeal is a "constructive alternative" to the situation which now prevails. Not only would it leave intact all the constitutional and statutory prohibition in the States, not only would it leave intact the Federal power to protect dry States, but it would revive all the temperance legislation which the Eighteenth Amendment has suppressed, and would for the first time in over ten years empower the people of the populous regions to protect themselves against the most gigantic industry ever known in the underworld.

June 8, 1932

II. CONSERVATIVE TEMPER OF THE ASSEMBLING REPUBLICANS

Absence of economic insurgency; prohibition and Vice-President Curtis

Chicago, June 12

The great puzzle here at Chicago is the total absence of any evidence of economic insurgency. At every other convention the Western Progressives have been on hand to do battle.

If they are here this year they are keeping themselves well hidden and nobody I have talked with has seen any signs that they will produce a program and challenge the conservative control of the party. Yet presumably this is the year of years when they might be expected to be particularly active.

Surely it is astonishing that in the midst of such great economic distress there should be no rumbling here of social discontent. The Administration leaders to whom I have spoken ascribe this strange state of affairs to two things: they say, first, that the drift of opinion in America as in England and in Germany is strongly to the Right because the great majority of the people is more concerned with defending and preserving what it has left than it is hopeful of much better things from experiments; they say too that this state of mind has been confirmed by the record of the Democrats in the House and by the sterility of the progressive proposals throughout the depression. They may be quite wrong, of course, on all counts. The discontent may exist and be awaiting expression; it may be that conservative Republicans are too deaf to hear the discontent and that the progressive Republicans are too bewildered to express it.

The fact remains that on the eve of the convention everybody is proceeding on the assumption that nothing important is to be decided here except the manner in which the party will take note of the popular revulsion against the Eighteenth Amendment. There are, besides, a few daring rebels who would like to displace Mr. Charles Curtis with somebody or other.

The conflict over the prohibition plank appears to have reduced itself to the question whether to be misleading or frank. It is generally admitted that public sentiment has turned radically against prohibition as it now exists. The Anti-Saloon League has lost its power to dictate the plank and the drys are clearly on the defensive. But there are still many drys. And therefore there is one school of politicians, said to be inspired from the White House, who are in search of a formula which will taste dry to the drys and wet to the wets. In one way or another they would like to offer the people a chance to vote on prohibition without definitely giving the people a chance to make their vote effective. This might be done, they seem to think, by proposing a referendum in the States or by calling State conventions together to debate the question.

Their opponents say that they are not interested in any vote which cannot decide the question. There can be no vote to decide the question except a vote to elect State conventions for the specific purpose of ratifying or rejecting a Twentieth Amendment which repeals the Eighteenth. They say that any other vote is meaningless, that it could have no more effect than the taking of another poll by the *Literary Digest*. Whatever there is of fervor and forthrightness here at Chicago is centered on this issue. On every other issue the delegates appear satisfied to let the Administration proceed in accordance with its philosophy and by means of such schemes as Mr. Hoover may from time to time improvise.

There are some troubled consciences when the name of Vice-President Curtis is mentioned. As rational men the delegates I have talked with admit that the chief reason for having a Vice-President is that there should be a man ready to replace the President. They realize that Mr. Curtis is fourteen years older than Mr. Hoover, and it is not claimed, I believe, by any one, unless it be Mrs. Gann, that Mr. Curtis even in his palmy days was any wonder. They realize that his accession to the Presidency during the next four years would probably necessitate something like a regency, for he was never fit for the office and time is not adding to his qualifications.

Yet they cannot think of anybody to put in his place.

For the eminent old men are not available and the more distinguished younger men are either too ambitious or too little known. The great charm of Mr. Curtis is that by renominating him nobody's feelings will be hurt. If he is renominated that will be the reason why.

June 13, 1932

III. THE UNHAPPY REPUBLICANS AT CHICAGO

Want of enthusiasm for Mr. Hoover; discouragement over prohibition

Chicago, June 13

As between the Federal officeholders and the professional politicians who make up the Republican convention and the Administration in Washington, the relationship is like an old marriage that has become sour and stale. There is not any respectable ground for a divorce, and it would cause much useless inconvenience to arrange a separation now. So they are holding the family together. Yet nothing remains between them of romantic love, nor of friendly interest, nor even of the little courtesies. I have seen just one picture of Mr. Hoover in Chicago, and that was an oil painting in the back of a store window on Michigan Boulevard. At the Congress Hotel, where the party has its headquarters, I have yet to see a single poster or banner designed to inspire the Republican hosts with Mr. Hoover's countenance. This cannot be mere economy. It cannot even be parsimony. It must be sheer absent-mindedness brought on by the dreary necessity of going through with an arrangement that has lost its charm.

So far as I can make out, the professionals take the view

that they can do nothing here at Chicago to affect the result in November. If the party is to win, it must win because events bring the Republican voters back to the standard. What those events might be nobody knows. Some think there is a drift back to Hoover because the tendency of public sentiment is conservative. Some think he may yet improvise a brilliant stroke, not unlike the moratorium, but more successful or at least luckier. All of them count heavily on Democratic mistakes.

But among the professionals the principal calculation, I am told, is a discounting of defeat, and a determination to hold on to the party organization for 1936. There have been several unspectacular, inside and technically political decisions arrived at already which indicate strongly that what is being done here is to set things in order for probable defeat in 1932 so that it will be Mr. Hoover and his friends, rather than the professionals, who will suffer the consequences. If by some chance the party wins in November the professionals will naturally rejoice. But win or lose, they seem determined to make secure their own control of the organization.

Their new-found friendliness to the cause of repeal of the Eighteenth Amendment is only in part, I think, a response to the change in public sentiment. On the basis of immediate expediency it is very dangerous to the Republicans to desert the prohibitionists. For by all past experiences the drys will be more enraged at the Republicans if they desert a little than at the Democrats if the Democrats are wringing wet. The drys will vote for wet Democrats in order to defeat Republican deserters, or at least they will refuse to vote at all or they will put up third candidates who will attract an important part of the dry vote.

It is hard to see how the Republicans can fail to lose heavily this year, whatever stand they take on prohibition. They are caught in 1932 as the Democrats were in 1924 and

1928 between the irreconcilable dry and the irreconcilable wets. Even if the two platforms are identical it seems almost certain that the Republicans must suffer the consequences of dry disaffection. For the dry Democrats have become accustomed to the idea of a wet Democracy, but the dry Republicans thought until this week that they owned their party.

All of this does not add to the joy of the occasion. The more farsighted professionals accept the situation as irremediable, and say to themselves that whatever the consequence this year, in the long run it is more important to hold on to the ardent young Republicans who are wet, the big campaign contributors who are wet, and the urban masses in the East who are wet than it is to try to hold the party together by giving the drys their prohibition and the wets a compromise of prosperity.

June 14, 1932

IV. SENATOR DICKINSON'S KEYNOTE SPEECH

Its intellectual dishonesty; partisanship on the public relief problem

Chicago, June 14

In the production of his speech Senator Dickinson obviously was determined that he would at all costs sound a triumphant keynote. This compelled him to omit all reference to the two-car garage and all explanations as to why after eleven years of Republican rule "our nation is in the midst of its most perilous economic crisis." The Senator just jumped right into the midst of the crisis and then devoted his energies to asserting that every act of Mr. Hoover's has been superb.

The historians admit that even Abraham Lincoln made a few mistakes, but if the Senator's story is to be believed Herbert Hoover has been invincibly right from start to finish. Such infallibility previously has not been known on earth, and when Mr. Hoover has this speech called to his attention by one of his secretaries he will feel either that the speech is nonsense or that the office of President of the United States is a paltry thing for one who has such cosmic genius.

A good sample of the quality of this speech is to be had by looking at what this official spokesman for the Republican party had to say on a subject still being debated in Congress —public works as a means of relieving unemployment. Discussing the early days of the depression, Senator Dickinson pointed with pride to the fact that "Congress, under Republican leadership, patriotically coöperated by increasing appropriations for public improvements of all character and by making available additional sums for road building," and that "the President enlisted the coöperation of the states and their subdivisions in extending and speeding up their programs of public construction, including highway improvements." All of this spending was done under Republican auspices. The Senator acclaimed it as a great achievement.

But about fifteen minutes later he reached that section of his speech where he had to denounce the Democrats and there he pointed with horror to the Democrats who "proposed billions in bond issues for unnecessary and unproductive public works." When the Republicans spent money in 1932 "upwards of a million persons, who would otherwise have been idle, were given gainful employment." When the Democrats proposed to spend money in 1932 they were acting on the theory that you can "squander yourself into prosperity."

This is not an intellectually honest performance, but if nothing were involved except Senator Dickinson's personal reputation it would not greatly matter. But, of course, this speech was approved, if not by the President himself, then certainly by some one who has authority to represent him. And when that fact is realized it suddenly is brought home to one that this keynote address is a reversion to the crudest kind of partisanship and a deliberate, reckless abandonment of any pretense that the Administration desires national coöperation in dealing with the crisis.

I cite the two quotations about public works as a mere illustration. The address from start to finish is based on the assumption that the Democrats contributed almost nothing to the relief program and that no further assistance from them is needed or desired. Looked at from this point of view, the Senator's speech is not the mere routine campaign buncombe to which the nation is so cynically accustomed, but a grave rupture of that precarious national unity upon which our safety may for many more difficult months continue to depend.

It is hard to understand how Mr. Hoover dared to permit his spokesman to forget so completely the interests of the nation and to make such an unpatriotic speech. For after this speech, so jealous and so grasping, the Democrats who have been coöperating with the President would be more than human if they did not feel that Herbert Hoover was a rather difficult man to coöperate with.

June 15, 1932

V. THE REPUBLICAN PROHIBITION PLANK

Mr. Hoover's secret dictation; muddling the question

Chicago, June 15

The Resolutions Committee has been sitting for several days trying to improvise a prohibition policy. The product of its labors is a plank which, amid elaborate hemming and hawing and much solemn protesting, proposes to scrap national prohibition as we have known it since 1920 and to substitute for it some sort of new but largely undefined Federal system. It will be debated late this evening at the convention.

The affair over the prohibition plank has disclosed once more the peculiar weakness of Mr. Hoover as a political leader. Until a short time before the convention assembled he seems to have taken no position on the question. Then it transpired that the repealers were very strong and that the convention if left to itself would take a radical position. Thereupon, without giving any public expression to his own convictions, Mr. Hoover set out to dictate through secret channels what the convention should do. The result is that he has displeased everybody and is accumulating all the blame for all the different disappointments.

It would have been possible for him to speak out clearly and promptly. He did not do that.

It would have been possible for him to stand aside and let the convention make its own policy. He has not done that. He was afraid to take the lead and he has been afraid not to dictate. Whatever the result he will get no thanks from anybody, and he is in grave danger of being regarded as a deserter by the drys, and by the wets as an unreliable convert.

A straightforward, open and decisive policy, whether it was wet or dry, would have been ever so much better politics. Truly it is the timid who muddle the world.

June 16, 1932

National prohibition abandoned; a greater victory than the wets realize

Chicago, June 16

Under cover of a smoke-screen of dry slogans, the Republican party has abandoned national prohibition. So

effective was the smoke-screen that it may take some time
before the drys realize how complete was their defeat and
the wets how imposing was their victory. In the convention
hall itself the galleries, which were full of wets, booed and
howled while the wet cause was winning, and the drys on the
floor applauded fervently the decision which marked the
end of the Republican party's adherence to national prohibition.

What is it that the Republicans have declared? They have
declared that Republicans in the House and the Senate
should vote for a resolution submitting a Twentieth Amendment to the states. They have pledged themselves to specify
that the ratification of this new amendment shall be considered not by state legislatures but by specially elected State
conventions "adequately safeguarded so as to be truly
representative." This can mean only one thing, that they
pledge themselves to see that these State conventions are
more truly representative than are most of the State legislatures. In other words, they declare that the over-representa-
tion of rural districts and the under-representation of cities,
which is characteristic of most Legislatures, shall not prevail
in the state conventions. This pledge is, from the point of
view of the practical difficulties of ratifying a new amendment on prohibition, an incalculably important victory for
the wets.

The Twentieth Amendment which the Republicans propose to submit to these state conventions would supersede
and, therefore, would in fact repeal the Eighteenth Amendment. The essence of the Eighteenth Amendment is that it
prohibits and does not merely give Congress the power to
prohibit the manufacture and sale of liquor. The new
Twentieth Amendment would take prohibition completely
out of the Constitution. Whatever the phrase makers may
choose to call it, this is repeal, and it constitutes an absolute

victory on the fundamental principle for which the opponents of the Eighteenth Amendment have always contended.

The Twentieth Amendment would not only repeal constitutional prohibition but it would deny to Congress the power to impose legislative prohibition. For the Republicans have committed themselves to the principle that the States may legalize liquor, not merely beer and wine, but all liquor, if they wish to do so.

The Twentieth Amendment would, however, grant certain powers over the liquor traffic to the Federal government. These powers would be of two kinds. There would be a grant of power to Congress to make laws and to set up enforcement machinery to protect dry states against the invasion of liquor from the wet states. There is no dispute as to the desirability of giving Congress this power. The only difference of opinion is whether it is necessary to amend the legislation in order to provide the power. Some think that the old Constitution vests in Congress all the authority needed; some deny that it does. There can be no possible objection to reaffirming the power if it exists or of granting it if it does not; it is generally agreed that Congress should have the power to protect dry states against invasion. Senator Morrow, who made a profound study of this problem, advocated an amendment which "would vest in the Federal government power to give all possible protection and assistance to those states that desire complete prohibition against invasion from the states that do not."

But the Republican platform goes further and proposes to vest more power in Congress. Here the language of the platform is vague, but what the authors probably had in mind was to give Congress the power to declare principles to which the states must conform in legalizing liquor. Their intention, it appears, is to give Congress the power to say that no state may, for example, legalize a system under which liquor is sold for consumption in public places, or conceivably that no state may legalize a liquor traffic conducted for private profit.

Here is matter for considered debate, and I for one can see no point in making a snap judgment. I should like to see a draft of the amendment which the President would accept as conforming to the language of his platform.

The main point is that this new amendment can go no further than to grant Congress the power to regulate. It cannot prohibit. It cannot give Congress the power to prohibit. It cannot embed any particular kind of regulation in the Constitution. Since the new amendment can only be a grant of power, it must substitute for the iron inflexibility of the present system a flexible system responsive to public opinion such as prevails in all other civilized countries. The worst that Congress could do under the new amendment could be corrected at any time by a majority vote of Congress.

The wets would be unreasonable if they refused to consider this proposal and to examine carefully the arguments for it which Secretary Mills set forth so cogently in the debate.

I left the convention hall early Thursday morning feeling that the anti-prohibitionists had won so great a victory so suddenly that they have not yet adjusted their minds to their new position. The wet galleries were certainly as fanatical and as ignorant and as intolerant as the drys ever were in the days when they were in the saddle. There is danger here, and the wet leaders should stop and consider.

They should remember that it is one thing to fight resolutely to win and another to refuse to make peace with your opponent. It is true that the wets have only won one battle in a campaign which must be fought out in Congress and in the states. But they are in the ascendant and they will make a great mistake if they take a stand which offers the drys no choice but to resist to the bitter end or to surrender abjectly. My view is that on the moot point of this platform —whether or not to grant Congress power to determine the principles upon which the states may legalize liquor— there is no sacrifice of principle in a conciliatory attitude. There is nothing in the proposal to grant Congress a limited power to regulate the liquor traffic which any self-respecting opponent of the Eighteenth Amendment and of the policy of prohibition need hesitate to consider with an open mind.

June 17, 1932

VI. THE DEMOCRATIC ALIGNMENT ON THE EVE OF THE CONVENTION

The South and West against the East; Governor Roosevelt an instrument rather than a leader

Chicago, June 26

The main alignment in Chicago is between a coalition of Southern and Western Democrats on one side and of Eastern Democrats on the other. The balance of power lies in the central states such as Ohio, Indiana, Illinois and Missouri. If these states throw in their lot with the Roosevelt coalition, the Governor will almost certainly be nominated and the battle in November will be fought on the pattern of the McKinley-Bryan contest of 1896. The Democrats would then stake everything on the theory that Governor Roosevelt, holding the South and the border states, could make a fairly clean sweep of the territory between the Mississippi and the Rockies, and then pick up enough strength in rural Indiana, Ohio, and Illinois to win the election.

This is the basic conception of the Roosevelt leaders. It accounts for their otherwise inexplicable behavior in riding roughshod over the Eastern delegates. They are not counting on the East, and while they would, of course, like to carry some Eastern states, they believe they can win the nomination and the election without the Eastern states. Holding that belief, they are disposed to make a thorough job of it by removing from the councils of the party the Raskob-Shouse-Smith-Ritchie faction.

The risks of this strategy are clear enough, but apparently the Roosevelt leaders have in their own minds discounted them. Along the lines they have decided to pursue the Roosevelt leaders are prepared to lose the Al Smith vote in the great cities, to lose the support of many conservative Democrats, and to send back to the Republicans those business men who would, if they had the chance, like to vote against Mr. Hoover. They are counting on general discontent, especially in the rural sections, to overcome that spirit of caution born of anxiety which is the main reliance of the Republicans.

An examination of the results in 1896, when Bryan lost by only ninety-five electoral votes, and in 1916, when Wilson won, though he failed to carry any large Eastern state except Ohio, will show the basis of the Roosevelt calculation. Bryan would have won in 1896 had he carried Illinois, Indiana and Minnesota. Wilson would have been easily, instead of narrowly, elected in 1916 had he carried Illinois, Indiana, Iowa and Minnesota. Therefore, the fundamental question in the Roosevelt strategy is whether Governor Roosevelt is stronger than Bryan or Wilson, whether President Hoover is weaker than McKinley and Hughes, in the central regions of the country. If the Roosevelt forces proceed as they plan, that will be the question which has to be decided between now and next November.

It is evident that Governor Roosevelt is not the leader of the forces behind him. He is being used by them. The seasoned politicians from the South have few illusions as to his personal capacity. Many of the most powerful among them say frankly that he is not their personal choice and that they would greatly prefer Newton D. Baker of Ohio. But they have two interests which transcend their interest in selecting the fittest man available to be President of the United States. One is the determination to avoid a deadlock like 1924 and the other is an almost hysterical desire to depose the Raskob-Smith leadership in the high command of the party.

The irregulars from the West, of whom Senator Wheeler of Montana is perhaps the most conspicuous, are also concerned to use Governor Roosevelt. I do not know what private assurances they have from him, but publicly they have had no progressive doctrine from him that has any teeth in it. They admit this. Their view is that, nevertheless, Governor Roosevelt has the kind of enemies he would have if he were a thoroughgoing progressive, and that, though he may be weak in his convictions, his sympathies lean in their direction. Evidence that he is vacillating tends curiously enough to reassure rather than to disturb them, and it may be assumed that they count heavily on controlling him because they look upon him as pliant.

Unless the unexpected happens this week, the great question to be decided at Chicago is how far the left wing of the Roosevelt following will force the right wing to go. The right wing, consisting of the seasoned politicians, will wish to preserve the appearance of party harmony and to take measures which would deprive the Eastern Democrats of an excuse for bolting the ticket. The left wing, consisting of the Western insurgents, will wish to depart from Chicago with the scalps of the Easterners in their belts and with Governor Roosevelt their nominal leader, but in fact their prisoner.

The great conflicts scheduled to be fought out in the convention may conceivably upset the whole Roosevelt strategy, but if they do not do that they will, nevertheless, test the balance of forces within the Roosevelt coalition. It is from this point of view that the Shouse-Walsh contest for permanent chairman, the fight over abrogating the two-thirds rule, the debates over the economic planks in the platform, and the choice of a Vice-President may acquire their chief significance.

June 27, 1932

VII. SENATOR BARKLEY'S KEYNOTE SPEECH

A world outlook partially grasped; the Jeffersonian tradition on prohibition

Chicago, June 27

Senator Barkley did not fail to observe the rules of etiquette long since established for keynote addresses. The rules require that the orator should pretend to believe that the opposing party is without a redeeming virtue and that his own party is superb, superior and sublime. It also is the rule that the orator must never use one adjective if he can think of three adjectives or make any statement except in superlative terms. A keynoter must never say that two and two make four. He must always say that the great patriotic double integer when conjoined by the Democratic party or the Republican party with the noble, patriotic double integer is a quadruple blessing or curse to all the people of this broad and fertile and smiling land. It is essential to the ritual that the orator should behave as no man ever would behave if he were trying to persuade a company of reasonable men; in at least every sixth paragraph he must work himself into a frenzy where a stranger, not knowing the artificiality of his efforts, naturally would wonder whether it were safe to let him go home alone.

Yet through the rumble of the rhetoric one could hear a few notes in Senator Barkley's speech which differentiate the Democratic policy from the Republican. As set forth two weeks ago, the Republican view of the world crisis is that the United States must recover by adhering to a policy of sound public finance within a framework of economic isolation, whereas the Democratic doctrine is that recovery must come by a policy of sound public finance within a framework of coöperation and freer trade. It is, of course, unfortunate and embarrassing that Senator Barkley himself has such a shabby record on the tariff, but the views he presented, as distinguished from what he has practiced, constitute a line of policy which is fundamentally different from that of the Republicans. Provided only that the Democrats nominate a candidate who can be trusted to lead his party effectively in accordance with this doctrine, the issue will be joined on a matter of great importance.

In so far as the keynote address represents the views of the dominant elements of the Democratic party, it is a matter of extraordinary interest that they have chosen to stand not upon some policy of monetary manipulation or artificial stimulation of business, but upon the thesis that the way to recovery is through the restoration of trade by the lowering of domestic tariffs and by international coöperation. This is an enlightened choice. It will enable the Democrats to argue with great effect that although the Republicans pledged their allegiance to the maintenance of the gold standard, it is only along the lines of this Democratic policy that the gold standard can again be made workable in the modern world.

With equal directness Senator Barkley dealt with prohibition by proposing that the Democratic party return to the Jeffersonian tradition. He declared without weasel words of any kind that the convention should recommend to Congress the passage of a resolution repealing the Eighteenth Amendment and submitting it to conventions elected by the people of the states. It is impossible to deal more simply or more straightforwardly with the issue, and this statement should please every one who has been wondering whether political parties would ever again be intellectually candid on controversial issues.

The effectiveness of the keynote speech was about exhausted after Senator Barkley had dealt with the tariff and prohibition. On the need for banking reform he was not only vague but timid; on the subject of economy he was bold in words but feeble in substance, omitting all mention of the plain fact that substantial economies in the Federal government can now be had only by reducing subsidies and grants to veterans and to other special interests; on the subject of the farmer he was, to my mind at least, quite unclear.

When all this has been said, it is nevertheless something, it is more than the ordinary, to find a party willing to declare itself so plainly on two issues that are as vital and as controversial as prohibition and the tariff.

June 28, 1932

VIII. THE FEELING IN FAVOR OF
NEWTON D. BAKER

*Illusory fears of a long deadlock; sentiment for
Baker behind other commitments*

Chicago, June 28

Although there are some who profess they fear a deadlock like that of 1924, the position today is fundamentally different. In Madison Square Garden the Democratic party was irreconcilably divided into two factions, one of which was passionately attached to McAdoo and the other to Smith. Both sides felt that they were fighting for principles that were sacred and could not be compromised. There is no such conflict in Chicago today. Smith is not here to win the nomination for himself, and Roosevelt's supporters are in the main people who like him, who sympathize with his intentions, who thought he was probably the most available candidate, but are in no sense fanatically devoted to him.

The convention is able, therefore, to turn from Roosevelt and Smith to some one else without hopeless embarrassment and disappointment. The way out of the danger of a deadlock is open. It is not only open, but it is attractive. For all through these various delegations there is an astonishingly strong though quiet conviction that the party can unite on a man who is stronger than any of the leading contenders. That man is Newton D. Baker of Ohio. My impression is that he is the real first choice of more responsible Democrats than any other man, and that he is an acceptable second choice to almost every one. Although there is not a single delegate instructed to vote for him, he is the man who, once pre-convention pledges have been fulfilled, could most easily be nominated.

The strength of Baker derives from an almost universal confidence in his ability and in his character. He is profoundly trusted. As to other men, it is necessary to guess whether they have the qualities of mind and heart needed in a world crisis. But Baker has been tested in a world crisis. He has piloted a ship in a great storm. It is not necessary to ask whether he can organize men for action. He has organized more men for action than any other living American. It is not necessary to ask whether he has the mind to grasp quickly the truth hidden in great complex problems. Every year the testimony has grown more compelling as to the effectiveness with which he improvised a great army and maintained its independence against all the entanglements of a war conducted by a coalition on foreign soil. No one has to ask himself whether Baker has the power to make decisions amidst danger and confusion. No one has to ask whether he is brave. No one can doubt that he has a calm judgment, and that in the fevers of a crisis he has shown himself to be cool, serene, patient and resolute.

I have heard it said here by a man who is a leading supporter of Governor Roosevelt that Mr. Baker owed it to his party and to his country to come forward months ago and seek the nomination. There are some who cannot believe that any man who has the Presidency within his reach should sit still and do nothing to obtain it. They wonder whether it is possible that any man in this day and age does not seek to promote his own advancement. The truth, as I know it to be, can best be stated by saying that Newton Baker is congenitally incapable of working for his own glory. This quality of his nature was confirmed by the ordeal of the war where he saw at first hand not only the glories of the Presidency but its awful responsibilities. Difficult as it is to believe that there are such men in public life, the truth is that he is an authentic example of a man who does not seek the office.

His great and varied abilities combined with his extraordinary purity of motive have made a deep impression upon all kinds of Democrats in this convention. Whether they can and will get free of their commitments in order to nominate him, I do not know. But this much I do know: if they unite on him, they can do so not in the spirit of weary compromise, but with the conviction that they are choosing their most experienced, their most eloquent, their most widely trusted man.

June 29, 1932

IX. THE BELLIGERENT ELEMENT IN THE ROOSEVELT CAMP

*A majority of Roosevelt's following out of control;
their eagerness to humiliate the Smith-Raskob
element*

Chicago, June 29

Thus far, up to the actual balloting for candidates, the significant struggle here has taken place within the Roosevelt forces. There is and always has been a decisive majority of delegates enlisted under the Roosevelt banner. But it has never been certain and it is not now certain who it is that controls that majority. For it has not been Governor Roosevelt himself who has controlled his own majority.

Thus it is evident that he was pushed into the ugly and expensive and wholly unnecessary struggle to defeat Mr. Jouett Shouse. He was pushed also into the fight to abrogate the two-thirds rule. It has been conflict within the Roosevelt camp rather than the attacks from the outside which has provided all the drama of the convention and has raised whatever threat there has been made to the Roosevelt cause. If the Governor has vacillated, it has been because he could not control his own majority.

Had Mr. Roosevelt been the leader of his own forces, it is plain that he would not have reneged on his consent that Mr. Shouse should be elected permanent chairman. What possible difference did it make to Franklin Roosevelt who presided over a convention in which he has a clear majority? Even an unscrupulous enemy in the chair could do him no harm with his own majority to protect him. The presiding officer has no power to influence the result. If Governor Roosevelt was to be nominated, the power of Mr. Shouse would have been terminated and Governor Roosevelt and his friends would have taken immediate possession of the machinery of the party. With nothing real at stake, Governor Roosevelt had every reason for not antagonizing Mr. Shouse's friends, who are powerful politicians in all sections of the country.

Why, then, was the Governor forced into the fight against Mr. Shouse? The answer is that a powerful group of his Western and Southern supporters had determined to wipe out as dramatically as possible all vestiges of the Raskob-Smith influence. The fight against Shouse was made in order to obliterate the memories of the campaign of 1928 when those Westerners and Southerners were compelled at great risk to their own personal careers to support Al Smith and to accept John Raskob. Mr. Shouse, being a Smith-Raskob man, was made a sacrificial victim to prove that they had purged themselves of the sins of 1928. The rite was not performed in the interest of Governor Roosevelt. It was done at his expense in the local interests of the politicians who are supporting him.

The movement to abrogate the two-thirds rule was of a different character. It was not a cool and selfish calculation. It was rather a small stampede led by hot-headed and inexperienced men among the Roosevelt chieftains. It was the action of men who, having a majority, were afraid they could not hold it together if they did not use it quickly. It is almost certain that they underestimated the strength of their own majority. For about thirty-six hours they stampeded Governor Roosevelt, and only when the caucuses showed that the plan to seize the nomination by a coup had failed was he willing or able to persuade them that they must abandon the project.

If Governor Roosevelt has had reason to worry this week, it has been because his own supporters were running away with him rather than because his avowed opponents were so

formidable. The open opposition has been a collection of
Chinese armies capable of producing disorder, but not of
winning a war. All that remains to be demonstrated as the
balloting begins is whether they will produce enough prolonged disorder to demoralize the Roosevelt majority and
create the kind of confusion in which a new combination
of leaders might rise to power.

June 30, 1932

X. THE DEMOCRATIC PLATFORM: A RETURN
TO WOODROW WILSON

*The Cleveland and Wilson philosophy; a platfrom
of liberal reform*

Chicago, June 30

On Wednesday night when the platform was read to the
convention there occurred one of the most remarkable
changes of mood which I have ever seen in a great popular assembly. The rancors of factionalism were for the moment forgotten and the delegates suddenly felt happy and at
peace with themselves and the world. They were doing what
they had evidently long believed without daring to say it,
and the sense of relief at being delivered from the bondage of
their fears acted upon them like a strong, cool wind after
a sultry day. They became hopeful, good natured and generous, and when Al Smith appeared before them they gave
him a reception which, though it had no political significance, had in it a note of lusty human liking for him as a man.

The resolutions committee has done the best job in any
national convention for at least twenty years. It has written a platform which is brief because, in the main, it is
honestly intended that it should be candid, and while it

contains some ambiguities and some vote-catching devices and some inaccuracies, it is more honest, more clear-headed and more courageous than the platform of any major party since the end of the war. Its authors were really aware of the fact that the country has become very impatient with the ordinary buncombe of politics and will respond to plain speech.

The basic philosophy of the platform was supplied by a group of elder statesmen who have survived from the Wilson administration. The main themes of the platform are those of the Cleveland and Wilson Democracy; they represent a revival of what can with fair accuracy be described as old-fashioned American liberalism. There are exceptions here and there, but in its central inspiration the platform conforms more closely to the kind of individualism which Woodrow Wilson called the "New Freedom" than it does to the kind of collectivism which progressives like Senator La Follette believe in, and, in certain of his moods, Governor Roosevelt himself.

Thus the platform starts with a declaration for drastic economy and for a balanced budget to maintain the national credit and a sound currency. It does not contemplate a currency inflation in the spirit of Bryanism or an expansion of governmental activity to create a new social order, as progressives with a collectivist philosophy advocate. The general attitude is favorable to retrenchment and laissez-faire, to competition among small producers rather than to planned and centralized establishments. The intention is to repeal government favors rather than to increase positive government activity. The power of the government is involved to protect the small producers, the small depositors, the small tradesmen, so that they may work out their own salvation. A Communist would say that the ideal of the platform is not conservative, but in the exact sense of the word reactionary; that what the platform looks to is a return to the simpler, freer capitalism of a generation ago.

It is a truly Jeffersonian platform, not merely as to liquor but in its economic philosophy. It is a platform which Gladstone and the Victorian liberals in England would have understood: its ideals are the peace, retrenchment and reform of the pre-war world, of that simpler world for which, though it may be irrevocably gone, most Americans instinctively yearn. Therefore, the platform should prove to be very popular with the voters and rather difficult to live up to.

Thus, for example, in dealing with the banking problem one looks in vain for any far-reaching commitment to reconstruct the banking system. The platform confines itself to suggesting that depositors in suspended banks be helped to realize more quickly on the assets, that national banks be more rigidly supervised, that security affiliates be abolished and that speculation be frowned upon. There is no suggestion that our banking system is archaic and needs to be radically reconstructed. Yet surely, if the crisis has taught us anything, it is that a new national banking system is imperatively needed. Such a new banking system cannot, however, be established within the framework of the old States' Rights philosophy.

The platform is the handiwork of men composing the right wing of the Roosevelt following. The only important exception is the prohibition plank, which in all its fundamentals was dictated by Al Smith and adopted because the wet sentiment was irresistible. It is a platform which comes from men like Senator Cordell Hull and Colonel House rather than from Senators Wheeler, Dill and Huey Long. It would seem to indicate that in the determination of party policy it is the Wilson rather than the Bryan tradition which is just now dominant.

July 1, 1932

XI. DURING THE INTERMISSION

The breathing-space; time for the final bargaining

Chicago, July 1

The author of this dispatch is no more fit at this moment to write about the struggle to nominate a President than the delegates are to make a nomination. He is, as they are, so stupefied by oratory, brass bands, bad air, perspiration, sleeplessness and soft drinks that the fate of mankind is as nothing compared with his longing for a bath, a breakfast and a bed. We have been given the third degree, and no man who has been through what we in Chicago have been through since about 9 o'clock Wednesday evening will ever again have difficulty in realizing how a blameless man, if he were tortured enough, might be persuaded to confess that he had stolen the crown jewels and eloped with Cæsar's wife.

With such shreds of mentality as remain with me, I think I can dimly remember that some time before dawn on Friday the Roosevelt managers decided to proceed with the balloting and settle the matter. I recall, too, that we were informed in the press gallery that the Roosevelt bandwagon would start at the end of the first ballot. I can also recall that when their bandwagon did not start the Roosevelt managers wanted to adjourn in order to have time to find out what they had to offer whom, particularly what they had to offer Speaker Garner, Mr. Hearst, Governor White of Ohio and Mayor Cermak of Chicago in order to obtain the votes necessary to save mankind. It also remains in my memory that at this point in the proceedings Mayor Hague of Jersey City and the other allied generals wanted to continue balloting on the theory, it would seem, that no man can betray you when he is asleep.

However, by about o o'clock this morning it had been amply demonstrated that unless somebody betrayed somebody else there never would be a nomination. So as this is being written the delegates are in bed and their bosses, if they come from the Northeast, their leaders if they come from the South and West, are trying to negotiate the great betrayal which is now absolutely essential to a successful conclusion of these proceedings.

It may be that before these lines are printed the matter will have been arranged by the bosses and the leaders or that at any rate the convention will somehow have found a way to break out of jail. Nothing that can now be arranged or decided will please all the delegates. That alone appears at this hour to be fairly certain. All else would be vain prophecy, and prudently I refrain from guessing what tomorrow morning's newspapers will say, knowing that though the ancient oracles often pretended to be in an inspired stupor, here in Chicago every one is really stupefied and no one is inspired.

July 2, 1932

XII. THE NOMINATION OF ROOSEVELT

Breakup of the opposition; Mr. Roosevelt's probable troubles with his friends

Chicago, July 3

The anti-Roosevelt coalition broke up at the appropriate point when California and Texas went over to the majority. The Garner candidacy never had any vitality and the Garner delegates had no good reason for separating themselves from the other Roosevelt states in the South and West. That Mr. McAdoo was able to make the announcement which prevented a deadlock must have seemed to him dramatically just, for in 1924 he was himself the victim of the kind of deadlock which the opposition was trying to organize. It was also fitting that he should proclaim the victory of the Roosevelt forces. They were the same forces which supported him eight years ago and Bryan thirty-six years ago. These forces had a decisive majority at all times, and they control the Democratic party in the nation. The minority could try to argue with them. It had no power to prevent them from imposing their will on the convention.

It is just as well that the decision was reached quickly. For just underneath the surface an appalling amount of bitterness had developed. The Roosevelt delegates were being persuaded that the opposition to Governor Roosevelt's nomination arose entirely from sectarian or economic interests, and the Roosevelt managers encouraged this belief. As passions were aroused the conviction grew that there was no such thing as a disinterested and liberal objection to the Governor on the ground of his qualifications. This conviction was reinforced by the brutal intolerance of the galleries and by the pressure exerted by men connected with public utilities and banks. Had the convention been deadlocked for a few more ballots there would have been an explosion of resentment which would have produced the utmost confusion and fury throughout the country. The temper of the opposition was also reaching a point where the fires of 1928 were again blazing and there was extreme danger that wounds would have been inflicted that could not soon have beeen healed.

Governor Roosevelt is the nominee of a majority which imputes to him an attitude of mind which is not normally his own. They have read into his phrases, and have assumed from the bitterness of some of the Eastern opposition that, like Bryan, he is their champion and that he has no other allegiances. There is bound to ensue a continual pushing and pulling among his advisers. Thus Governor Roosevelt owes his platform to the Wilson liberals, but he owes his nomination to the descendants of Bryan and to the living influence of William Randolph Hearst. At the moment of his triumphant nomination on Friday night it was Mr. McAdoo, who has a promise of Hearst support for the Senate in California, who took the center of the stage, and it was former Senator Reed, of Missouri, the bitterest of all Wilson's enemies, who delivered a keynote address in which he denounced Wilson's ideas. Franklin D. Roosevelt will need all his strength to manage his friends. There are deep antagonisms among them, and he will not find it easy to satisfy them all or to keep the peace among them.

Perhaps the most important thing to be said at this moment is that the independent voter need be in no hurry to take his position in this campaign. We shall see many things before November. We are now at a point where no one can any longer devote himself to promoting the ideal candidate. The choice is narrowed to Hoover, Roosevelt and Thomas among candidates and to the Republican, the Democratic and the Socialist parties as they are now controlled. Those who can find in any one of these men or in any of these parties the ideal of their heart's desire are fortunate indeed. The rest of us will, I imagine, spend the next few months realizing that John Morley was right when he said that politics was the science of the second best.

July 4, 1932

· XI ·

THE SOCIAL SCENE: PERSONALITIES
OF THE DAY

I. THE UNDERWORLD

*Our sense of impotence before organized crime; two
great traditions which make for lawlessness*

OF the great emotions aroused by the kidnaping of the
Lindbergh baby, little seems to remain except a feeling of
dull defeat. Men and women continue to hope that somehow the kidnapers will be moved to relent and restore the
child, but in regard to the condition of general insecurity of
which the deed is a heartbreaking symbol there is a kind
of despairing impotence.

The people know that they are beset by organized criminals
who operate on a scale which has horrified the civilized
world. They know that unless they master this evil it will
master them. They know that a generation of city children
is growing up in an atmosphere where racketeering has become an established institution. These children hear their
elders complain and do nothing. Or they see their elders
acquiesce and pay tribute. They even hear the racketeers
admired for their cunning. Thus new recruits are enlisted
and in a vicious circle the evil perpetuates itself.

The most destructive phase of the whole thing is the
feeling of the ordinary man that he is impotent and defeated.
For unless he can translate his indignation into action, he

will lose it and become demoralized, and the public spirit upon which everything else depends will evaporate in words. What, for example, could be more devitalizing than the conduct of the Administration in this matter? The President on the day he was inaugurated declared that crime was increasing and that confidence in rigid and speedy justice was decreasing; he announced that a remedy for these evils was "the most sore necessity of our times." And then what happened? He appointed a commission. The commission investigated. The commission reported. The President dismissed a vital part of the report, and then the excitement was over. The great war against crime was forgotten and the authority of the government impaired by the humiliating exhibition it had given of starting something which it could not finish.

We may quite pertinently ask ourselves what there is in our national life which paralyzes our efforts to deal with this problem. We cannot expect, I think, that a nation of pioneers and immigrants, who have lost touch with the established habits of the past and are still restless and unsettled in their constantly changing environment, should have attained the degree of order and discipline that exists among some of the older nations of the West. But we might reasonably hope that we would not sink into a defeatist attitude before the barbarism in our midst. There must be some reason why we are so continually frustrated when we seek to arouse ourselves into action.

My own notion is that we are constantly frustrated by two traditions which we deeply cherish.

The first is our almost instinctive belief that the laws must represent not merely a reasonable adjustment of human interests but what the majority of the voters regard as the highest and noblest ideals. Thus American legislation makes no concession to the weakness of human nature. Our laws are written by men who have pleased their constituents by writing into law innumerable declarations of moral faith, and taken as a body the American statute books are an encyclopedia of moral perfection. They outlaw not only all crimes and frauds but also all the vices and peccadillos and impure thoughts of man.

So thoroughly imbued are the American people with the idea that the law must express moral perfection that a proposal to modify prohibition is widely regarded as propaganda for drunkenness, a proposal to modify the laws against other sins is regarded as an invitation to a carnival of licentiousness. As a result, the American people have insisted upon outlawing human propensities in which they rather generally indulge. They have pushed into the underworld activities which in all other civilized countries are regulated by custom and convention. And by their moral fervor as lawmakers they have made a large part of the people allies and clients of lawbreakers.

But not only do the American people insist that the written law shall be uncompromising with unrighteousness; they insist at the same time that the government which executes these laws shall be weak. The same voters and the same lawmakers who enact laws that no despotism has ever been able to enforce are jealous to the point of absurdity at intrusting the executive and judiciary with power. It is fair to say, I think, that we have the strongest laws and the weakest government of any highly civilized people. Nowhere else, I think, are the police of a great city like New York under the control of politicians who are locally elected. Nowhere else, I think, are judges so tied to fluctuating political majorities and nowhere else are they so ignominiously entangled with legislative rules.

The American distrust of the executive and of the judiciary, which expresses itself in a refusal to give them authority and dignity, is, I suppose, an inheritance from the struggle of the colonies against the crown. Whatever its origin, there can be little doubt that Americans unconsciously think that the preservation of their liberty is bound up with the weakness of the executive and judiciary.

These two ingredients of our national mind account in large measure, I think, for the rise of the underworld and for our impotence in combating it. By passing excessive laws we put a premium on lawlessness; by refusing power to the government we stultify the execution of the laws. These, too, are the reasons why our efforts at reform expire so quickly. Any reform that amounts to anything requires modification of laws which embody exorbitant moral aspirations and a grant of power which must look like an infringement of liberty.

The American people are as yet unprepared to give up their right to have laws which express their faith in moral perfection. They are unprepared to establish governments which have authority and power if that means giving up a measure of liberty and democracy. But until they are prepared to alter their basic prepossessions in these respects they will continue to have majestic laws and immense lawlessness.

April 1, 1932

II. THE LINDBERGH CASE AND THE NEWSPAPERS

The dilemma of editors; news that interferes with the detection of crime

The kidnaping of the Lindbergh baby has presented a difficult case to conscientious American newspaper editors. They have had, on the one hand, to consider the enormous interest of their readers in every conceivable fact and rumor and, on the other hand, the repeated requests of Colonel Lindbergh that the publication of clues and of news of his movements be avoided so as not to interfere with the recovery of the child. Last week the United Press invited a large number of newspaper editors to express their opinions as to the policy which ought to be pursued in reporting the case. These opinions are, as might be expected, so varied that no clear judgment emerges which might be considered the verdict of the newspaper profession.

It is often said that hard cases do not make good law. The Lindbergh case is certainly a hard case. What makes it a hard case is the fact that the need for secrecy surrounding the negotiations to ransom the child arise out of a fear that publicity will frighten away the kidnapers. The request for secrecy rests upon the assumption that the ransom of the child involves not only money but immunity. It is a national humiliation that the life of a child should depend upon so abject a surrender to the forces of organized crime. Therefore, while there is no doubt that American sentiment would be virtually unanimous on a willingness to surrender to the kidnapers in order to recover the child, responsible editors must hesitate at the thought of agreeing to any general rule of the profession which would establish a precedent compelling them to become accomplices after the fact in crimes of this sort.

It follows that the request for secrecy to permit dealings with the kidnapers must rest solely upon an appeal to the sympathy of the editors and their public. They can be asked to coöperate on no other ground than that the recovery of the child is poignantly desired by the American people. It is not their duty to contribute toward the immunity of the kidnapers. It simply happens to be a rather revolting necessity. What the press is asked to do, looked at from the vantage

point of high public policy and of morals, is akin to lying
like a gentleman to save a friend. It is bad in the abstract
to lie. It is bad in the abstract to suppress news in order to
countenance crime. But there are times when only a cad
will be so great a prig that he won't lie for his friend, and
there are times when newspapers have to act on simple
human intuitions and compromises rather than upon abstract principles.

The moral problem is simplified by the fact that no newspaper that I know of has taken the Spartan position that
the child should not be ransomed at the price of immunity
to the kidnapers. It is tacitly agreed that the immunity should
be granted if the child can thereby be recovered. Consequently, the question whether to print all the news obtainable
is reduced to a question of self-interest. The Lindbergh case
is a great news story and under the competitive conditions
prevailing among newspapers there is a tangible sacrifice
when any newspaper suppresses precisely those parts of the
story which are most interesting.

Nevertheless, once a newspaper accepts the conclusion that
the child should be recovered at any price, including the
compounding of the felony, it ceases to have any moral justification whatever for printing any clue which might interfere with the negotiations. To agree that the kidnapers may
go scot free, but to insist in the name of the freedom of the
press upon the right to publish everything, is to swallow a
camel and strain at a gnat. It is to abandon the principle
that the law must not be nullified and to invoke a principle
of liberty which happens to be profitable.

I have said that the Lindbergh kidnaping is a hard case
and, therefore, it does not make a good precedent. Were the
facts in the case a little different, a much more important
and general problem in newspaper policy would be raised.
Let us suppose that instead of trying to ransom the child

with gold and immunity, we were dealing merely with the efforts of the police to catch a gang of criminals. That is, after all, the normal situation when a crime has been committed. Kidnaping, because a child becomes the hostage for the safety of the criminals, is a crime of a very special sort. In other crimes there is no doubt as to the necessity of relentless pursuit.

How far, under normal conditions, is it the function of the press to engage in the pursuit and to give publicity to all the clues it can lay its hands on? The American newspaper tradition is quite different from that of other countries. Our newspapers feel free to publish what they can find out and it is the habit of the police, chiefly because they like to stand well with the newspapers, to make the pursuit of criminals difficult by giving criminals all kinds of advance information. When a sensational crime has been committed the American detective works in a blaze of publicity. It is difficult to avoid the feeling that this is one of the important reasons why we have such a large number of unsolved crimes. It can not be good for the detectives to be thinking of the headlines and of the good will of the city editor, and it must be very helpful to the criminal to be kept so well informed about the plans of his pursuers.

My own notion is that when the American people finally arouse themselves to take action against lawlessness, one of the many things they will have to attend to is the practice of printing news which might interfere with the detection of a crime. I think I appreciate the importance of a free press. But I am quite unable to believe that the press would be less free if some reasonable restraint were put upon its right to make instantaneous copy out of clues which are vital to the detection of a crime.

April 21, 1932

III. THE PLACE OF THE SUPREME COURT IN AMERICAN LIFE[1]

Its work in bridging the future and past; imminence of great changes involving new decisions by the courts

In the vast range of his powers there are few in which the President exercises so far-reaching an influence on the nation's history as in the selection of judges of the Supreme Court. When he makes these appointments he deals not with the emergencies of the moment but with the future, which no man can clearly foresee. For though the business of the court is to decide particular cases before it, it is through these cases that it adjusts not only the relations of the individual to the separate states and to the United States, of the states to one another and to the Union, of the three branches of the government to each other, but also acts as the guardian and promoter of acceptable and workable compromise between the past and the present, between settled traditions and the evolution of public purposes.

It is not enough, therefore, that the court should be composed of competent and upright judges. It is essential that its deliberations should be infused with prophetic and creative willingness to administer the Constitution, as Mr. Justice Holmes has said, "not simply by taking the words and a dictionary but by considering their origin and the line of their growth," realizing that these legal texts "have called into life a being the development of which could not have been foreseen completely by the most gifted of its begetters," and that, therefore, cases "must be considered in the light of our whole experience. . . ."

[1] Written just after the resignation of Justice Oliver Wendell Holmes, to whose seat President Hoover appointed Judge Cardozo of the New York State Court of Appeals.

At this moment, it is important it be not forgotten that we stand upon the threshold of great changes in American life. There is a crisis in the world and for the time being our energies are absorbed in meeting it. But a crisis cannot be permanent; it must resolve itself somehow—whether according to our plans or by sheer force of brute circumstances will depend upon the amount of intelligence, courage, and collective discipline that can be mustered in time. The crisis will, nevertheless, pass. And however it passes, it will leave us with the urgent necessity and the compelling desire to reconsider many established things and to experiment with new forms of collective effort. For only the blind imagine that we shall find ourselves back where we were in the post-war "normalcy" or in the pre-war innocence. The processes of history are cumulative and irreversible, and when the tension of the crisis relaxes, we shall find ourselves in one of the great eras of reorganization and pioneering.

It would be naïve to think that men can or will be satisfied with the kind of life which they now have. They know, and every one knows, that invention and technical skill have opened up possibilities of security and plenty which are to a grievous extent unused or perverted. The awful paradox of our time, that there should be want in the midst of abundance, is self-evident proof that the prevailing political and economic arrangements and policies and methods of administering affairs are deeply and seriously at fault. A period of great changes is not merely indicated. It is certain.

In such a period it is crucial whether or not change is continuous with the past, whether there is a sudden break with established wisdom or the use of that wisdom to season new enterprise. Of all the Western peoples the English-speaking nations have been the most successful in finding ways to preserve and yet to change. Their secret is their sense of the law, which in their great periods they have looked upon not as an iron frame, but as a garment which can be cut and altered so that it always covers them and yet allows them to move freely.

It is the business of the Court in our political system to oversee this cutting and alteration of the garment that it may always fit comfortably and endure. That has been the work of the judges from Marshall to Holmes and those who see ahead ought to hope ardently for a true successor in that great line.

January 21, 1932

IV. PROGRESSIVES AND CONSERVATIVES IN TIME OF CRISIS

The mind of the nation; conservative changes needed for the immediate juncture, progressive ideas for the future

To read the *Congressional Record* with even moderate diligence is a not inconsiderable punishment, for on an ordinary day our legislators have no difficulty in producing up to two hundred columns of print. Now, of course, even the most conscientious student of affairs is not required to read every word of all this. He can skip a good many things. Nevertheless, the *Congressional Record* is worth the trouble, for it is the only central place where the diverse opinions of the American people are brought together.

It is, of course, clear that the important division of opinion is not between Republicans and Democrats but between conservatives and progressives. It is no less clear, I think, that what divides the two groups is a difference of feeling toward the established financial and industrial powers: the conservative feeling is that the country must work with and through the existing powers to set the economic machine running again; the progressive feeling is that the existing powers have forfeited the right to the confidence of the country by failing to avert the breakdown of the economic machine.

It was to this progressive feeling that Governor Roosevelt was appealing when he said the other night that the Hoover Administration "can think in terms only of the top of the social and economic structure" and that it had forgotten or did not wish to remember "the infantry of our economic army." The rejoinder of the New York *Times* in asking him whether he had ever seen "an infantry which did not need commanders" reflects the conservative feeling. The essential difference is over the question of confidence in the existing commanders.

In proposing measures to meet the immediate emergencies of the crisis the initiative has lain with the conservatives. It is they who have brought forward the Reconstruction Finance Corporation, it is they who worked out the Glass-Steagall bill, it is they who have insisted that a balanced budget in the government was the basis for an expansion of credit in private industry. The progressives have had no agreed program to deal with the immediate emergency. They have had a program to relieve suffering, though even here they have been divided; thus Governor Roosevelt has described the proposals to produce an inflation by great bond issues devoted to public works as an example of "the habit of the unthinking to turn in times like these to the illusions of economic magic."

The attention of the progressives is not centered upon the emergency but upon reforms designed to correct the causes which have produced it. Thus they are either skeptical or hostile as to measures to arrest the deflation of values and to stabilize credit. They are greatly concerned with measures which would in the future prevent the frenzied finance of the boom and the host of evils which have resulted from over-expansion, from over-capitalization and from the fantastically complicated concentration of power through financial manipulation. Thus far the conservatives have shown no adequate response which avowed that they too appreciated the need of reforms. Partly because of their preoccupation with immediate necessities, but in the main because of their innate conservatism, they have failed to convey to the country any adequate sense that they realize that a far-reaching reconstruction has become necessary.

Thus there is no meeting of minds. There is only an exchange of epithets and a glowering resentment. The progressives, without an immediate program, are deadlocked with the conservatives, who have no far-reaching program. The position may be illustrated by the controversy over the Glass bill to amend the banking laws. This bill in certain of its central provisions is a drastic attempt to prevent the kind of credit inflation which preceded the crash. The bill as drafted would, if enacted today, accentuate the deflation, which is already excessive. The conservatives have quite properly opposed it. But in opposing it they have failed to make clear what they must all know, that a great reform of the banking system, comparable with that which resulted in the formation of the Federal Reserve system itself, has become imperative. For it is inconceivable that the country will not seek and apply remedies for the demonstrated weaknesses and evils of the existing banking structure. But because Senator Glass and his followers are preoccupied with the need for long-range reforms to the exclusion of the immediate emergency, whereas the conservatives and the bankers are preoccupied with the immediate emergency to the exclusion of deeper reform, there is confusion, misunderstanding and destructive conflict.

In a realistic view of the situation it is plain, I think, that the time is too short and the crisis is too urgent to make serious reforms in the economic system and then set it going again. It must be set going again long before the desirable reforms can be invented, debated, enacted and introduced, or else there will be a breakdown on such a scale as no sincere progressive would care to face.

On the other hand, the conservatives must expect suspicion and resentment to mount higher and higher unless they have the intelligence to see that an era of anarchic acquisitiveness like that of the last decade must inexorably inaugurate an era of far-reaching reforms. The nation's experiences up to and through the great depression of the nineties produced the issues which culminated in the reforms of Theodore Roosevelt and Woodrow Wilson. In all human probability something of the same sort will happen again, for it is an illusion to suppose that there will soon be another boom in which all this suffering and anxiety will be quickly forgotten. The issues which are gradually crystallizing out of the bewilderment and complaints of the people will endure and will provide the subject matter of public life for a long time to come.

April 12, 1932

V. THE DEFECTS OF OUR REPRESENTATIVE SYSTEM

Disillusionment with Congress; local interests vs. the general good

The last ten years have been a period of disillusionment with the working of elected governments. Both in the crisis of the war and in the crisis of reconstruction the democratic system has seemed again and again to present almost insuperable difficulties to wise and prompt decisions. That has been the universal experience, and the behavior of Congress during the last few months has added new distrust to the doubts which were already in the air.

The chief complaint against Congress, and it is well founded, is that it does not succeed in representing the national interest, that its members are preoccupied with their own special interest in reëlection, and that to this end, in the effort to placate, cajole, and even to bribe their constituents, they will as a general rule sacrifice every other consideration. Thus it has been plain throughout the debates on the tax bill and on the appropriations that what was moving the individual members was not loyalty to the national interest as a whole but an extreme sensitiveness to the demands and wishes of groups of voters.

Many explanations have been current as to why this demoralization prevails. It has been suggested that the term of office is too short, that a Congressman is no sooner seated than he must start preparing for reëlection. It has been suggested that the direct primary has shattered party responsibility and made Congress a place where each member must shift for himself. It has been pointed out that the custom of selecting Congressmen solely from the districts where they live deprives the country of the services of able men.

These are, it seems to me, sound criticisms of our system, and no doubt it would be improved if the term of office were longer, if the party system were revived, and if able men could be elected from districts in which they do not necessarily reside. But the trouble is really deeper than these reforms imply. The trouble is that the country has abandoned the conception of representative government and is trying to deal with enormously complex problems through an assembly of mere delegates. The American people has forgotten that if it is to have good government it must elect men, not to perform errands for their constituents, but to use their judgment freely, and freely to speak and act upon that judgment.

The real problem at Washington today was stated with perfect clearness by Edmund Burke some years before the American Republic was founded. This is a good time to turn back to Burke, who was one of the wisest men of his century and among the profoundest political thinkers of the tradition which we inherit. Burke's constituency was the city of Bristol, and in 1774 he and Cruger were the two Whig candidates. Cruger had told the voters that if they elected him he would do what they desired. Burke abjured this doctrine and in his speeches plainly told the voters that he would not be their slave. He was anxious to meet their wishes. He would prefer their interest to his own. But "his unbiased opinion, his mature judgment, his enlightened conscience he (as a representative) ought not to sacrifice to you, to any man, or to any set of men living. These he does not derive from your pleasure; no, nor from the law and the constitution. They are a trust from Providence for the abuse of which he is deeply answerable. Your representative owes you, not his industry alone, but his judgment; and he betrays instead of serving you, if he sacrifices it to your opinion."

That is the heart of the matter. This conception of the relation between the representative and his constituents rested upon Burke's conviction as to what a national legislature ought to be: "Parliament," he said, "is not a *congress* of ambassadors from different and hostile interests; which interests each must maintain, as an agent and advocate, against other agents and advocates; but Parliament is a *deliberative* assembly of *one* nation, with *one* interest, that of the whole; where, not local purposes, not local prejudices, ought to guide, but the general good, resulting from the general reason of the whole. You choose a member, indeed; but when you have chosen him, he is not a member of Bristol, but he is a member of *Parliament*. If the local constituent should have an interest, or should form an hasty opinion, evidently opposite to the real good of the rest of the community, the member for that place ought to be as far as any other from any endeavor to give it effect."

This is the ideal of representative government. You may say that it is suitable to a race of heroes and of saints. Perhaps. But this is the ideal, and as long as we profess to be living under representative government it is useful to recall it.

May 17, 1932

VI. THE QUESTION OF A PLANNED SOCIETY

Governor Roosevelt's vague Atlanta speech; the difficulty of a planned society—the choice of objectives

In taking his stand in favor of what Mr. Stuart Chase and Mr. George Soule and others are calling a Planned Society, Governor Roosevelt has sought to identify himself with the aspirations and necessities of the times we live in. Few can contemplate the paradox of poverty in the midst of plenty without feeling that the modern industrial order must somehow be managed more consciously than it has been in the past. Few can look upon the results of the haphazard greed of the recent past without feeling that our highly integrated economy cannot be operated by a preponderantly competitive and acquisitive individualism. There will be little serious dissent among thoughtful men on these generalities. Some, to be sure, will regret the passing of laissez-faire. Many will be highly skeptical as to whether we possess the wisdom and disinterestedness for a high degree of conscious control over human affairs. But few will deny that far-reaching controls must and will be attempted.

All this the Governor sees and proclaims, and if he were looking forward to no more active a duty than lecturing and writing essays, one might say that it is useful, though very easy, to point out in a large and vague manner the general direction which mankind will probably take. But as Governor Roosevelt aspires to lead the march, it is pertinent to inquire whether he shows any signs of knowing where he is really going and what he is really talking about.

The Atlanta speech does not, it seems to me, show any sign whatever that Franklin D. Roosevelt has ever come to grips with the doctrine of "planning." For a planned society will not come into being by accumulating a collection of blueprints. Somebody must be given power to execute the plans, and Governor Roosevelt did not give even a hint as to who those somebodies should be and how they should be chosen. A planned society, furthermore, is one in which the somebodies have power not only over all men's property but over all men's careers. Otherwise they cannot execute their plans. But Governor Roosevelt, if he understands this, does not, as we shall see in a moment, care to face the sacrifice of liberty which his doctrine implies. Finally, a planned society must, as he said, be planned for clearly defined objectives. Yet except in terms so general as to be empty of meaning, Governor Roosevelt made no attempt to define these objectives. The reason he did not define them is that "objectives" is simply a new name for issues which divide men.

In Russia and in Italy the question of who is to exercise the power to plan has been answered by the establishment of militarized dictatorships. This is obviously not Governor Roosevelt's notion. For only a few weeks ago he publicly thanked God that the American ideal of public man was George Washington and not Mussolini or Lenin. He is equally clear that the bankers and captains of industry won't do. Who then is to exercise the centralized power which every sincere planner recognizes as necessary? That is a difficult question to answer, but the problem is not honestly faced if it is ignored. Ruling out dictators and the present overlords of finance and business, whom does he substitute? Elected officials? Presidential appointees?

This is no academic question. We are confronted with it right now. For the attempt is being made to plan and manage credit, the most decisive element in the economic order. To whom does Governor Roosevelt wish to intrust this power? To Congress, as so many of his supporters proposed when they voted for the Goldsborough Bill? To the Administration in office, as was the case during 1928 and 1929? To an "independent" body responsive to the opinion of commercial and financial interests? To ask these questions is not "to confuse purpose with method," as the Governor so blandly suggests, but to test the reality and the sincerity and the significance of vague purposes by concrete standards.

The second question—which concerns the power to manage not only property but lives—can fortunately be discussed in the light of a concrete illustration offered by the Governor himself. He pointed out, as an example of planlessness, that the normal schools are turning out more trained teachers than the schools can absorb. He complained that this "oversupply" would not exist if we had "the wit or the forethought to tell" the teachers that their profession is "gravely oversupplied." Does the Governor really think that "telling" young men and women that a profession is oversupplied will keep them out of it? Does he not realize that each young person will still believe that there is room for *him?* If Governor Roosevelt is going to "plan" the supply of teachers, he will have to do more than tell things to young men and women. He will have to make it difficult for them to enter the normal schools by raising the requirements or by fixing quotas or by some other device which will rule out the excess numbers. That might be done in respect to teachers and other professions. But what does Governor Roosevelt propose to do about the oversupply of miners, shopkeepers, stenographers, wheat farmers and the rest? Does he propose to "tell" them how they may attempt to earn their living? Or does he propose to have a public agency decide that for them?

This brings us to the third question—the "definite objectives" for which the plans are to be made. The moment this question is asked we are face to face with the contentious issues which every one, whether he calls himself a planner or not, is struggling with. Are you going to plan your wheat farming, your cotton farming, your copper mining, your automobile production, for the domestic market alone or for export as well? It will make a world of difference in your plans which way you answer these questions. If you decide for the domestic market alone, you will have to make some very far-reaching plans for your permanently unemployed farmers, miners and industrial workers. If you decide for exports, how do you propose to be paid? By accepting imports or by lending money abroad?

No one can even begin to "plan" the American economic system who has not answered these questions and settled them decisively. But these are the questions which all the world is debating: these are the questions on which all the chief problems of tariffs, international finance, and foreign affairs turn. "Planning" is no answer to them. Planning can only take place after they are answered. In other words, planning is not a substitute for statesmanship. It is dependent upon it.

It is here, if I may say so, that the American advocates of planning need to do some more realistic thinking. They have been misled, I think, by a false analogy between engineering and politics into thinking that human society can be planned the way an ocean liner, for example, is planned. They overlook the fact that in an engineering product the "objectives" are clear and definite, and only methods have to be devised, whereas in a human society it is the objectives which divide men into parties, sects, classes and nations. The issues in politics that matter are almost always about objectives.

That is why the only actual experiment in a planned society is being made by men who do not tolerate differences of opinion about objectives. The Russians are at least realists. If you do tolerate differences as to fundamental policy, a planned society in the full sense of the word is impossible. For any important change in policy will upset the premises on which your plans are based.

May 25, 1932

VII.   CRISIS   AND   RENEWAL

The purgative effects of a great depression; incentives to new energy and enterprise

In the past ten years there has appeared a large literature prophesying the end of our civilization. Sometimes there is an accent of hope in the promise of a wholly new and infinitely better order of human life and at other times there is a dull foreboding of decadence and deterioration. Thus there are those to whom Russia has become what America was in the nineteenth century: the land of the future where the ancient pains of the world are to be cured. And there are also those who have no hope and who take a kind of pleasure in the grim jest that the last depression of this magnitude is known as the Dark Ages and persisted for five hundred years.

They are agreed, however, on the thesis that the chief characteristic of our time is the breakdown of established things. An overwhelming array of facts can be adduced in support. The Great War ended in the collapse of the European empires and of those remnants of the feudal system which had survived the revolutions since 1789. Since the War there has been a breakdown of a very large part of the financial obligations and of the economic organization to which men have been accustomed. There has been a vast disillusionment not only with the existing order but with its idealism over liberty, democracy, nationalism, and progress. One could go on endlessly, for here is endless material, pointing out the variety and the extent to which there have broken down, or been overthrown, or rejected, the things which the pre-war generations held to be most precious or most certain.

Yet I suspect that when enough time has passed to bring this present into perspective, the historians will see a renewal of energy where we see a breakdown of achievements, and that they will see continuity where we see abrupt change.

For what is the chief human fact behind all this liquidation of old arrangements, of old prestige, of old reputations and of old interests? Is it not the clearing away of rigid accumulations and of the hardened consequences of misjudgments that would, if they endured, block and constrict the enterprise of the generation which is now on the threshold of life? This is a hard time for those who are irrevocably committed to these establishments. It is a cruel and bitter time for those who are the present victims of disorder. But for the young and for those who are free in spirit it is a time of liberation and of opportunity. For them there remains, come what may, their own energy, and the richness of the earth, the heritage of invention and skill and the corpus of human wisdom. They need no more. Their paths will be more open, and what in one light is a vast breakdown of hopes is in another light the clearing away of debts and rigidities and pre-emptions that would choke them on their way.

In this large sense depression and crisis are not the collapse of our system, but a furious purge. Conceivably a system can be devised which would be stable without accumulating an insupportable burden of vested interests. But until such a system comes into being there is in every society as we know it a fatal tendency to accumulate too many obligations, to let arrangements become rigid, to let those who have retired from active life acquire too large claims, to let the grip of the place holders become too strong, to let seniority and privilege block the advance of youth and enterprise. So there must come inevitably a time of liquidation.

The changes which ensue bring new faces and new formulæ and sometimes new symbols, and there is for a while a great liberation of energies. But the new men in their turn began to accumulate and to become set, and so the enduring changes are far smaller than the apparent ones. The new men are less free than they thought, and they must compromise their wishes with the inexorable necessities of man's existence on this planet and his ancient constitution. So the permanent forms of human life and of national existence change far less than it would seem that they must change when everything seems to be moving; for while nothing human is eternal, it is also true that nothing in the deeper patterns of human relations is easily altered.

Thus no one springtime lasts very long, and no winter; and though nothing endures, the sap rises again to renew mortality.

July 22, 1932

VIII. DWIGHT W. MORROW[1]

An exemplar of sincerity in public life; the superior importance of human relationships over human institutions

Dwight Morrow entered American public life at a time when all political values were inflated and unreal. The war propaganda had dislocated the sense of truth and had brought into being marvellously effective devices for selling things at more than they were worth. It was the appearance, not the reality, that counted, and the politician, ambitious to succeed, surrounded himself not with the wisest counsellors but with the smartest press agents. It was the function of these press agents to create a fictitious public character for the multitude to gape at, and the utmost care was taken by the politician never under any circumstances to let his private and real thoughts disturb the carefully built up fiction.

This radical insincerity was regarded in the post-war years as the only practical politics. The effects were devastating. The public man himself became so preoccupied with maintaining his public personality that he tended to lose what personality and what personal conviction he may have had. He became so interested in the "reaction" to what he was doing that he lost sight of what he was doing. Plain speaking and honest thinking being at a discount, the public was fooled and yet knew it was being fooled. The younger gener-

[1] Senator Dwight W. Morrow died suddenly on October 6, 1931.

ation who first encountered public life in this period turned
from it in cynical disgust, and among the people generally
there was less faith in the character of the government than
at any time within memory.

The historic achievement of Dwight Morrow was that
he broke through these conventions of insincerity in public
life and raised a standard of intrinsic worth to which men
could repair. Like the greatest teachers, he taught by example. When the demonstration had been made, as in Mexico and in his campaign for Senator, the artificial and syn-
thetic careers which had looked so important seemed
inexpressibly tawdry. Morrow did nothing to promote his
popularity; it gathered about him from all quarters and from
every station in a kind of deep murmur of implicit confidence
and deeply felt need. For the rise of Morrow in the esteem
of the American people was like an awakening out of a daze
of appearances and a rediscovery of the solid, honest substance of real things.

No man of our time has had the complete trust of so many
different kinds of people. What were the qualities which
made this man trusted in Wall Street and in Moscow, at the
Vatican and among the Mexican revolutionists, among hard-
boiled politicians and among star-eyed reformers? Was it
because he succeeded in being all things to all men? On the
contrary, it was because he based his whole public life on the
deep principle that the one common thing to which all the
warring sects of man must in the end submit is the truth
itself. From this principle he derived the working hypothesis
of his career which was to assume that every man was interested in the truth.

He knew quite as well as the most sophisticated among us
how often men, when left to their own devices, will deceive
themselves and others. Nevertheless, he proceeded on the
assumption that they intended to be honest, and by the very

force of the assumption made them justify him. That was, I believe, the inner secret of his marvellous successes as a negotiator. By divesting himself of all weapons but these which could promote understanding, his adversary had either to disarm too or feel wretchedly uncomfortable at having to be a deliberate villain. Here, at the heart of his power, Dwight Morrow had possession of an ancient, mystical insight into human character which the merely worldly can never know. Thus because he touched the deeper chords of their natures all sorts of men trusted him. They loved him because he had the essential human wisdom which remembers always all the octaves of the human spirit. It is a kind of wisdom which is almost submerged by the raw efficiency of our machine-made ways. He had it, and with it he turned not away from the world to a contemplative religious life, but to the management of the most immediate and practical affairs.

The peculiar genius of Dwight Morrow lay in the fact that he kept a mystical faith in men without losing his own intellectual standards. The commonest outcome of mysticism is muddle-headedness; the visionary can see nothing but the white light of the mystery, and for the rest his speech runs out into rhetoric and his actions into eccentricity. Dwight Morrow kept his mind by using it incessantly, so incessantly that it was sometimes exhausting to others and to himself. He lived at a pitch of mental activity many stages above that of the normal actively-minded man. His brain never stopped going and it never was aimless. It fed voraciously on anything and everything that came within the range of his attention, everlastingly purposeful, endlessly raising questions, forever finding explanations and solutions. He had the incandescence of genius and he never rested.

The acquired character of his mind, as distinguished from its native energies, was formed in the great tradition of English empirical thinking. Dwight Morrow was a genuinely learned man in the field of history, and had circumstances been different he might readily have been as eminent a scholar as he was a statesman. The history which he knew best was English and American history from the time of Cromwell. This meant that he knew intimately where were the roots of American institutions. Unlike most Americans of the present time, his mind was not severed from the past out of which this nation has come. He carried with him, as something known and understood, the central political tradition of American life, and in his own person he came to exemplify it. Those who have marveled that a successful banker should so quickly prove himself a successful statesman and an excellent practical politician will, I think, find a large part of the explanation there. Dwight Morrow did not come unprepared into public life. He came greatly prepared by the intimate acquaintance of a lifetime with the classic models of statecraft and politics. Thus the things which would have seemed new to an unread novice were through many precedents quite familiar to him.

Because of his loyalty to the Anglo-American tradition, it is impossible in our present intellectual confusion to classify him under such conventional labels as conservative or progressive. In a time when conservatives are for the most part high protectionists he was a free trader by deepest conviction; in a time when progressivism is enchanted with the prospect of regulating mankind from central places, he was a resolute believer in decentralization, preferring the evils of liberty to those of authority. But though the pattern of his thought was the classic liberal view of human affairs, he had no disposition to impose his ideas.

This is, perhaps, the aspect of the man which was most inscrutable to many who watched him. Although he had enormous prestige, it did not interest him to use his influence to promote causes and instigate political movements. Some ascribed this diffidence to his alleged political inexperience. It should really be ascribed to his ultimate wisdom about human affairs. It was this wisdom which made him put relatively small value upon specific laws, arrangements, policies, and the greatest store upon weaving thread by thread the fabric of common understanding. For he was of those who believe that men make institutions, and that all depends at last, not on the forms of things, but on the intrinsic quality of men's dealing with each other.

Thus it was in the art of honest dealing that he was a master, and an example to his country.

October 7, 1931

IX. EDISON: INVENTOR OF INVENTION [1]

A discoverer whose works insured the popular acceptance of science; the need for a better control of inventions and their results

It is impossible to measure the importance of Edison by adding up the specific inventions with which his name is associated. Far-reaching as many of them have been in their effect upon modern civilization, the total effect of Edison's career surpasses the sum of all of them. He did not merely make the incandescent lamp and the phonograph and innumerable other devices practicable for general use; it was given to him to demonstrate the power of applied science so concretely, so understandably, so convincingly that he altered the mentality of mankind. In his lifetime, largely because of his successes, there came into widest acceptance the revolutionary conception that man could by the use of his in-

[1] Thomas A. Edison died on October 17, 1931.

telligence invent a new mode of living on this planet; the human spirit, which in all previous ages had regarded the conditions of life as essentially unchanging and beyond man's control, confidently, and perhaps somewhat naïvely, adopted the conviction that anything could be changed and everything could be controlled.

This idea of progress is in the scale of history a very new idea. It seems first to have taken possession of a few minds in the seventeenth and eighteenth centuries as an accompaniment of the great advances in pure science. It gained greater currency in the first half of the nineteenth century when industrial civilization began to be transformed by the application of steam power. But these changes, impressive as they were, created so much human misery by the crude and cruel manner in which they were exploited that all through the century men instinctively feared and opposed the progress of machines, and of the sciences on which they rested. It was only at the end of the century, with the perfecting of the electric light bulb, the telephone, the phonograph, and the like, that the ordinary man began to feel that science could actually benefit him. Edison supplied the homely demonstrations which insured the popular acceptance of science, and clinched the popular argument, which had begun with Darwin, about the place of science in man's outlook upon life.

Thus he became the supreme propagandist of science and his name the great symbol of an almost blind faith in its possibilities. Thirty years ago, when I was a schoolboy, the ancient conservatism of man was still the normal inheritance of every child. We began to have electric lights, and telephones, and to see horseless carriages, but our attitude was a mixture of wonder, fear, and doubt. Perhaps these things would work. Perhaps they would not explode. Perhaps it would be amusing to play with them. Today every schoolboy not only takes all the existing inventions as much for granted as we took horses and dogs for granted, but, also, he is entirely convinced that all other desirable things can and will be invented. In my youth the lonely inventor who could not obtain a hearing was still the stock figure of the imagination. Today the only people who are not absolutely sure that television is perfected are the inventors themselves. No other person played so great a part as Edison in this change in human expectation, and finally, by the cumulative effect of his widely distributed inventions plus a combination of the modern publicity technique and the ancient myth-making faculty of men, he was lifted in the popular imagination to a place where he was looked upon not only as the symbol but as the creator of a new age.

In strict truth an invention is almost never the sole product of any one mind. The actual inventor is almost invariably the man who succeeds in combining and perfecting previous discoveries in such a way as to make them convenient and profitable. Edison had a peculiar genius for carrying existing discoveries to the point where they could be converted into practicable devices, and it would be no service to his memory, or to the cause of science which he serves so splendidly, to pretend that he invented by performing solitary miracles. The light which was born in his laboratory at Menlo Park fifty-two years ago was conceived in the antecedent experiments of many men in many countries over a period of nearly forty years, and these experiments in their turn were conceivable only because of the progress of the mathematical and physical sciences in the preceding two centuries.

The success which Edison finally achieved in his specific inventions demonstrated the possibility of invention as a continuing art. Mr. Hoover, in his tribute printed yesterday, pointed directly to this fact as constituting the historic importance of the man, when he said that Edison "did more than any other American to place invention on an organized basis of the utilization of the raw materials of pure science and discovery." Because of Edison, more than of any other man, scientific research has an established place in our society; because of the demonstrations he made, the money of taxpayers and stockholders has become available for studies the nature of which they do not often understand, though they appreciate their value and anticipate their ultimate pecuniary benefits.

It would be a shallow kind of optimism to assume that the introduction of the art of inventing has been an immediate and unmixed blessing to mankind. It is rather the most disturbing element in civilization, the most profoundly revolutionary thing which has ever been let loose in the world. For the whole ancient wisdom of man is founded upon the conception of a life which in its fundamentals changes imperceptibly if at all. The effect of organized, subsidized invention, stimulated by tremendous incentives of profit, and encouraged by an insatiable popular appetite for change, is to set all the relations of men in violent motion, and to create overpowering problems faster than human wisdom has as yet been able to assimilate them. Thus the age we live in offers little prospect of outward stability, and only those who by an inner serenity and disentanglement have learned how to deal with the continually unexpected can be at home in it. It may be that in time we shall become used to change as in our older wisdom we had become used to the unchanging. But such wisdom it is impossible to invent or to make widely and quickly available by mass production and salesmanship. It will, therefore, grow much more slowly than the inventions which ultimately it must learn to master.

October 20, 1932

X. BRIAND

*His work in helping pacify Europe; its coincidence
with the economic boom* [1]

Geneva, March 8

In a tribute published here in Geneva, Salvador de
Madariaga says that what made Briand the directing spirit
of the march towards the promised land of peace was that
he had faith. That is a just appraisal. The fame of Briand
does not rest very particularly on definite and tangible
achievements, but rather upon the recognition that during
his long time as Foreign Minister of France he really wished
to make peace with Germany.

He achieved some actual solutions of specific problems.
But they are not a measure of him. The deep esteem in
which he is held rests upon the memory of the six years from
1924 to 1929, when Europe and the world thought that the
losses of the war and the blunders of the peace would be
washed away by the tides of prosperity. During that period
the tempered idealism of Briand was immensely convincing
and reassuring; partial solutions had the air of being final,
and provisional arrangements had the appearance of perma-
nence. The essential goodness of Briand's intentions and
the popular credulity of that era of false recovery combined
to create an atmosphere of optimism which was soothing,
expansive, and deceptive.

The European fame of Briand really begins with his
attack in 1924 on the Nationalistic bloc which had governed

[1] Aristide Briand died in Paris on March 7, 1932, three weeks before his
seventieth birthday. Entering Parliament in 1902, at the age of forty, he had
been twenty times a Cabinet Minister, eleven times Premier, and in his last
years the foremost representative of international peace in Europe—sharing
the Nobel peace prize with Stresemann in 1926.

France since just after the war. It was the victory of the parties of the Left in the election of May, 1924, that gave Briand the power he exercised for the six succeeding years, and one may say that the beginning of the end of his influence was the defeat of his Cabinet in the autumn of 1929. After that he continued to hold office, but plainly his power was waning. The German elections of September, 1930, in which the Hitlerites made such sensational gains, weakened him decisively. The German attempt to form a customs union with Austria in the late winter of 1931 was utterly destructive to his influence. His ill-judged candidacy in the Presidential elections was the final blow. After that the Briand period was over.

Is it a coincidence that Briand's great work as a pacifier of Europe corresponded so exactly with the period of tremendous foreign investment in Germany? It was in 1924 that the German currency was stabilized and the capital markets of the world opened to Germany. In the five following years Germany had a great boom and paid reparations punctually. It was in 1928 that the boom ended after the stoppage of foreign lending, and by September, 1930, Germany was in the throes of depression and in political turmoil.

The correspondence is too close to be overlooked: there can be little real doubt that the apparent political progress in Franco-German relations between 1924 and 1928 represented not so much actual reconciliation of real differences as a temporary obliviousness to realities under the spell of the credit inflation. Easy money is a good painkiller. Thus what really brought the Briand-Stresemann period to an end was the drying up of credits to Germany and the great fall in prices which completely upset all the expectations upon which the Young Plan on the one hand and the private credits on the other had been based.

It is interesting to speculate whether a continuation of

the boom would have washed away Franco-German differences. That was the premise of M. Briand's policies and
the Young Plan. Expanding trade and a rising standard
of life were to render reparations tolerable and negligible.
In a common prosperity there was to be a growing collabora-
tion. Had the boom continued it might have worked, but
since for many reasons, high among them reparations and
excessive borrowing, the boom had to collapse, it might as
well be admitted that while the intentions of the policy were
excellent its premises were unsound.

The problem of world readjustment is much deeper and
more complex than even the best of the statesmen of the
post-war decade dared to admit. We are undergoing the
travail of that readjustment now and it will carry us far beyond the policies discussed in the last decade. Yet the name
of Aristide Briand will remain of good report. For men
will recall that he made hatred a little less patriotic and good
will a little more fashionable. And because of that he will
be well remembered by many millions whose instincts it is
to forget that they ought to dislike their neighbors.

March 9, 1932

XI. OLIVER WENDELL HOLMES

A tribute on his retirement

There are few who, reading Judge Holmes's letter of resignation, will not feel that here they touch a life done in the
great style. This, they will say, is how to live, and this is how
to stop, with every power used to the full, like an army rest-
ing, its powder gone but with all its flags flying. Here is the
heroic life complete, in which nothing has been shirked and
nothing denied, not battle or death, or the unfathomable

mystery of the universe, or the loneliness of thought, or the humors and the beauties of the human heritage. This is the whole of it. He has had what existence has to offer, all that is real, everything of experience, of friendship and of love, and the highest company of the mind, and honor, and the profoundest influence—everything is his that remains when illusion falls away and leaves neither fear nor disappointment in its wake.

It is impossible for the layman to do justice to Holmes the jurist. But even the layman, if he has read some of the opinions and has lived among the generations of lawyers whom Judge Holmes has influenced, must be aware that he is one of that small number who have determined not merely the course of the law but the premises and quality of legal thinking. For this great judge is one of the true philosophers of the English-speaking world, and it is the part of the philosopher to show men not so much what to think as how. This is his immortality. He has altered the casts of thought. And not only for lawyers. In the days to come, when only scholars remember the cases he decided, he will live on with Emerson and with William James and with a very few others in whom the American spirit became articulate and ripened into distinction. He has the gift of delivery. I have no doubt that his prose is the purest American writing of our time, and I am not sure but that in the American anthology his wisdom, so firm, so graceful, so spare, so clean, will be cherished as a tonic to the will of man above any thus far uttered on this continent.

It is a delight to honor him, and to express, while he is within hearing, a little something of the esteem in which he is held. He himself, however, has said, speaking more than thirty-five years ago to the undergraduates of Harvard College about the calling of the thinker, what now in the fulfillment of his life should be said of him. "Your education begins when you . . . have begun yourselves to work upon the raw material for results which you do not see, cannot predict and which may be long in coming—when you take the fact which life offers you for your appointed task. No man has earned the right to intellectual ambition until he has learned to lay his course by a star which he has never seen—to dig by the divining rod for springs which he may never reach. In saying this, I point to that which will make your study heroic. For I say to you in all sadness of conviction that to think great thoughts you must be heroes as well as idealists. Only when you have worked alone—when you have felt around you a black gulf of solitude more isolating than that which surrounds the dying man, and in hope and in despair have trusted to your own unshaken will—then only will you have achieved. Thus only can you gain the secret isolated joy of the thinker, who knows that, a hundred years after he is dead and forgotten, men who never heard of him will be moving to the measure of his thought— the subtile rapture of a postponed power, which the world knows not because it has no external trappings, but which to his prophetic vision is more real than that which commands an army. And if this joy should not be yours, still it is only thus that you can know that you have done what it lay in you to do—can say that you have lived and be ready for the end."

January 14, 1932

INDEX

A

Accord of Confidence, most promising political event, 179

Acquisitiveness, as a moving force, 2–3, 28–29; run wild, 247; resentment against era of anarchic, 327

Administration, devitalizing conduct of, 316; Governor Roosevelt on, 325
See also Hoover

American Legion, calls for a dictatorship, 30–31

Alabama, post-Civil War debts repudiated by, 162

Angly, Edward, his devastating classic, 16

Anti-Saloon League, loses its power to dictate, 287

Apathy, moral, in high places, 27

Arkansas, state debt repudiated by, 162

B

Baker, Newton D., favored by Southern politicians, 300; Democratic pre-convention feeling for, 303–305

Balfour Declaration, 165, 172

Bank of France, opposed to credit expansion, 20

Banking, reform in, Democratic timidity on, 303, 310; Senator Glass and reform of, 325, 326

Bankruptcy, tariff reduction as causing, 48; widespread, in trade war,

176; national, Britain's near approach to, 212–215

Barkley, Senator A. W., robs his party of its chief issue, 281, 282; his convention keynote speech, 301–303

Basle committee, its report on reparations, 24, 25, 164

Bear market, Senate investigation of, 50–52

Bewilderment, spiritual, aggravated in U. S., 27

Bitterness, developing, in Democratic convention, 313–314

Bonds, foreign, marketing of, 57; tax-exempt, for public relief, 82–83, 87–91; taxation vs. issue of, 94–98; repudiated by American states, 159, 160–164

Bonus, 29, 102, 108; and cheaper money, 123–126

Bonus army, Congress and, 131–133

Boom, post-war, assumptions of, 16

Borah, Senator W. E., makes best argument against national prohibition repeal, 284

Borrowing, mania for, 8–10

Brandeis, Justice Louis D., quoted, 16

Briand, Aristide, his work, 345–347

Brookhart, Senator S. W., in investigation of N. Y. Stock Exchange, 52

Bruening, Dr. Heinrich, causes of his fall as chancellor, 236–239

Bryanism, a new, Democratic Party and, 265, 269, 270; absent from Democratic platform, 309–310

Date Due

APR 3 '97			